THE
BEST
OF
SPORTS
ILLUSTRATED

THE
BEST
OF
SPORTS
ILLUSTRATED

Oxmoor
House.

Copyright 1990 The Time Inc. Magazine Company

Published by Oxmoor House, Inc.
1271 Avenue of the Americas
New York, New York 10020

SPORTS ILLUSTRATED is a registered trademark of
The Time Inc. Magazine Company.

ISBN: 0-8487-1039
Library of Congress Catalog Card Number: 90-62247

Manufactured in the United States of America
Third printing 1991

THE BEST OF SPORTS ILLUSTRATED

Senior Editor: MORIN BISHOP
    Editorial Assistants: STACEY HARMIS, ROXANA LONERGAN
    Copyreader: PAMELA ROBERTS
    Reporter: STEFANIE KRASNOW
Director of Photography & Research: GERALDINE HOWARD
    Photo Editor: LORNA BIEBER
    Photo Researchers: JOHN BLACKMAR, JANINE JONES,
        STELLA KRAMER, ZOE MOFFITT
Production Manager: JERRY HIGDON
    Associate Production Manager: RICK LITTON
    Production Assistant: TERRY BESTE
Designer: STEVEN HOFFMAN
    Design Assistants: MAGDALENA DESKUR, VICTORIA LOWE

The following material is excerpted from SPORTS ILLUSTRATED
and is used by permission of the authors and publishers acknowledged:
"Kentucky: May: Saturday" by William Faulkner. Printed by
    permission of Random House, Inc., publishers of Essays,
    Speeches and Public Lettersin which this selection appears.
    Copyright 1955 by Estelle Faulkner and Jill Faulkner Summers.
"There Have Been Shootings In The Night" by Kenny Moore.
"Nasty Little Devil" by Bil Gilbert.
"Where Am I? It Has To Be a Bad Dream" by Darryl Stingley
    with Mark Mulvoy. An excerpt from the bookHappy To Be
    Alive(Beaufort Books, Inc.). Copyright 1983 by Darryl Stingley.
"The Curious Case of Sidd Finch" by George Plimpton.
"Ali and His Entourage" by Gary Smith.

Special thanks to PETER HERBERT, Deputy Art Director, and to the
staff of the Sports Illustrated Picture Collection for their cooperation.

Cover photograph (Muhammad Ali vs. Sonny Liston, 1965): Neil Leifer

To order SPORTS ILLUSTRATED magazine, write to:
SPORTS ILLUSTRATED, Subscription Service Department,
P.O. Box 60001, Tampa, Florida 33660-0001

Contents

INTRODUCTION
6

THE GOLDEN AGE
1954-1962
8

THE AGE OF AUDACITY
1963-1975
70

THE ERA OF FREEDOM
1976-1983
154

THE SELLING OF SPORT
1984-1990
212

PHOTOGRAPHY CREDITS
268

INDEX
270

INTRODUCTION

SPORTS HAVE UNDERGONE SOME DRAMATIC CHANGES

since SPORTS ILLUSTRATED first hit the newsstands and mailboxes in 1954. The games expanded their reach as television propelled them into homes across the land. Ever richer players began to shift locations as they never had before and the era of stable dynasties came to an end. New faces appeared—black faces, women's faces—to diversify the countenance of sport. The evils that afflicted the rest of society became evident in the athletic world as well: drug abuse, violence, cheating to win. SPORTS ILLUSTRATED covered all these developments, sharpening its focus over the years to become what it is today—the authoritative voice on America's spectator sports and the athletes who play them. Through all the changes, certain qualities have endured: a respect for great writing, an appreciation of the power of a vivid photograph, an undiminished appetite for the joy and grace that typify our games at their best. It has been quite a ride. Sit back and savor where we've been.

— **MARK MULVOY,** *Managing Editor,* SPORTS ILLUSTRATED

1954-1962

The

GOL

THE
GOLDEN
AGE

BY RON FIMRITE

Golden Age? Yes, but that is a distinction generally conceded to the Roaring '20s, when for better or worse, sport was transformed from an innocent diversion into a national obsession, when mythic heroes—Ruth, Grange, Dempsey, Tilden, Jones—bestrode the land. The '20s were golden in the further sense that, seemingly all at once, there were vast sums to be made from previously trivial pursuits. But the years of our magazine's beginnings were golden too and, it seems to me, even more lustrous because the changes wrought on sport then would prove more profound and enduring. The '20s may have propelled our games onto center stage as mass entertainment, but the second Golden Age stretched their very boundaries from coast to coast, brought hitherto unseen "big league" action, through the wondrous instrument of television, into private homes and, most significantly, opened wide the gates of our playing fields to those who had been shut off from them for too long. A Golden Age? Why yes, for this was a time when sport developed something it had been notably lacking in previous decades—a conscience. And it reached this high ground well ahead of the rest of the country.

A second generation of black athletes had come to sport by 1954. And this time around, their presence was more than merely symbolic. They had a new freedom to become their own distinct and identifiable personalities. Jackie Robinson had been the pathfinder, a hero for the ages. The "First Negro." The new black athletes eschewed such distinction; they were merely stars—and stars of the first magnitude. It no longer made much sense to lump such divergent characters as Willie Mays and Henry Aaron into the same safe category of "Negro Athlete." If Ernie Banks was exuberant, Maury Wills was analytical. If there was an old school for black players, then Frank Robinson was a notable truant. Stereotypes were being shattered beyond recognition. An old-guard New York press had invented a personality for Mays when he burst upon the baseball firmament in the early '50s. He was to be the child-like southern Negro who spent his off hours gamboling with the kids of Harlem in back-street stickball games. When he moved west to San Francisco in 1958, Mays proved himself to be quite a different person. Far from being naive, he was complicated, moody, even calculating—a far more interesting character than the one advertised.

There were comparable sociological breakthroughs in almost every sport. The National Football League had featured black stars before, notably Marion Motley and Joe Perry, but none who changed attitudes as dramatically as Jim Brown, the arrogant, rebellious and supremely gifted new star. Brown played the game his way, asking no privileges, and he played it better than anyone ever had. Off the field he was resolutely his own man, the devil take the hindmost.

And what of basketball? This was the time, remember, of Bill Russell, Wilt Chamberlain and Elgin Baylor. The NBA, long the province of playmaking whites, seemed to evolve almost overnight into a personal confrontation between the two great black centers, Russell and Chamberlain. Chamberlain was the irresistible force, Russell the immovable object. Far from being brothers in race, they were bitter opponents for the whole of their long and glorious careers. Baylor was no center. He was the Nijinsky of the periphery, the player who introduced "hang time" to a game previously confined to jumping, not soaring. And he would soon have a legion of imitators, beginning with the equally brilliant Oscar Robertson.

At a time when it was necessary to employ federal troops to enforce anti-segregation laws elsewhere in the nation, blacks in ever-increasing numbers were rising to prominence in sports. Althea Gibson, in 1957, became the first of her race to win a Wimbledon tennis championship. Milt Campbell became the first black to win an Olympic Games decathlon, in 1956, Rafer Johnson the second four years later. Wilma Rudolph became the heroine of the 1960 Olympics, winning three gold medals in the sprints while an 18-year-old boxer, Cassius Marcellus Clay, captivated the world television audience.

But blacks weren't the only new stars. Scores of foreign athletes would appear to shake us to our parochial boots. Ingemar Johansson of Sweden knocked out Floyd Patterson in June of 1959 to become the first non-American to hold the heavyweight championship in 25 years. Two years later, Gary Player of South Africa became the first foreign golfer ever to win our Masters tournament. And tennis's brightest new players were the Australians: Lew Hoad, Ken Rosewall and Rod Laver. Not that we weren't capable of some surprises of our own. In the 1960 Olympics, the U.S. hockey team pulled off one of the biggest upsets in sports history by defeating the Canadians and the Russians for the gold medal. Yes, you could believe in miracles then, too.

In almost every sport, giants suddenly appeared. Not much later, we would call them "superstars." The best of these newcomers would be the equal of any superstars in sports history. In golf, we would have, first, Arnold Palmer and then Jack Nicklaus. Willie—later, with advancing maturity, Bill—Shoemaker was already being acclaimed in the late '50s as the greatest jockey of modern times. Baseball may never see Mays's equal, or football, Brown's. Has there ever been a better hitter than Ted Williams, whose oft-interrupted career finally ended in 1960, with, of course, a home run in his last at-bat? Stan (The Man) Musial, another survivor from the previous generation, would continue banging line drives through 1963. But Aaron and Mickey Mantle would prove more than adequate successors to the older stars.

MARCH 19, 1956

SPORTS ILLUSTRATED

25 CENTS
$7.50 A YEAR

IN THIS ISSUE
THE FABULOUS
CABO BLANCO CLUB
IN COLOR

MARLIN CHAMPION
ALFRED GLASSELL JR.

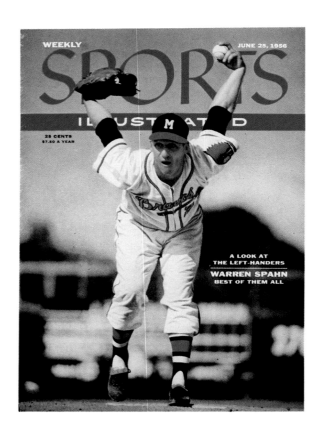

Sports were more dynastic then. The Yankees would win four more World Series in this Golden Age, and the Mantle-Maris Yanks of '61 rated comparison with the Ruth-Gehrig champions of the old Golden Age. The Celtics of Russell, Bob Cousy, Bill Sharman, K.C. Jones et al., would begin an astonishing string of eight straight NBA championships in 1959. Before he became a Celtic, Russell would lead his University of San Francisco team to successive NCAA titles and 55 straight wins. The Montreal Canadiens would win five NHL titles in a row, from 1956 through 1960. And the power struggle in the NFL among the Browns, Lions, Giants and Colts would soon be resolved by a dominant team from Green Bay under new head coach Vince Lombardi.

There were performances in those years that will be remembered forever. Don Larsen pitched a perfect game for the Yankees against the Dodgers in the fifth game of the 1956 World Series, but the Pirates' Harvey Haddix would achieve-even more astonishing perfection on May 26, 1959, when he kept the Braves off base for 12 innings. Alas, he would lose the game one inning later on a two-base error and the only hit he allowed.

But the most memorable and least popular achievement of the time belonged to Roger Maris, a powerful young slugger for the Yankees who on October 1, 1961, hit his 61st home run of the season, thereby demolishing baseball's most revered record, the one nobody was supposed to beat, the one held by the Babe. Even after Maris had surpassed this supposedly inviolate standard, the baseball establishment sought to deprive him of the honor. Maris, the argument persisted, had hit two of his 61 homers after his team's 154th game, this being baseball's first 162-game season, the end product of the American League's expansion to Minneapolis-St. Paul and Los Angeles. The Babe had hit his 60 within the conventional 154-game format. Maris's record was, therefore, an aberration. Commissioner Ford Frick seemed to agree with the critics, affixing a demeaning asterisk to the new numbers in the record book. Maris, a far more sensitive man than his detractors would allow, never seemed to recover from what should have been his finest hour. He would never hit more than 33 homers again, finishing a downsliding 12-year major league career with only eight, 13, nine and five in his last four seasons. His career total of 275 was scarcely Ruthian. Maris was one hero of the new Golden Age who was victimized by a ghost from the old one.

And yet, because of television, many million more Americans saw Maris hit home runs than ever saw the Babe. The almighty tube was the true owner of the new era. It could make or break any sport and even, as with the Roller Derby, introduce a new one. Television stirred up a tremendous revival of interest in boxing during the early '50s with its Wednesday and Friday night fight broadcasts. At the same time, it killed off the smaller arenas where young boxers had for generations developed their craft. The introduction of closed-circuit matches in this period—particularly those of the great champion Rocky Marciano—brought to an end those monumental big-gate outdoor fights in the summer. The gate for big fights henceforth would be calculated according to TV revenues, not by turnstile count. There would be no more "live" boxing crowds of 120,000, as there had been in the earlier Golden Age for the first Dempsey-Tunney fight, in Philadelphia. Television also brought major league baseball into the hinterlands, but it brought financial ruin to the once-flourishing minor leagues, forcing big league franchises to dip into their own treasuries to revive the wilting bushes.

But nowhere was the impact of the new medium more apparent than in the National Football League. Here was a sport that before television had been played almost exclusively in the industrial cities of the east and the middle west and had attracted a relatively small and specialized audience. College football had been king until the mid-'50s, when the tube took command and revealed to an unsuspecting public the much more polished skills of the professionals. The NFL soon became a television attraction to rival *I Love Lucy,* especially so after the 1958 Colts-Giants championship game in Yankee Stadium, an incomparable thriller SI called "The Best Game Ever Played." In 1960, the league hired as its new commissioner a young public relations dynamo from California who recognized instinctively that the warming relationship between television and the NFL could become a marriage made in heaven. It was this man, Pete Rozelle, who pressed upon the owners the revolutionary concept of having every team share equally in the burgeoning network revenues that gave the league financial security for the first time. It was a form of capitalistic socialism that ultimately made it possible for the likes of Green Bay and Minneapolis to compete with New York and Los Angeles in the marketplace. Television also spawned a competing league, the AFL, in 1960 that, when absorbed into the NFL a decade later, created the monolith that is pro football today.

But television was not solely responsible for the spread of major league sports to all parts of the country, for in 1954, Boeing introduced its 128-foot-long "707," the first commercial jet passenger plane in the U.S. Technology once again had shrunk the landscape. Four years after the introduction of the jetliner, the National League Giants and Dodgers moved out of New York and Brooklyn, to San Francisco and Los Angeles respectively. Two years after that, the NBA's Lakers transferred from Minneapolis to Los Angeles, to be followed by an American League expansion team in 1961.

The new Golden Age was, then, a time of furious innovation. Television and jet travel had broken down previously impenetrable geographic barriers. Blacks had taken their rightful place in the sports community. The new 24-second clock had transformed professional basketball from a deliberate game into the whirlwind spectacle it has been ever since. The new batting helmets made standing at the plate a somewhat less perilous experience. Old legends had been replaced by the new. Ah, but this was a revolution in firmer control of itself than most. Indeed, the age is nearly as significant for what it did not have as for what it did. There were no designated hitters, no three-point shots, no interminable instant-replay reviews and no labor strikes or lockouts. Team owners considered themselves sportsmen, not CEOs, and players were wage-earners like the rest of us, not multimillionaires.

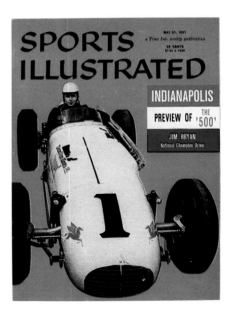

A Golden Age? Certainly. Maybe the best of them all. But then again, the past always seems such a happy place. Pity we can only visit it in memory.

1954

The Winner's Circle

Baseball: New York Giants
NFL: Cleveland Browns
College Football: Ohio State/UCLA
NHL: Detroit Red Wings
NBA: Minneapolis Lakers
College Basketball: La Salle
Masters: Sam Snead
U.S. Open (golf): Ed Furgol
British Open: Peter Thomson
PGA: Chick Harbert
Australian Open: Mervyn Rose
French Open: Tony Trabert
Wimbledon: Jaroslav Drobny
U.S. Open (tennis): Victor Seixas
Australian Open: Thelma Long
French Open: Maureen Connolly
Wimbledon: Maureen Connolly
U.S. Open (tennis): Doris Hart
Kentucky Derby: Determine
Preakness: Hasty Road
Belmont: High Gun
Indianapolis 500: Bill Vukovich
World Cup: West Germany

It is just a month after SI's inception when Willie Mays makes his over-the-shoulder catch against Cleveland's Vic Wertz to help the Giants to victory in Game 1 of the World Series. The ball would have been a home run in most parks; in the cavernous Polo Grounds, it is just a 460-foot out.

SPORTS ILLUSTRATED isn't the only legend born in '54. The year also marks the debut of a future star named Arnold Palmer, a young golfer from Latrobe, Pa., just seven months out of the Coast Guard, who wins his first major tournament with a victory in the U.S. Amateur.

Alabama's Tommy Lewis (42) adds a bizarre footnote to football history when he comes off the bench—literally—to tackle Rice's Dickie Moegle, who is flying up the sidelines for an apparent touchdown in the Cotton Bowl. The officials award the touchdown to Rice, and the Owls go on to win, 28–6.

England's Roger Bannister becomes SI's first Sportsman of the Year by breaking the four-minute mile, in May—with a 3:59.4 at Iffley Road track in Oxford (left)—and then doing it again, in August, with a 3:58.8 at the British Empire Games to defeat Australia's John Landy.

When Maureen (Little Mo) Connolly wins her third Wimbledon at the age of 19, she seems poised to dominate women's tennis for years to come. But she suffers an accident while riding her horse, and her leg is crushed, ending her tennis career forever.

The Senate condemns Joe McCarthy   Swanson introduces the TV dinner

1955

The Winner's Circle

Baseball: Brooklyn Dodgers
NFL: Cleveland Browns
College Football: Oklahoma
NHL: Detroit Red Wings
NBA: Syracuse Nationals
College Basketball: San Francisco
Masters: Cary Middlecoff
U.S. Open (golf): Jack Fleck
British Open: Peter Thomson
PGA: Doug Ford
Australian Open: Ken Rosewall
French Open: Tony Trabert
Wimbledon: Tony Trabert
U.S. Open (tennis): Tony Trabert
Australian Open: Beryl Penrose
French Open: Angela Mortimer
Wimbledon: Louise Brough
U.S. Open (tennis): Doris Hart
Kentucky Derby: Swaps
Preakness: Nashua
Belmont: Nashua
Indianapolis 500: Bob Sweikert

The electrifying Jackie Robinson gets only four hits for the Brooklyn Dodgers in the Bums' first World Series triumph, but his aggressive style of play—including a steal of home in the first game—inspires his teammates to victory. The batting star is Duke Snider, who has four home runs and seven RBIs in the seven-game win over the Yankees.

Gordie Howe (second from right) leads Detroit to the Stanley Cup title for the second straight year as the Red Wings defeat the Montreal Canadiens in seven games. Howe, who is the top playoff scorer with 20 points, will go on to set the alltime NHL scoring record and earn six MVP awards, but he will never win the Cup again.

Eddie Arcaro and Nashua don't win the Kentucky Derby, but they finish in front in almost every other important contest, including the Preakness, the Belmont and a match race (below) with Derby winner Swaps in August. Nashua's 6½-length win over his rival makes him a nearly unanimous choice as Horse of the Year.

Rosa Parks refuses to give up her seat on an Alabama bus

1955

All seems in order as the drivers dash to their cars for the start of the LeMans Grand Prix (left), but disaster strikes just 32 laps later, when Pierre Lavegh's Mercedes barrels into the earthen bulwark around the track and hurtles into the air, sending lethal bits of wreckage into the crowd. The death toll will number 87.

Bill Russell celebrates after San Francisco's 77–63 victory over La Salle for the NCAA title. Russell was a dominant force throughout the season, averaging 21.4 points and 20.5 rebounds per game. He will repeat the feat in his senior year, leading the Dons to their second straight title and an undefeated 29–0 record.

Disneyland opens in Anaheim, Calif.   James Dean dies at 24

21

1956

The Winner's Circle

Baseball: New York Yankees
NFL: New York Giants
College Football: Oklahoma
NHL: Montreal Canadiens
NBA: Philadelphia Warriors
College Basketball: San Francisco
Masters: Jack Burke
U.S. Open (golf): Cary Middlecoff
British Open: Peter Thomson
PGA: Jack Burke
Australian Open: Lew Hoad
French Open: Lew Hoad
Wimbledon: Lew Hoad
U.S. Open (tennis): Ken Rosewall
Australian Open: Mary Carter
French Open: Althea Gibson
Wimbledon: Shirley Fry
U.S. Open (tennis): Shirley Fry
Kentucky Derby: Needles
Preakness: Fabius
Belmont: Needles
Indianapolis 500: Pat Flaherty

It is a season of dreams for Mickey Mantle, who finally fulfills all the expectations of the demanding Yankee fans. His numbers: 52 homers, 130 RBIs and a .353 batting average, good enough to make him one of only 14 men to win baseball's coveted Triple Crown.

Dashing Lew Hoad of Australia dominates men's tennis, winning three of four major tournaments. His countryman, Ken Rosewall, is his main rival, losing to Hoad in the finals of both Wimbledon and the Australian Open but getting his revenge by defeating Hoad in the U.S. Open to prevent him from completing the Grand Slam.

Cancer takes the life of Babe Didrikson Zaharias and robs the world of one of its finest athletes. Among her many accomplishments: gold medals at the 1932 Olympics in the javelin and the 80-meter hurdles and a silver medal in the high jump. She becomes a professional golfer in 1947, winning 12 major tournaments, including three U.S. Opens.

Yogi Berra joyfully leaps into the arms of pitcher Don Larsen after Larsen's perfect game against the Dodgers gives the Yankees a 3–2 lead in the World Series. Larsen is an unlikely hero, having lasted only into the second inning in Game 2, but manager Casey Stengel's gamble pays off in the fifth game as Larsen delivers his masterpiece.

Quarterback Jimmy Harris (right) helps to send Texas to a 45–0 drubbing, its worst defeat since 1908. The Sooners go on to enjoy a banner season as they roll to a 10–0 record and a national champion-ship, beating Notre Dame 40–0 in South Bend and dominating their conference opponents by an embarassing average score of 49–7.

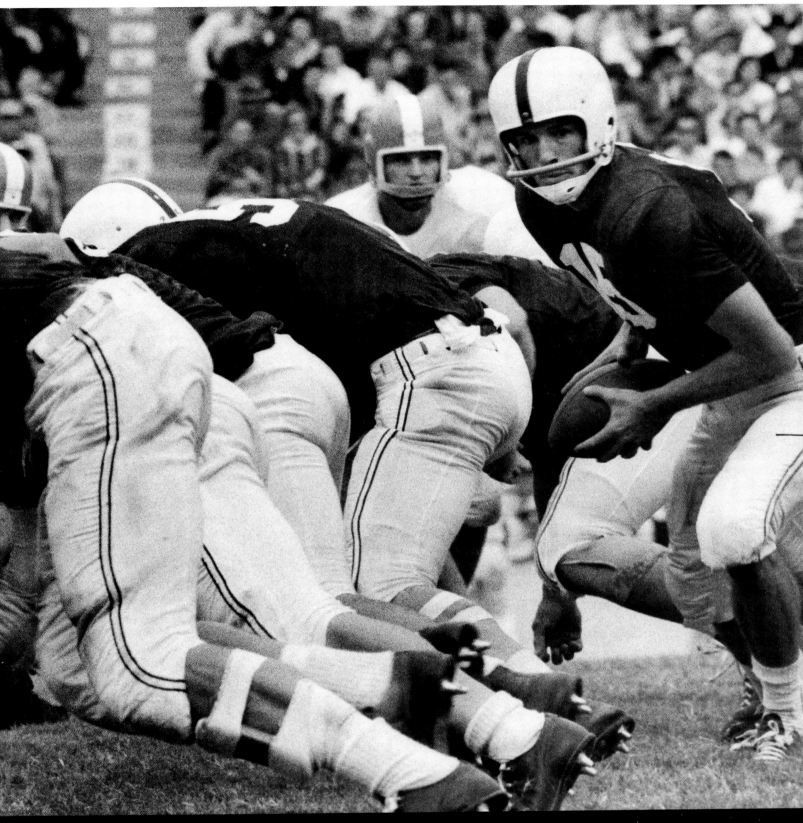

Revolution breaks out in Hungary, prompting a Soviet invasion

Toni Sailer of Austria becomes the first man to win all three Alpine events (slalom, giant slalom and downhill), at the Olympics in Cortina. A broken bootstrap just minutes before his downhill run nearly costs Sailer the medal—neither he nor any member of the Austrian team has a spare—but a friendly Italian trainer saves the day, and Sailer finishes his run 3.5 seconds faster than his closest opponent.

Bobby Morrow becomes the first man since Jesse Owens in 1936 to earn gold medals in both the 100- and 200-meter dashes, winning the latter in a world-record time of 20.6 seconds (right). It is a clean sweep for the U.S. in the 200 as Americans Andrew Stansfield and W. Thane Baker finish second and third respectively.

Grace Kelly marries Prince Rainier of Monaco   Nasser seizes the Suez Canal

26

1956

Tenley Albright strikes gold at the Winter Games in Cortina, becoming one in the long line of successful American figure skaters who have charmed Olympic audiences with their grace and style. But Albright was tough and smart as well: She overcame polio at the age of 11 and later went on to medical school and a career as a surgeon.

Israel reaches a ceasefire agreement with its Middle East neighbors

1957

The Winner's Circle

Baseball: Milwaukee Braves
NFL: Detroit Lions
College Football: Auburn/Ohio State
NHL: Montreal Canadiens
NBA: Boston Celtics
College Basketball: North Carolina
Masters: Doug Ford
U.S. Open (golf): Dick Mayer
British Open: Bobby Locke
PGA: Lionel Herbert
Australian Open: Ashley Cooper
French Open: Sven Davidson
Wimbledon: Lew Hoad
U.S. Open (tennis): Malcolm Anderson
Australian Open: Shirley Fry
French Open: Shirley Bloomer
Wimbledon: Althea Gibson
U.S. Open (tennis): Althea Gibson
Kentucky Derby: Iron Liege
Preakness: Bold Ruler
Belmont: Gallant Man
Indianapolis 500: Sam Hanks

Henry Aaron, just 23, stands at the plate in Milwaukee during a regular-season game against the St. Louis Cardinals. Hammerin' Hank's magnificent season (44 homers, 132 RBIs) will be capped by a brilliant World Series: Aaron will lead all players with 11 hits, three homers and seven RBIs in the Braves' seven-game triumph over the Yankees.

Althea Gibson becomes the first black tennis player to win Wimbledon, beating Darlene Hard 6–3, 6–2 in the finals. Two months later she will win the U.S. Open, and will go on to win both events in 1958 as well. Long retired now, Gibson continues to lend her support to recreational tennis programs for disadvantaged youth.

An embarassing moment in an otherwise shining career: Willie Shoemaker mistakes the 16th pole for the finish line and stands up aboard Gallant Man (below, center), thereby giving the Kentucky Derby to Iron Liege. Shoemaker will later redeem himself by riding Gallant Man to victory in the Belmont Stakes.

30

1957

Sugar Ray Robinson lands a body blow to the belly of Gene Fullmer in a middle-weight bout that will earn him the championship for the fourth time. He had lost the title to Fullmer in January; in September he will lose it again, to nemesis Carmen Basilio, a defeat he will avenge in '58 to win a record fifth title.

Acrobatic rookie Bill Russell (above) snares a rebound in the NBA finals against St. Louis. By the time the seven-game Celtic triumph is in the books, Russell will have averaged 24.4 rebounds per game during the playoffs. The Hawks will return the favor in 1958, but Russell's Celtics will go on to win the next eight in a row.

Blacks enroll at Central High in Little Rock, Ark.   The Frisbee is a soaring success

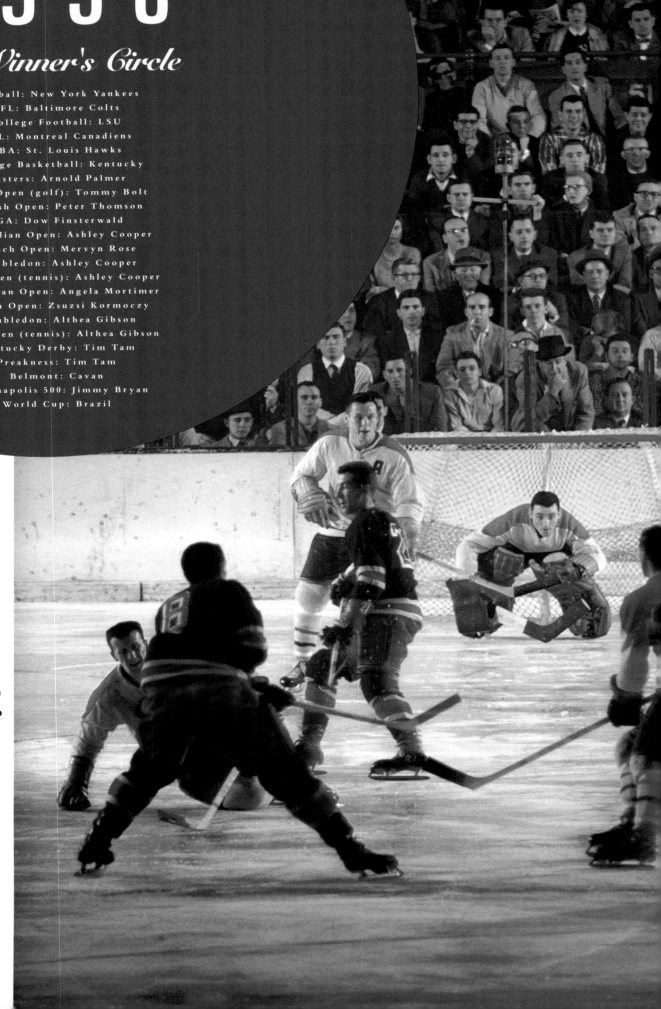

1958

The Winner's Circle

Baseball: New York Yankees
NFL: Baltimore Colts
College Football: LSU
NHL: Montreal Canadiens
NBA: St. Louis Hawks
College Basketball: Kentucky
Masters: Arnold Palmer
U.S. Open (golf): Tommy Bolt
British Open: Peter Thomson
PGA: Dow Finsterwald
Australian Open: Ashley Cooper
French Open: Mervyn Rose
Wimbledon: Ashley Cooper
U.S. Open (tennis): Ashley Cooper
Australian Open: Angela Mortimer
French Open: Zsuzsi Kormoczy
Wimbledon: Althea Gibson
U.S. Open (tennis): Althea Gibson
Kentucky Derby: Tim Tam
Preakness: Tim Tam
Belmont: Cavan
Indianapolis 500: Jimmy Bryan
World Cup: Brazil

The Montreal Canadiens, led by innovative goalie Jacques Plante, win their third straight Stanley Cup, defeating the Boston Bruins in six games in the finals. Plante, who leads the league with a goals-against average of 2.11, will revolutionize goaltending during the following season by becoming the first man to wear a goalie mask in competition.

Baseball is shocked when popular Brooklyn catcher Roy Campanella (left) is paralyzed from the waist down after his car skids on a patch of ice, hits a telephone pole and overturns. During his 10-year career, Campanella led the Dodgers to five World Series and won the National League's Most Valuable Player award three times.

The Yankees win yet another World Series—their seventh in 10 years—as Hank Bauer (below) leads the way with 10 hits, four homers and eight RBIs in the seven-game series with the Milwaukee Braves. It is a rare moment in the sun for the quiet Bauer, who is often overshadowed by the multitude of superstars in the Yankee lineup.

The normally volatile Tommy Bolt—famous for abusing his golf clubs the way John McEnroe would later torture his racket—keeps his cool long enough to post a three-over-par 283 to win the U.S. Open. Leading after two rounds, Bolt refused to wilt, calmly firing a one-over-par 141 for the last 36 holes to repel challenges from Julius Boros, Gene Littler and a young pro from South Africa named Gary Player.

1958

With the LPGA title already in her possession, Mickey Wright sets her sights on the Women's Open, where she will decimate the competition, finishing five strokes ahead of Louise Suggs in second, averaging 30 putts per round and some 240 yards per drive. Wright will go on to win a total of 13 major tournaments in her long career.

Elvis Presley is drafted   Khrushchev becomes Soviet premier

1959

The Winner's Circle

Baseball: Los Angeles Dodgers
NFL: Baltimore Colts
College Football: Syracuse
NHL: Montreal Canadiens
NBA: Boston Celtics
College Basketball: California
Masters: Art Wall
U.S. Open (golf): Billy Casper
British Open: Gary Player
PGA: Bob Rosburg
Australian Open: Alex Olmedo
French Open: Nicola Pietrangeli
Wimbledon: Alex Olmedo
U.S. Open (tennis): Neale Fraser
Australian Open: Mary Carter-Reitano
French Open: Christine Truman
Wimbledon: Maria Bueno
U.S. Open (tennis): Maria Bueno
Kentucky Derby: Tomy Lee
Preakness: Royal Orbit
Belmont: Sword Dancer
Indianapolis 500: Rodger Ward

Phil Hill is the embodiment of laid-back as he reclines against his trusty Ferrari, but two weeks later, he will be competing in the 12-hour race at Sebring, Fla., one of motor racing's most grueling events. Hill and his codrivers will be up to the task, averaging 80.26 mph over the 977.6 miles of rain-swept track to finish a full lap ahead of the second-place team.

Ingo-mania sweeps the U.S. as handsome Ingemar Johansson of Sweden and his girlfriend Birgit Lundgren become media darlings. His celebrity soars even higher when he floors Floyd Patterson with a right hook in the third round of their title fight to become the first non-American heavyweight champ since 1934. Alas for Ingo, he will lose the rematch in '60.

Halfback Ernie Davis (below) follows the blocking of 230-pound teammate Roger Davis before bursting up the sideline for a 57-yard touchdown in Syracuse's 44–0 rout of West Virginia. The Orangemen will go on to the national title, and Davis will win the Heisman Trophy two years later. Tragically, he will die of leukemia in 1963, his professional promise left unfulfilled.

Johnny Unitas looks downfield for his favorite target, Ray Berry (82), as he leads the Colts against the Giants in a rematch of 1958's dramatic title game. The Colts come out on top once again as Unitas takes over the game in the fourth quarter, rolling out for one touchdown and hitting rookie receiver Jerry Richardson with another en route to a 31–16 victory.

1959

Shed a tear for poor Harvey Haddix of the Pittsburgh Pirates, whose defeat to the Milwaukee Braves will go down in history as the epitome of a tough loss. Haddix pitches 12 perfect innings before an error, a sacrifice, an intentional walk to Hank Aaron and a single by Joe Adcock make him a 1–0 loser. For the record, Lew Burdette, who allowed 12 hits but no runs, was the winner.

Castro seizes power in Cuba   The hula hoop sets the nation swinging

1960

The Winner's Circle

Baseball: Pittsburgh Pirates
NFL/AFL: Philadelphia Eagles/Houston Oilers
College Football: University of Minnesota
NHL: Montreal Canadiens
NBA: Boston Celtics
College Basketball: Ohio State
Masters: Arnold Palmer
U.S. Open (golf): Arnold Palmer
British Open: Kel Nagle
PGA: Jay Hebert
Australian Open: Rod Laver
French Open: Nicola Pietrangeli
Wimbledon: Neale Fraser
U.S. Open (tennis): Neale Fraser
Australian Open: Margaret Smith Court
French Open: Darlene Hard
Wimbledon: Maria Bueno
U.S. Open (tennis): Darlene Hard
Kentucky Derby: Venetian Way
Preakness: Bally Ache
Belmont: Celtic Ash
Indianapolis 500: Jim Rathmann

Norm Van Brocklin, playing in his 12th and final season, leads the Philadelphia Eagles to the NFL title, throwing for 2,471 yards and 24 touchdowns in just 12 games. After knocking the New York Giants out of the race with back-to-back wins, the Eagles upset the Green Bay Packers in the championship game 17–13 as rookie Ted Dean runs in from the Green Bay five-yard line with the game-winning score.

A young student from Ohio State expresses a wish to remain an amateur golfer in the Bobby Jones mold. He is known to his friends by the unflattering nickname of Blob-o or Whaleman. He is also a whale of a player, winning the U.S. Amateur in 1959 and '60, and finishing two strokes behind a guy named Palmer in the U.S. Open. His name: Jack Nicklaus.

Twenty years before the Miracle on Ice, there is another U.S. Olympic hockey team that astounds the world. Led by brothers Billy and Bobby Cleary, the Americans upset the Soviets 3–2 (below), then, helped by a between-periods suggestion from the Soviet captain that they take some oxygen, defeat the Czechs 9–4 in the gold medal game.

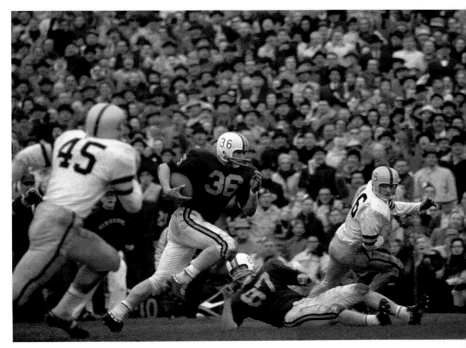

1960

The scoreboard sets the scene for perhaps the most dramatic moment in World Series history as the Pirates' Bill Mazeroski hits a solo home run (see ball above the scoreboard) against New York's Ralph Terry to break a 9–9 tie and beat the Yankees in the bottom of the ninth inning of the seventh game. Pittsburgh, without a Series win since 1925, celebrates wildly.

Minnesota fullback Roger Hagberg bursts up the middle for the 42-yard touchdown run that will put the Gophers in front by nine points en route to a 27–10 win over top-ranked Big Ten rival Iowa. Hagberg gains 103 yards on 15 carries in the win; it will propel Minnesota and long-suffering coach Murray Warmath to an 8–2 season and the national title.

The FDA approves the Pill   Chubby Checker turns to the Twist

Wilma Rudolph sprints to gold in the 100-meter Olympic finals with a wind-aided time of 11.0 seconds. Rudolph will also win gold medals in the 200-meter dash and the 4 x 100-meter relay. Born in rural Tennessee, Rudolph overcame polio, double pneumonia and a case of scarlet fever as a child that forced her to wear a brace on her left leg until she was 11.

Running in only his third marathon and given little hope of victory by the experts, barefoot Abebe Bikila of Ethiopia lopes toward the Arch of Constantine and a gold medal. A member of Haile Selassie's Imperial Bodyguard, Bikila will become the first black African to win an Olympic marathon, running the course in a world-record time of 2:15:16.2.

The Belgian Congo fights for its independence   Kennedy is elected president

1960

Jake LaMotta tells a Senate subcommittee that he took a dive in '47

1961

The Winner's Circle

Baseball: New York Yankees
NFL/AFL: Green Bay Packers/Houston Oilers
College Football: Alabama
NHL: Chicago Black Hawks
NBA: Boston Celtics
College Basketball: University of Cincinnati
Masters: Gary Player
U.S. Open (golf): Gene Littler
British Open: Arnold Palmer
PGA: Jerry Barber
Australian Open: Roy Emerson
French Open: Manuel Santana
Wimbledon: Rod Laver
U.S. Open (tennis): Roy Emerson
Australian Open: Margaret Smith Court
French Open: Ann Haydon
Wimbledon: Angela Mortimer
U.S. Open (tennis): Darlene Hard
Kentucky Derby: Carry Back
Preakness: Carry Back
Belmont: Sherluck
Indianapolis 500: A.J Foyt

Bill Russell powers the Celtics to another NBA title, this time leading Boston to a five-game final-series triumph over the St. Louis Hawks. Once known only for his defense, Russell has now developed an impressive offensive arsenal as well, averaging 19.1 points per game in the playoffs to go with his 299 rebounds, an incredible average of 29.9 per game.

A jubilant Bear Bryant is carried off the field after Alabama beats Auburn 34–0. The Crimson Tide will go on to a perfect 11–0 record and win the national title, Bryant's first. He had been a miracle worker wherever he went, transforming floundering programs at Kentucky and Texas A&M before arriving in Tuscaloosa in 1958 to take over a team that had fallen to 2–7–1 in the previous season.

The brilliant Soviet high jumper Valeri Brumel pours himself over the bar for a world record-tying jump of 7' 3" at a meet in Madison Square Garden. Brumel will go on to set a world record of 7' 5¾" in 1963 and win the gold medal at the '64 Olympics in Tokyo. But he will seriously injure his right leg in a motorcycle accident the following year and never participate in international competition again.

1 9 6 1

Roger Maris looks skyward as homer No. 60 heads out of Yankee Stadium to tie him with Babe Ruth for the single-season home run record. Five days later, in the season's last game, Maris will send a fastball from Boston's Tracy Stallard into Yankee Stadium's rightfield stands for the record-setting 61st.

The original man in black is Gary Player, who lets out a whoop after sinking a 25-foot putt for a birdie during the third round of the Masters. He will falter in the final round, shooting a two-over-par 74, but will still finish with an eight-under 280, good enough to keep him a stroke ahead of Arnold Palmer and Charles Coe and make him the first non-American to win the Masters.

The Berlin Wall is erected   The U.S. invades the Bay of Pigs

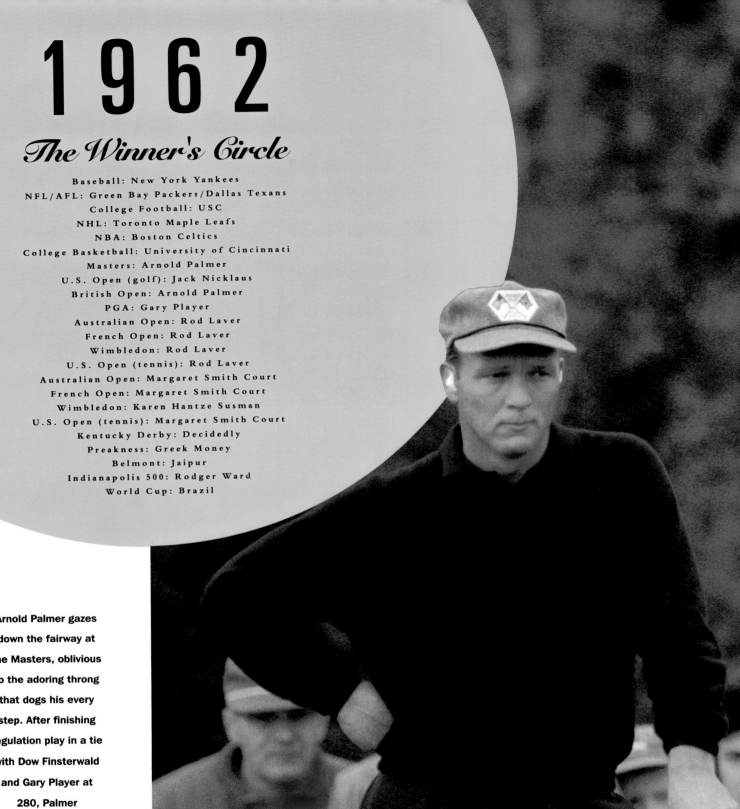

1962

The Winner's Circle

Baseball: New York Yankees
NFL/AFL: Green Bay Packers/Dallas Texans
College Football: USC
NHL: Toronto Maple Leafs
NBA: Boston Celtics
College Basketball: University of Cincinnati
Masters: Arnold Palmer
U.S. Open (golf): Jack Nicklaus
British Open: Arnold Palmer
PGA: Gary Player
Australian Open: Rod Laver
French Open: Rod Laver
Wimbledon: Rod Laver
U.S. Open (tennis): Rod Laver
Australian Open: Margaret Smith Court
French Open: Margaret Smith Court
Wimbledon: Karen Hantze Susman
U.S. Open (tennis): Margaret Smith Court
Kentucky Derby: Decidedly
Preakness: Greek Money
Belmont: Jaipur
Indianapolis 500: Rodger Ward
World Cup: Brazil

Arnold Palmer gazes down the fairway at the Masters, oblivious to the adoring throng that dogs his every step. After finishing regulation play in a tie with Dow Finsterwald and Gary Player at 280, Palmer dominates the 18-hole playoff, firing a four-under-par 68 to finish three strokes ahead of Player and nine ahead of Finsterwald. It is the third of four Masters that Palmer will win.

Rocket Rod Laver becomes the second man—the first was Don Budge in 1938—to win tennis' Grand Slam. Using perhaps the most powerful serve-and-volley game in history, the Australian redhead beats Roy Emerson for the Australian, French and U.S. titles and sweeps Martin Mulligan away in three sets to capture Wimbledon.

USC quarterback Pete Beathard rolls to his left during the Trojans' 25–0 victory over Notre Dame. The win is just one peak in a season of highlights as USC streaks to an undefeated record and the national title, the first for coach John McKay. The Trojans' perfect mark is sorely tested in the Rose Bowl as Wisconsin stages a furious comeback but falls short in the 42–37 USC win.

1962

Sonny Liston dispatches Floyd Patterson with a devastating series of punches in the first round, and a new heavyweight champ is crowned. In spite of persistent questions about his unsavory connections, Liston reigns for two years, amassing a sizable reputation as a puncher of almost mythic proportions. It will take a young man from Louisville to do the debunking.

Third baseman Frank Thomas throws wide; first baseman Marv Throneberry can't reach it. It's just another error for the bumbling New York Mets, who raise incompetence to an art form in their debut season. Under the pained gaze of manager Casey Stengel, the Mets commit 210 errors and stumble to a 40–120 record, still the worst in major league history.

John Glenn orbits the earth   The Cuban missile crisis raises the peril of nuclear war

With his business behind him and his car underfoot, Sugar Ray Robinson is the very picture of the gentleman of leisure. Has there ever been a more elegant champion?

SI *Favorites*

KENTUCKY: MAY: SATURDAY
William Faulkner reports from the Kentucky Derby

SPORTSMAN OF THE YEAR: 1955
Robert Creamer profiles Johnny Podres

DUEL OF THE FOUR-MINUTE MEN
Paul O'Neil covers the Bannister-Landy matchup

THE SAVERS VS. THE SPOILERS
Coles Phinizy speaks up for Alaskan wildlife

THE HEAVEN BELOW
Clare Boothe Luce goes skin-diving

THE MOST EXCITING FIVE MINUTES
Tex Maule reports from the 1960 Olympics

SUGAR'S SHOW ROLLS ON
Gilbert Rogin vists Sugar Ray Robinson

12 DAYS BEFORE THE MAST
Rogin learns to hate ocean sailing

YOU LOVE WOODY OR HATE HIM
Roy Terrell examines the world of Woody Hayes

KENTUCKY: MAY: SATURDAY

BY WILLIAM FAULKNER

While attending the 1955 Kentucky Derby at SI's request, novelist William Faulkner learned that he had won the Pulitzer Prize. His joy did not prevent him from filing this memorable piece that recorded his impressions of Kentucky and its premier sporting event. Just for the record, the race was won by Swaps.

This saw Boone: the bluegrass, the virgin land rolling westward wave by dense wave from the Allegheny gaps, unmarked then, teeming with deer and buffalo about the salt licks and the limestone springs whose water in time would make the fine bourbon whiskey; and the wild men too—the red men and the white ones too who had to be a little wild also to endure and survive and so mark the wilderness with the proofs of their tough survival—Boonesborough, Owenstown, Harrod's and Harbuck's Stations; Kentucky: the dark and bloody ground.

And knew Lincoln too, where the old weathered durable rail fences enclose the green and sacrosanct pace of rounded hills long healed now from the plow, and big old trees to shade the site of the ancient one-room cabin in which the babe first saw light; no sound there now but such wind and birds as when the child first faced the road which would lead to fame and martyrdom—unless perhaps you like to think that the man's voice is somewhere there too, speaking into the scene of his own nativity the simple and matchless prose with which he reminded us of our duties and responsibilities if we wished to continue as a nation.

And knew Stephen Foster and the brick mansion of his song; no longer the dark and bloody ground of memory now, but already my old Kentucky home....

[Two days before the race]

Even from just passing the stables, you carry with you the smell of liniment and ammonia and straw—the strong quiet aroma of horses. And even before we reach the track we can hear horses—the light hard rapid thud of hooves mounting to crescendo and already fading rapidly out. And now in the gray early light we can see them, in couples and groups at canter or hand-gallop under the exercise boys. Then one alone, at once furious and solitary, going full out, breezed, the rider hunched forward, excrescent and precarious, not of the horse but simply (for the instant) with it, in the conventional posture of speed—and who knows, perhaps the two of them, man and horse both: the animal dreaming, hoping for the moment at least it looked like Whirlaway or Citation, the boy for that moment at least that he was indistinguishable from Arcaro or Earl Sande, perhaps feeling already across his knees the scented sweep of the victorious garland.

And we ourselves are on the track now, but carefully and discreetly back against the rail out of the way: now we are no longer a handful clotting in a murmur of furlongs and poles and tenths of a second, but there are a hundred of us now and more still coming, all craning to look in one direction into the mouth of the chute. Then it is as if the gray, overcast, slightly moist post-dawn itself had spoken above our heads. This time the exercise boy is a Negro, moving his mount at no schooled or calculated gait at all, just moving it rapidly, getting it off the track and out of the way, speaking not to us but to all circumambience: man and beast either within hearing: "Y'awl can git out of the way too now; here's the big horse coming."

And now we can all see him as he enters the chute on a lead in the hand of a groom. The groom unsnaps the lead and now the two horses come on down the now empty chute toward the now empty track, out of which the final end of the waiting and the expectation has risen almost like an audible sound, a suspiration, a sigh....

[Minutes before the race]

And this too: the song, the brick mansion, matched to the apotheosis: Stephen Foster as handmaiden to the Horse as the band announces that it is now about to be the one 30 minutes past 4 o'clock out of all possible 4 o'clocks on one Saturday afternoon of all possible Saturday afternoons. The brazen chords swell and hover and fade above the packed infield and the stands as the 10 horses parade to post—the 10 animals which for the next two minutes will not just symbolize but bear the burden and be the justification, not just

of their individual own three years of life, but of the generations of selection and breeding and training and care which brought them to this one triumphant two minutes where one will be supreme and nine will be supreme failures—brought to this moment which will be supreme for him, the apex of his life, which, even counted in lustra, is only 21 years old, the beginning of manhood. Such is the price he will pay for the supremacy; such is the gamble he will take. But what human being would refuse that much loss, for that much gain, at 21?

Only a little over two minutes: one simultaneous metallic clash as the gates spring. Though you do not really know what it was you heard: whether it was that metallic crash, or the simultaneous thunder of the hooves in that first leap or the massed voices, the gasp, the exhalation—whatever it was, the clump of horses indistinguishable yet, like a brown wave dotted with the bright silks of the riders like chips flowing toward us along the rail until, approaching, we can begin to distinguish individuals, streaming past us now as individual horses—horses which (including the rider) once stood about eight feet tall and 10 feet long, now look like arrows twice that length and less than half that thickness, shooting past and bunching again as perspective diminishes, then becoming individual horses once more around the turn into the backstretch, streaming on, to bunch for the last time into the homestretch itself, then again individuals, individual horses, the individual horse, the Horse: 2:01⅕ minutes.

And now he stands beneath the rose escarpment above the flash and glare of the magnesium and the whirring film of celluloid immortality. This is the moment, the peak, the pinnacle; after this, all is ebb. We who watched have seen too much; expectation, the glandular pressure, has been too high to long endure; it is evening, not only of the day but the emotional capacity too; Boots and Saddles will sound twice more and condensations of light and movement will go through the motions of horses and jockeys again. But they will run as though in dream, toward anticlimax; we must turn away now for a little time, even if only to assimilate, get used to living with, what we have seen and experienced. Though we have not yet escaped that moment. Indeed this may be the way we assimilate and endure it: the voices, the talk, the airports and stations which we scatter back to where our old lives wait for us, in the aircraft and trains and buses carrying us back toward the old comfortable familiar routine like the old comfortable hat or coat: porter, bus driver, pretty stenographer who has saved for a year, scanted Christmas probably, to be able to say "I saw the Derby," the sports editor who, having spent a week talking and eating and drinking horse and who now wants only to get home and have a double nightcap and go to bed, all talking, all with opinions, valid and enduring:

"That was an accident. Wait until next time."

"What next time? What horse will they use?"

"If I had been riding him, I would have rode him different."

"No, no, he was ridden just right. It was that little shower of rain made the track fast like California."

"Or maybe the rain scared him, since it don't rain in L.A.? Maybe when he felt wet on his feet he thought he was going to sink and he was just jumping for dry land, huh?"

And so on. So it is not the Day after all. It is only the 81st one.

Excerpted from an original story published in
Sports Illustrated, *May 16, 1955*

SPORTSMAN OF THE YEAR: 1955

BY ROBERT CREAMER

When Johnny Podres tossed a shutout against the Yankees in the seventh game of the 1955 World Series, he fulfilled the dreams of his hard-working family as well as those of frustrated Brooklyn fans everywhere. Robert Creamer, later the author of an acclaimed biography of Babe Ruth, told the story in his piece naming Podres as Sportsman of the Year.

The grandfather of Johnny Podres climbed out of the mines of czarist Russia and came to America in 1904, the year after Cy Young and the Boston Red Sox beat Hans Wagner and the Pittsburgh Pirates in the first World Series.... He was 24, and he had been working in the mines for 10 years.

In America he found his way to an iron-mining community in upstate New York in the rough foothills of the Adirondacks near Lake Champlain, married a Lithuanian girl and took his broad back and big hands down into the mines again. Forty-six-years, two wives and eight children later he came out of the mines for the last time....

Consider Joe Podres, son of old Barney and father of Johnny, the Sportsman of the Year. Like his father, he went down into the mines in his youth.... He worked all week and played ball on Sundays, or whenever the local team could schedule a game. He was a topflight semiprofessional pitcher for 25 years, until he reluctantly retired three years ago at the age of 43. Sports earned him no money to speak of ... [but] it provided the key that opened the way for his son to make come true a modern version of one of those old legends of beggars and-kings and gold pots in the cabbage patch that were told for centuries by miners, farmers, peasants and other wishful Old World dreamers.

Today, even the dream is different. It does not deal with beggar boys becoming kings, or knights on white chargers. The boy kicks a football along Gorky Street and imagines himself booting the winning goal for Spartak in Dynamo Stadium in Moscow. He belts a hurley ball along the rich turf with a stick of Irish ash and thinks how grand it would be in Corke Park in Dublin saving the All-Ireland title for Cork. He stands on the edge of a street in a village in Provence as the Tour de France wheels by and sees himself pedaling into Parc des Princes Stadium in Paris, miles ahead of Louison Bobet. He throws a ball against the battered side of a house and dreams of pitching Brooklyn to victory in the World Series....

And so, when the country boy from the small mining village stands alone on the mound in Yankee Stadium in the most demanding moment of one of the world's few truly epic sports events, and courageously, skillfully pitches his way to a success as complete, melodramatic and extravagant as that ever dreamed by any boy, the American chapter of the International Order of Frustrated Dreamers rises as one man and roars its recognition.

Excerpted from an original story published in
SPORTS ILLUSTRATED, *January 2, 1956*

DUEL OF THE FOUR-MINUTE MEN

BY PAUL O'NEIL

In May of 1954, Dr. Roger Bannister of England became the first man to break the four-minute mile. Six weeks later, Australia's John Landy became the second. In August, just in time for SI's premier issue, came the long-anticipated duel between the two men, in the British Empire Games. Their meeting was historic: For the first time, two runners broke the four-minute barrier in the same race.

The art of running the mile consists, in essence, of reaching the threshold of unconsciousness at the instant of breasting the tape. It is not an easy process, even in a set-piece race against time, for the body rebels against such agonizing usage and must be disciplined by the spirit and the mind. It is infinitely more difficult in the amphitheater of competition, for then the runner must remain alert and cunning despite the fogs of fatigue and pain; his instinctive calculation of pace must encompass maneuver for position, and he must harbor strength to answer the moves of other men before expending his last reserves in the war of the homestretch....

At first glance they seemed like an odd pair of gladiators. Like most distance men both look frail and thin in street clothes. Landy has a mop of dark, curly hair, the startled brown eyes of a deer, a soft voice with little trace of the Australian snarl, and a curious habit of bending forward and clasping his hands before his chest when making a conversational point....

[Bannister] too would be the last man in the world to be singled out of a crowd as an athlete. He is stooped and negligent in carriage; he has lank blond hair, a high-cheeked, peaked face, and a polite and noncommittal upper-class British voice....

[The race begins and all eyes are on the two men.]

As Landy moved, Bannister moved too. They ran Landy first, Bannister second at the end of the stretch and the duel had begun. "Time for the first lap," the loudspeakers grated as they entered the turn, "fifty-eight seconds." Then bedlam began too. It increased as Landy moved away—five yards, ten yards, fifteen yards—in the backstretch of the second lap, and Bannister let him go. "It was a frightening thing to do," said the Englishman later, "but I believed he was running too fast. I had to save for my final burst and hope I could catch him in time."

Landy's time was 1:58 at the half. The groundwork for a four-minute mile had been laid. The field had faded far to the rear. The duelists ran alone in front with Landy still making the pace. But now, yard by yard, easily, almost imperceptibly Bannister was regaining ground. He was within striking distance as they fled into the last, decisive quarter amid a hysterical uproar of applause. He stayed there on the turn. Two hundred yards from home, Landy made his bid for decision and victory. But Bannister refused to be shaken, and with 90 yards to go he lengthened his plunging stride. He came up shoulder to shoulder, fought for momentum, pulled away to a four-yard lead and ran steadily and stylishly through a deafening clamor to the tape. He fell, arms flapping, legs buckling, into the arms of the English team manager a split second after the race.

Excerpted from an original story published in
SPORTS ILLUSTRATED*, August 16, 1954*

THE SAVERS VS. THE SPOILERS

BY COLES PHINIZY

SI's commitment to the environment is as old as the magazine itself, reflecting the belief that a proper enjoyment of the outdoors includes an awareness of its fragility. In 1961, associate editor Coles Phinizy traveled to the Alaskan wilderness and filed this report on the threat to that majestic and challenging land.

Two hundred years ago, before bigger ideas were thrust upon them, the Indians of southeast Alaska believed that the creator of all things was a large black raven. If by chance a Great Raven does have the final say when this world ends, the human race will be in for it. The raven is by nature tidy and efficient, gregarious but still free, living from day to day raucously confident that when one carcass is picked clean, another will turn up. No Alaskan raven would ever, like a man or beaver, spend its short life gnawing and toiling for the future, stockpiling surpluses in untidy hummocks about the land. Most of the world has been appropriated for human use so that more and more men can be packed into large urban wallows, like brood sows on a collective farm. No raven in its right mind would approve of this. Unless men mend their ways, on Judgment Day the Great Raven will consign most of the human species to one of the lower levels of hell, along with the beavers and ground squirrels.

There have been a few men the Great Raven could accept—perhaps among the acceptable would be Kublai Khan and James Audubon, because they cared for birds; possibly also the poet Poe (he understood ravens), and quite possibly Biologist James Brooks, age 38, chief of the Game Division of the State of Alaska. In the confusion of the 20th century, it is doubtful whether Biologist Jim Brooks, or any one of his 19 widely scattered assistants, will ever achieve historical distinction as a conservationist, but they all deserve some reward in the hereafter, for they are responsible for a wilderness as challenging as any the great khans ruled or Audubon ever saw....

Because of its size and its elemental hostility to the casual advances of man, Alaska is today the last true U.S. wilderness, the last chance for man to prosper intelligently in free association with companion species. There is no doubt that with the increasing pressure of human population, the Alaskan wilderness, too, will go. Given the motive, the technicians will find a way to tame Alaska and cut it down to size.... The ducks and brant of the Kuskokwim flats will have no place to go, but they will have to go. And when they go, they will be gone forever....

Since the human race is the self-appointed proprietor of the whole land, in the final analysis the future of any wild species depends on the attitude of men toward it. Men do not tolerate any predator half so efficient as themselves, and on this count, the wolf is doomed. The brown bears and grizzlies of Alaska in time will be reduced to the status of public-park wards, desirable but innately

feared. The Alaskan has no objection to coexistence now, while there is plenty of room for men and bears, but he's not for integration—he doesn't want his kids going to school with bears. Even away from town, an Alaskan finding a grizzly or brown bear on his favorite fishing stream often will shoot it and conscientiously report the kill as self-defense. On the weekend the fisherman has left the tedium of his city work to re-create himself in the bear's world. But when the bear comes to the stream for the mutual purpose of fishing, the man presumes the bear is threatening him.

The mountain sheep and goats are reasonably secure for the future. They have a good reputation among people. They do not eat children. Moreover, their range is a rough one. People like

to visit it, the high ground of the sheep and goats, but few would want to live there. The Alaskan deer will do fairly well. When the need arises, the deer can be fitted into fairly small corners, persisting under wise management. The restless caribou will decline. They are getting their antlers tangled in the phone wires occasionally now, and when roads and other communication lines cut unnatural barriers across their land, the effect may be too much for them. The caribou will probably become park wards, to be harvested by hunters on a quota basis, as buffalo are now in some of the shooting galleries of the lower states.

The moose and black bear have some advantage over the others. They are acquiring the status of lovable bums who often show up in town, the bear usually heading directly for the city dump, the moose drifting around, eating shrubbery, chasing (and being chased by) dogs and children. The Alaskan may shoot a grizzly 100 yards from him on the stream, but he tolerates the moose that walks through his back fence and tramples his cabbage garden.... A construction worker living in a trailer telephones the Anchorage game office: every morning for a week a moose has chased him when he tried to get in his car to go to work. That was O.K., but now the moose is kicking in the side of his trailer. Can anything be done?...

The bear and moose that drift in and out of town are but a sliver of the total population, but the biologist must spend some time on them. "It is one of our ways," Jim Brooks said recently, "of encouraging the public to think of these animals as objects of value. We may never be able to produce people and bears on the same ground. We have limited manpower and still so much game that we cannot manage it fully. But we have the duty of keeping people aware that what they see today can go tomorrow, and is worth caring for, worth preserving now. Alaska is a place where all kinds come, among them the malcontents of crowded places to re-create their souls. If we sack Alaska, where do we go next?"

Excerpted from an original story published in SPORTS ILLUSTRATED, *January 16, 1961*

THE HEAVEN BELOW

BY CLARE BOOTHE LUCE

The amazing Clare Boothe Luce—war correspondent, playwright, ambassador, U.S. representative, managing editor of VANITY FAIR, wife of TIME founder Henry Luce—decided to take up skin-diving in her fifties. The result was a series of vivid articles for SI that describe the wonder of the undersea world.

How hard, how very hard, it is to tell anybody who has never been there about the underwater world. The Iron Curtain is, after all, a mere political figure of speech. But the Salt Curtain of the ocean's surface is a physical fact that separates two physically quite different worlds. Underwater techniques, sensations and sights all present real semantic and terminological difficulties for those who try to describe them to the uninitiate. It is not easy to communicate the physical experience of moving and breathing in a medium which is 800 times denser than air and which radically modifies, if not nullifies, the pull of gravity. Man, an erect animal, moves most naturally forward, in a vertical position on a horizontal plane. Underwater he moves most easily in a prone position, though he can also with facility walk or stand on feet or hands, and move up or down, forward or backward, in any position. He can imitate, however slowly or awkwardly, the motions of pipefish or crab, flounder, eel or octopus. Underwater he is relatively omnimobile.

His underwater visual experience is equally "unnatural." He moves in a world of constantly shifting perspectives. There are no horizons where the eye level shifts with every movement of your body. Even under optimum light conditions, you can seldom see clearly more than a hundred feet in any direction. The eye can measure distance only from point to point within that circle of visibility. Even the shallow-water scuba diver has the sensation at all times of circling at the heart of an enormous opaque fish bowl, whose globular, mysterious sides advance and recede with his own motions. He proceeds like a small chrysalis, silent in his sea-green cocoon and essentially alone, for his fellow divers seem to have an eerie habit of gliding away like gray ghosts through the green walls of his bowl into unseen bowls of their own. Looking up, he sees nothing but the opaque silver lid of the Salt Curtain....

The sensuous experiences of the underwater world are perhaps hardest of all to describe. In those "chambers deep, where waters sleep, and unknown treasures pave the floor," what fishes like flowers, what stones like trees! What crenelated walls, parapets, spires and grottoes the skeletons of coral make! What labyrinthine groves and gardens wave where the live coral are still building! The coral reefs are a golden girdle of dead and living cities, which dwarf in their age and beauty all the cities of man. For how many eons have they waited—must they still wait—for their Dante and Shakespeare?

Excerpted from an original story published in
SPORTS ILLUSTRATED, *August 11, 1958*

THE MOST EXCITING FIVE MINUTES

BY TEX MAULE

Tex Maule is best remembered for his coverage of pro football. But in the early years of the magazine, he wrote stories on track and field as well, including this memorable account of the decathlon showdown between Rafer Johnson and C.K. Yang, filed from the 1960 Summer Games in Rome.

His strong, cold face impassive, the big man pounded steadily through the dank chill of the Roman night. Two steps in front of him, Formosa's Chuan Kwang Yang moved easily. In the gap between them lay the Olympic decathlon championship.

Four other men were in the race, but none of the 50,000 people huddled against the cold in Rome's Stadio Olimpico saw them. They watched Rafer Johnson and Yang in their lonely, desperate race against time and each other, and as the race spun on and on they began to yell.

Johnson, his eyes fixed on the back of Yang's neck, did not hear them. To win this decathlon championship, he had to punch his big, magnificently muscled body through the fastest 1,500 meters of his life. Yang usually is 10 seconds better than Johnson in the 1,500; he had only to maintain this margin to win an Olympic gold medal.

Watching, knowing Johnson's limitations in this race, you kept expecting that two-step gap to widen. But Johnson has a relentless pride that goads him far beyond the limits of normal human endeavor, and now that pride kept him plodding doggedly behind Yang, a bigger, darker shadow of the handsome Chinese.

On the last lap Yang tried desperately to move away. He managed a slow spring down the backstretch, and Johnson moved easily with him. He kicked again off the turn into the last straight, and Johnson kept pace. The exhausted Yang's head wobbled. Once, despairingly, he looked back, and Johnson was still there; and he was there at the finish, 1.2 seconds behind Yang. Johnson ran this 1,500 meters (in 4:49.7) at the end of two days of extraordinarily taxing competition, six seconds faster than he has ever run before in his life. He finished the tensest five minutes of the entire Games—five minutes in which the tension grew and grew and grew until it seemed like a thin, high sound in the stadium—composed and relaxed and almost fresh....

Johnson's point total, 8,392, was well below the world record he set in the U.S. Olympic trials, principally because of a very poor performance in the high hurdles and mediocre ones in the javelin and discus. But in two of the last three events, under strong pressure from Yang, he produced career bests in both the pole vault and the 1,500 meters.

"All I could think of in that 1,500 meters was 'this is the last race I'll ever run in my life,'" he said later. He was preparing to leave the stadium, tired now, let down from the strain. Someone asked him if he were going to catch up on his sleep.

"No," said Johnson quietly. "Not right away. I don't think so. First I'm going to walk and walk and look at the moon and think about it."

Excerpted from an original story published in
Sports Illustrated, *September 19, 1960*

SUGAR'S SHOW GOES ON

BY GILBERT ROGIN

Gilbert Rogin, now the corporate editor of Time Inc. Magazines, worked in the SI ranks for 24 years before ascending to the position of managing editor in 1979. When he visited Sugar Ray Robinson, the former champion was in the declining stages of his brilliant career, one that had seen him win the middleweight title a record five times. But Robinson had just lost his crown in a lackluster bout and many were questioning why he continued fighting. Rogin's report offered a vivid portrait of the forces that drove him on.

"I'm such a blessed man," Ray Robinson is fond of saying. "God's given me Sugar Ray Robinson." Robinson's original name was Walker Smith Jr. "I gave it away where I started at," he says, "a skinny kid in a hole of a basement gym. I wasn't old enough to fight but this Robinson was and I took his name. I meant to give the guy's name back, but...." The Sugar part he earned. "'Sweet-looking boy you got there,' man told my manager, George Gainford. 'Sweet as sugar,' George told him." And, "doucement, doucement," Gainford would cry up to him from the corner of the ring in years gone by.

But not last week in Boston, where, fighting with the desperate, jerky violence of a character in an old silent film, Robinson lost his middleweight title, for the fifth time, to Paul Pender, a fireman from neighboring Brookline, Mass....

"That isn't Ray Robinson in there tonight," a fight manager had said at ringside. Will Robinson be in there another night? He is entitled to a rematch within 90 days if he wants it, and he said he did. "I been a winner and a loser," Robinson has said. "Other people lose, they go crazy. I always moved ahead." Moving ahead or backpedaling, losing or winning, Robinson remains one of the most fascinating men in sport, flamboyant, egocentric, an artist....

There is one image of Robinson as a suspicious and arrogant man. It is an image shaped by those who have tried to do business with him and found him an intractable if capricious bargainer. He is acutely sensitive to the harsh fact that Negroes and boxers are exploited, that it requires great wieldings of moxie to survive. "I was born into poverty," says Robinson. "I know what it is to need. Whatever's due me, I'll stand up and fight for." "We're both Taurus," says Evelyn, "bullheaded, stubborn, but we help people in trouble."

Indeed, Robinson is impulsively generous. "I've seen so many poor people all over the world," he says. "They're destitute. I can't say no. I've got tenants here three, four months behind in their rent [Robinson owns a number of apartment houses.] What am I going to do? Women, they have to work, support children. I met an old woman—Mom—in this barbecue place fumbling through pennies to eat those greasy ribs. I brought Mom into my club, introduced her to the crew. At least I know she eats. She must be up in her 70's...."

There is an image of Robinson as a man of flash, pose and exuberance whose hair is brushed by his valet and tied up in a pale flowered kerchief. It is his flourish, his mark. "He is an entertainer," says his mother. "He loves to get a laugh." But no matter how often he looks in the mirror he finds, beneath his glittering hair, himself: inaccessible, ambiguous, vulnerable.

There is an image of Robinson as the finest prizefighter of his age. It is an image flawed by the hard uses of time, but it was true, it was true....

His next stop was at Professor Hall's, where he has studied classical voice for a year and a half. (Robinson, when he retired from the ring for two years in 1952, had a brief, highly paid career as a song-and-dance man. The feeling was that, for a fighter, he was a first-rate hoofer.) Professor Jarahal Hall is a short, elderly man, with long, white hair parted in the middle, and a serene manner. His studio is in a small room in an old building in Harlem. Under his piano is a bongo drum. An electric heater glows orange in the corner.

"Don't jazz Handel," Professor Hall told Robinson when he came in. "You take him straight...."

Robinson sang Handel's *Ombra mai fu,* and *Il Lacerato Spirito* from Verdi's *Simon Boccanegra.* "That Italian," he said. "Nothing more beautiful." He knew the pieces by heart and wandered away from the piano, his eyes half-closed, to where the window looked out on the white winter street. His head was back on his broad neck the way a globe of the world sits on its standard.

It is the way he looks when he is fooling with the jump rope in Harry Wiley's Broadway Gym, where a sign on the wall says, "The gentleman boxer has the most friends," to which somebody has added in pencil "and the most losses." Not jumping the rope, but holding the handles carelessly with one hand, whirling it, slapping it against the floor, dancing abandoned, clowning, swaggering steps as Wiley, his trainer, whistles *Come to the Mardi Gras,* and maybe another whistler joins in tentatively, and Otis Woodward, his sparring partner, hits the bongo. And so they whistle together, and Robinson, strutting, ragging there, becomes a tenant of some distant stage, some old, gaudy night. The whistlers go surely from one song to another and Robinson, grinning, winking the while, plays his prancing part in the splendid belief that he can go on almost forever but watching the dedicated faces about him to see if they believe it, too. The bell on the electric roundtimer rings, and three go quickly to him. Two bend down on either side and massage his legs, and one holds up a towel. Robinson gives him his face and when the man takes the towel away he is grinning marvelously still.

When Robinson went to his cafe from the gym, a little, ragged kid stood in the entrance, holding out his hand. "Give me a dime, Sugar Ray," he said.

Robinson looked down at the wise face as if he saw Walker Smith Jr., who danced for pennies on the sidewalks of Detroit. "What did I tell you about begging?" he said and entered his place grandly, as if it were Versailles. A square clock on the wall, painted the same elusive color as his car, with gloved arms for hands, miniature ring posts and ropes, told him it was late.

Excerpted from an original story published in SPORTS ILLUSTRATED, *February 1, 1960*

12 DAYS BEFORE THE MAST

BY GILBERT ROGIN

When Gilbert Rogin embarked upon a transatlantic race aboard the 55-foot yawl Santana, it was assumed that he would return with romantic tales of the sea and its many charms. Instead he came back an unregenerate sailing-hater. This is the story that explains how he resisted the ocean's lure.

The ruts and tracks of life are made early, and mine never led to sea, so I don't know what others lose and find there. The oceans—Pacific, Atlantic, Indian and so forth—which call others like Roland passionately blowing on his horn are, to me, as oppressive as dark rooms full of old, heavy furniture. What can you say about the sea? "High interiors and kelpy bottoms"? Chekhov said that you can say nothing significant about the sea except that it is big. But the sea is also—out of sight of land and off maps—perfectly round. Sailors call it the round locker. Traveling, one remains in its center as though fixed with a pin.

Several weeks before crossing from San Pedro, Calif. to Honolulu on the 55-foot yawl *Santana*, in the Transpacific race, I was swimming at Key Biscayne, Fla. I wore a reed hat in the water that completely covered my face, the hat apparently floating, like an old bird's nest, on the Atlantic. Its brim, my horizon, was three inches from my lips. I moved within that silent shade, unaware of gain or tidal loss, and it was that way on the *Santana*. Her horizons were 20 miles off, but her sea and illusory progress were the same. *Santana* had the broad, variable sky for a hat: after sunset, great fires burning beyond the sea's melancholy rim, clouds and apocalyptic shafts and strokes of light, squalls with black manes of rain, a bos'n bird, its tail a knitting needle, fluttering about the masthead, never seen approaching or noticed departing, more omen than bird.

The sea, too, in itself is quiet. Even in the most remote part of the land you can hear something—an insect's minor progress, a dislodged stone. At sea the noise is from the boat, the junction of the boat with wind and water, sea or rain.

And, to a sailor's purposes, the ocean is empty. This is a catalog of all the living things we saw during our 12 days' passage. One whale blowing dispiritedly, its spout a feeble, windy fountain in its old, soft gray head. Flying fish. One came aboard; it was only an inch long but perfectly formed, its back as blue and shining as the sea it flew wildly out of, its eyes immense, round, blind in its dying, its wings, when we spread them, no larger than a bee's. A narrow, silver fish that washed into the cockpit at night; we shone the flashlight on it, held it speculatively and then threw it back, but it was already dead. A squid. It came in over the weather rail. I fished with it from the stern when the sun rose, but it was quickly torn from the hook. Three bugs; one on the underside of a hatch cover, another vanishing down a cockpit drain, the last in the fo'c'sle. Albatrosses with white faces like clowns. Shearwaters. Little petrellike birds. Bos'n birds. Spots of phosphorescence in the wake betraying anatomies. And one white bird searching like prudent Noah's dove. Many days we saw nothing.

I now sit in a hotel in Waikiki, with green mountains and the roar of air conditioners at my back. The sea is the other way, beyond the wall, but I feel its tug at night; I dream about boats, which I have never dreamed of before, and the bed and carpeted floor tilt like *Santana*'s decks. It is as if some fundamental remnant of the Pacific still washed in my bilges and responded like the tide. I am back, huddled in the cockpit in the dark with the starboard watch. We sit about it like old men with pale feet in a bathtub, past reflection and communication: all has been said and all seen; they stare at their toes because toes have no meaning. We have said nothing and won't; we are like preserves in a jar. It is an intimacy only of bodies. What have we in common but the heaving boat, a thermos of coffee and dreams of the islands? Of course, I speak for myself here, as always. We were four strangers meeting by convention like a Geneva commission, polite on account of manners or the unbearable consequences of violating, by honesty or rudeness, the equanimity of our confinement, desperately telling jokes one after another as though we were lost and blowing on our last fire, laughing uproariously, giggling, listening to cheap night music, when we could find it, on Babe's radio and, for hours in the cloudy nights, silent....

I have to remind myself. Things have a way of receding, like balloons astern or punchlines of the best jokes. Just now Wally phoned. He wants me on his starboard watch for the Acapulco race. He knows my sentiments, but he told me I'd think differently in a few weeks. Is this what they mean by sea change? But I have devised a means to remind myself. Next time they want to send me to sea I'll lock myself in the bathrom for 12 days with canned goods, Sterno, an electric fan and an alarm clock. I'll sit in the tub for hours, fully dressed, with the fan blowing across me, taking a cold shower. Then I'll go out, eat, undress and go back to the tub to sleep. Four hours later I'll put on my wet clothes, take another shower and so on.

What did I learn at sea? I know about endurance, but I do not class it as a virtue. What benefit is it to lie a few inches below the overhead in the fo'c'sle as the boat pitches and tosses so you have to hold tightly to the pipes or chains or be thrown; to lie there with a track meet going on overhead when the port watch changes sail; to listen to the seas washing over the foredeck and the ominous gurgling of the bow waves as the boat lifts its heavy head and sets it down? It's like living in a washing machine. Then they call you out, stumbling and cursing, your arm aching from hanging on while you slept, hopping about in a bizarre jig to try to get on your foul-weather gear, a suit notable for drying rapidly on the outside while remaining clammy as a cave's wall in the interior, then climbing up the companionway ladder and changing places, grunting greetings, with the port watch. I've known discomfort—and this discomfort was minor if prolonged—but discomfort is not a virtue, either.

I've known boredom, too, but never so total an apathy, where the bleakness and monotony of the sea seem to invade the mind, drown it, so that you cannot even rescue yourself with reveries, those comforting journeys. But my dreams at night, as though compensating, were extraordinarily vivid. Ask me what I did in real life when I was at sea and I will relate to you my dreams.

Excerpted from an original story published in SPORTS ILLUSTRATED, *January 16, 1961*

YOU LOVE WOODY OR HATE HIM

BY ROY TERRELL

For 19 years before becoming SI's third managing editor, in 1974, Roy Terrell worked as a writer and an editor for the magazine, frequently covering the events and personalities of college football. In 1962, he wrote this feature on Woody Hayes, the controversial curmudgeon of a coach at Ohio State. It is a portrait that stood the test of time as Hayes remained a maddeningly complex figure throughout his 33-year coaching career.

> When the One Great Scorer comes
> to write against your name
> He writes—not that you won or
> lost—but how you played
> the game.
> —Grantland Rice

> Rubbish.
> —Wayne Woodrow Hayes

Woody Hayes will be 50 years old next Valentine's Day, if he makes it, and sometimes you wonder. Football is a happy game, even in the Big Ten. Chrysanthemum sales boom, old grads have a good excuse to get squiffed, hardly anyone goes to class, and if the halfback gets a black eye his girl will kiss it. Only Woody Hayes must suffer. To him, football is less a game than a 20th century torture device, and on his own private rack, on a hundred Saturday afternoons in the vast stadiums of the Midwest, he has been subjected to agonies that would make your hair look like Harpo Marx's....

While the avalanche of sound from 80,000 hysterics rolls down on him, he stands alone, a short, powerful man with a barrel chest and a barrel stomach. It is cold, but he wears no coat. His hands are balled fists below his shirtsleeves, and perspiration streams from beneath the old gray baseball cap with the scarlet letter O, as in O-HI-O, that he has worn so long it now seems a part of his head. He prowls the sidelines like a bear in a pit, shouting in fury at the officials, snarling in frustration at his team, at his coaches, at himself. Deprive Woody Hayes of victory and he would die, just as surely as a man in space suddenly deprived of his oxygen supply; and so,

until victory is assured, Woody dies. With each Ohio State mistake, with each fumble and penalty and interception, he dies. It would be a pitiful sight were it not for one thing: at the rate at which Ohio State makes mistakes, no one should have to worry about burying Hayes for at least another 132 years....

....Success alone can never explain the passion that Hayes has been known to arouse. You either love him or you hate him, and if you happen to be one of the few with no opinion you may just as well form one, since he probably has an opinion about you. He has an opinion about everything else. If you choose to disapprove of Woody Hayes, there is a wide selection of reasons.

He drives his players with a ferocity that would make a Marine Corps drill instructor look like Mary playing with her lamb. The football that he coaches—the crunching up-the-middle trap and off-tackle smash—is about as inspiring as a radish. It has furnished the sport with a now-tired phrase—three yards and a cloud of dust—and so far as you can discover in Columbus, Knute Rockne, Gus Dorais and the forward pass have not yet been invented. His own faculty complains that Woody's football success is distorting the academic image of a great university, and Hayes, a professor himself, sometimes attends faculty meetings to roar denunciations of his detractors.

Reporters assigned to cover the Ohio State dressing room decide to bury their grandmothers on days when it appears that the Buckeyes might not win. If Hayes is a bad loser—he has refused to shake hands with an opposing coach who beat him—he is also a bad winner, sometimes heaping scorn and humiliation upon a defeated opponent's head. He has a temper like a toothless cat. Most damning of all, he always says what he thinks. In fact, Woody Hayes passes up more opportunities to keep his mouth shut in one year than most people do in a lifetime.

In the middle of a game he once ran 60 yards, probably a record for fat coaches, in order to accuse Big Ten officials of allowing the defense to play dirty football. "You're overofficiating the offense and letting the defense get away with murder," he snarled. "The Bible says turn the other cheek, but I'll be damned if I'll tell my kids to do that when they'll just get it fractured!"...

While talk of education sounds hypocritical on the lips of some coaches, no one can question Hayes's sincerity on the subject. "I've never heard him talk about how many All-Americas he's had, or how many undefeated teams," says another Big Ten coach, "but he'll drive you crazy telling you about all his boys who have become doctors and lawyers and dentists and engineers."...

"I don't guess there is anything that I believe in more than this university and the value of the education that a boy receives here," says Hayes...."Of the 27 freshmen who came here on football scholarships in the fall of 1959, 24 will be around this fall. Normally you can expect 40% of the students entering a big university to graduate. On the Ohio State football squad we graduate 70% to 80%. How can anyone condemn college football when they see a figure like that?...

The greatest speech that Woody Hayes ever made was delivered before an Ohio State alumni group last fall at the Hollenden Hotel in Cleveland. Arriving from the airport, Hayes was met in the hotel lobby by reporters. "The Ohio State Faculty Council has just voted 28 to 25 against letting the team go to the Rose Bowl," he was told. Hayes dropped his bag and walked out. For two hours he paced the streets alone, thinking what this meant to his players, who had been working for the championship and trip for four years, thinking what the decision meant to the Ohio State fans, to the school, to himself. When he finally arrived at the speaker's platform, he was remarkably composed, for Woody Hayes.

"I don't agree with those 28 no votes," he said, "but I respect the integrity of the men who cast them, if not their intelligence. I would not want football to drive a line of cleavage in our university. Football is not worth that."

Not everyone has fallen in love with Woody Hayes, even yet. He still pops off, he has a terrible temper, and defeat, when and if it comes, will jar him as before. This season he may not throw even one pass. But the old joke—"The football team should have a university of which it can be proud"—does not sound so absurd now.

Excerpted from an original story published in SPORTS ILLUSTRATED, *September 24, 1962*

The Age of
AUDA

1963-1975

CITY

THE AGE OF AUDACITY

BY LEIGH MONTVILLE

am the same age as Joe Willie Namath. I am one year older than Billie Jean King, one year younger than Muhammad Ali. This was my time. The years were my years, 1963 through 1975. The Age of Audacity. I was a foot soldier in the same army, a traveler on the same trip toward adulthood. The vehicle of choice, I believe, was a Volkswagen minibus that was painted in Day-Glo colors.

I sat in the back.

My first out-of-town assignment for a little Connecticut newspaper was Joe Willie's first day as a professional football player. The Peekskill Military Academy in New York. The rest of the New York Jets were already on the field. Joe Willie took his time. He walked across the grass from the locker room at a slow, even pace. A bunch of kids were around him. He was signing autographs....

I was 20 years old in 1963, a junior in college. I still used Stri-Dex medicated pads. I was 32 years old by the end of '75. I was married, the father of two kids. I owned a mortgage that I could not afford, two cars and an untreatable stretch of crabgrass. In the time that passed, I watched phenoms of my age become seasoned veterans of my age. Joe Willie became a millionaire and did ads for panty hose and popcorn poppers. My time.

I saw Julius Erving play when he was in college. He was the best-kept secret in basketball. The University of Massachusetts. He had an Afro the size of a beach ball. He would swoop past these startled kids and jam over their heads. No one had ever seen anything like it. You think Michael Jordan is amazing? Julius was a positive revelation. There would be no Michael Jordan today if there had never been a Julius....

When you are very young, a child, the players on the major league level are a collection of gods in a temple on a hill. They are keepers of grand secrets, cartoon characters who are larger than every day life. I once heard a relief pitcher, Joe Sambito, describe how he always had believed that the players simply lived at the ballpark, that Mickey Mantle and Roger Maris and all the rest of them went into the Yankee Stadium clubhouse to sleep, eat, maybe play a little bumper pool and reappear the next day. That is young. When you are old, even middle-aged old, the perspective changes. The players are talented kids coming off a conveyor belt that never stops. They are crops. Crops of kids. Coming from Iowa or someplace. Bigger, better, faster every year.

Ah, but when you are the same as the athletes—*your time*, a decade, perhaps, maybe 15 years—the games are best. These are *your* people. They have listened to the same music, watched the same movies, lived through the same historical events. *Your* people. The best of *your* people.

I saw Princeton with Bill Bradley at the Holiday Festival at Madison Square Garden. That's the old Madison Square Garden, on Eighth Avenue. I snuck into the game, sat on the stairs in the balcony. Bradley was fantastic. Princeton was playing Michigan, which was No. 1 at the time. Cazzie Russell was good, but I don't think Bradley missed a shot....

What happened in my time? There was a war in Vietnam. There was a party at Woodstock. Hair grew long and pants grew wide and imaginations suddenly added the strangest colors. The tromp-tromp of the Baby Boomers just kept going and going, this big bulge passing through the garden hose. There was peace and love and Abbie Hoffman and the Beatles and Jack Nicholson wearing a football helmet, riding along, with the wind blowing, on the back of Peter Fonda's motorcycle. What was the bumper sticker? QUESTION AUTHORITY. No other generation had ever grabbed its own time with such force or determination. Or so it seemed.

Sports was touched by all of this. Joe Willie slouched and spat tobacco juice into a paper cup and guaranteed what he would do. Muhammad did not step forward at the draft board in Houston and became a hero and a villain at the same time. Ken Harrelson wore something called a Nehru jacket and posed next to his circular water bed. Tommie Smith and John Carlos wore black gloves and raised their fists defiantly from the victory stand at Mexico City. The Oakland A's wore gold uniforms and white shoes and moustaches that made them resemble Saracen hordes invading some pitiful small town in search of plunder.

I was in Muhammad's dressing room the day before he fought Chuck Wepner in Cleveland. Muhammad was lying on a trainer's table. Around him were Billy Eckstine, Redd Foxx and James Brown, the soul singer. Muhammad kept asking Foxx to tell jokes. Foxx would tell a joke. Everyone would laugh. Muhammad would ask for another one. Foxx would tell another one. It was as if you had stumbled into the royal palace and were seated near the king as he put his court jesters to work. Would James Brown get up and sing next? Power and athletic greatness and funk seemed to have been molded together in one incredible place....

The old rules did not apply. The college and high school coaches saw this first when they asked their young warriors to run through the nearest cinder block walls. "Why?" the young warriors asked. This was revolutionary. A first. Was there a town in America that didn't have a controversy between a coach and a kid about the amount of hair that should be removed by the local barber? Was there a town where the coach won the argument? Logic became much

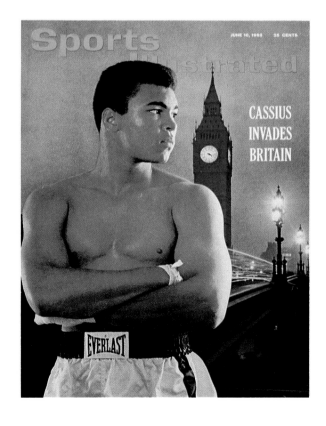

73

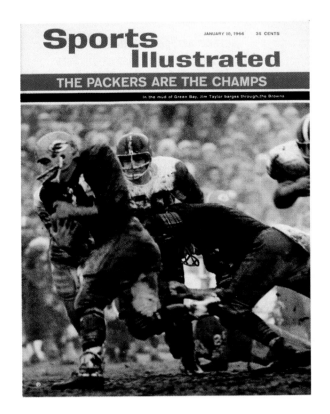

more important than the old rules.

The black athlete took control. More logic. If he could run faster, jump higher, score more often, then why wasn't he playing? He played. On all levels. The breakthrough that Jackie Robinson made in the '50s was finally extended to the lower tiers of the depth chart. A second-string outfielder or a backup wide receiver suddenly might be black. Sport probably became the first true equal opportunity employer. If you looked on the NBA court sometimes, you might notice that all 10 players were black. Logic.

I went with the New England Patriots to Birmingham, where they played an exhibition against the Miami Dolphins. The neighborhood around Legion Field was a ghetto. The houses were falling down, needed paint, needed just about everything. There was silence on the team bus as everyone looked at all of this. Finally, a black player in the back said, "Thank god for football."

Football—professional football—was the big game for the first time in history. I am not exactly sure how or why this happened, except it obviously had something to do with speed and pace and violence and action. Confrontation. The pastoral beauty of baseball was put into a vault for a while, filed away for later use in a less turbulent time. Professional football first captured the national attention for three hours on a Sunday afternoon, then expanded to a six-hour doubleheader, then took control of Monday nights as well. Monday night football! The voice of Howard Cosell was wallpaper in the average American home. Wallpaper with giant swirls and floral patterns.

Television and football seemed to be a perfect marriage. The game fit into the 21-inch screen as if it had been developed by network executives. Each year, there seemed to be another technological improvement that brought the viewer closer and closer to the action. The Green Bay Packers ruled in the beginning. The Pittsburgh Steelers ruled at the end. The Super Bowl was invented in the middle. It became almost a religious holiday.

The first Super Bowl I saw was Super Bowl III. I went to the press room before the game, and a man from the National Football League was distributing mimeographed sheets. The sheets contained quotes from the players about the upcoming game. Add adjectives and water, and an instant story could be concocted. What was this? I had the uneasy feeling I had landed at a sports event run by a Fortune 500 Corporation....

Advances in television technology also brought the athlete back to human dimensions. This happened in all sports. What do you have to say for yourself, champ? The champs finally could talk, and everyone else could listen. Players became personalities. They weren't rumors anymore, pictures on a tavern wall. They were residents of the family living room. Personalities. Power began to shift. The people who performed suddenly started to become stronger than the venerable old men who directed the work and counted the receipts. New leagues appeared in football, basketball and hockey. Options to be contemplated and explored.

I remember being in the office of Red Auerbach, the general manager of the Boston Celtics, when he was finishing a negotiating session with a draft choice named Dave Robisch. Red wound up by giving Robisch a pile of Celtics promotional items. A couple of key chains, some posters, maybe a towel, a plastic gym bag. All the giveaways from the past season. I remember thinking how all of this largess must have been impressive in the old days, but that it didn't seem to be working now. The guy looked at his key chains and the rest of the stuff like, "What the heck is this junk?" He ended up signing with the other league, the ABA....

The individual counted. This was the lesson of the time. Be outrageous. Be safe. Be what you want to be. Say what you want. Do what you want. Don't like the fans? Richie Allen scuffed the word *boo* in the dirt in Philadelphia. Tennis players wore colors other than white and talked back to the line judges. This was a time to flourish, to expand. Do what you want.

Hockey defensemen, led by Bobby Orr, now took the puck from one end of the rink to the other in mad dashes. The one-on-one game of the basketball playground invaded the colleges and the pros. Slam dunks became as common as free throws. Joe Willie passed whenever he damn well pleased. Reggie Jackson hit home runs and ran the bases as if he had liberated France all by himself. Why be dull? These were the children of rock 'n' roll. They knew how to strut.

I remember talking with Frenchy Fuqua, a running back for the Steelers. He wore shoes with high glass heels. Inside the heels was water. Inside the water were goldfish. One inside each heel of each shoe. Frenchy said the fish enjoyed the activity when he walked. I remember being inside the locker room of the Stanley Cup champion Boston Bruins one day after practice when the radio was turned loud and suddenly all of the players were singing and dancing to the words, "You're 16, you're beautiful, and you're mine." I remember listening to a golfer named Bill Mallon, a local guy who had made the PGA Tour, describe how he and his partner had the first tee times at some bank classic and decided to run from shot to shot to set a record for the fastest round of tournament golf ever played. The PGA officials were not amused.

I'll argue with anyone about *my* time, convinced as everyone is from every generation that he lived through the most important moments of all history. There'll never be another Joe Willie. There'll never be another Muhammad. Not even another Joe Frazier. Secretariat was the best horse there ever was. No one ever will go undefeated the way the Miami Dolphins did. No one ever will dominate college basketball the way Kareem Abdul-Jabbar and Bill Walton did. There will never be another chess player as good as Bobby Fischer. And Evel Knievel....

I stood on the edge of Snake River Canyon in 1974 when Evel took off in his red-white-and-blue rocket. There was a powerful whoosh of white smoke and everyone cheered. The rocket climbed into the air and then a parachute suddenly appeared. The flight had been altered. Evel had panicked. The rocket floated down on the same side of the canyon that it took off from. Everyone ran to their television sets. A hatch was opened. Evel appeared.

You can say what you want.

There'll never be another Evel Knievel.

U.S. OLYMPIC CHAMPION PEGGY FLEMING

1963

The Winner's Circle

Baseball: Los Angeles Dodgers
NFL/AFL: Chicago Bears/San Diego Chargers
College Football: University of Texas
NHL: Toronto Maple Leafs
NBA: Boston Celtics
College Basketball: Loyola (Ill.)
Masters: Jack Nicklaus
U.S. Open (golf): Julius Boros
British Open: Bob Charles
PGA: Jack Nicklaus
Australian Open: Roy Emerson
French Open: Roy Emerson
Wimbledon: Chuck McKinley
U.S. Open (tennis): Rafael Osuna
Australian Open: Margaret Smith Court
French Open: Lesley Turner
Wimbledon: Margaret Smith Court
U.S. Open (tennis): Maria Bueno
Kentucky Derby: Chateaugay
Preakness: Candy Spots
Belmont: Chateaugay
Indianapolis 500: Parnelli Jones

Court wizard Bob Cousy performs his magic one last time to lead Boston to yet another title before calling it quits. The hands aren't quite as quick as they once were, but Cousy still dazzles the crowd with his astonishing array of acrobatic moves, averaging 14.1 points and 8.9 assists per game as the Celtics beat Cincinnati in seven games and Los Angeles in six for the championship.

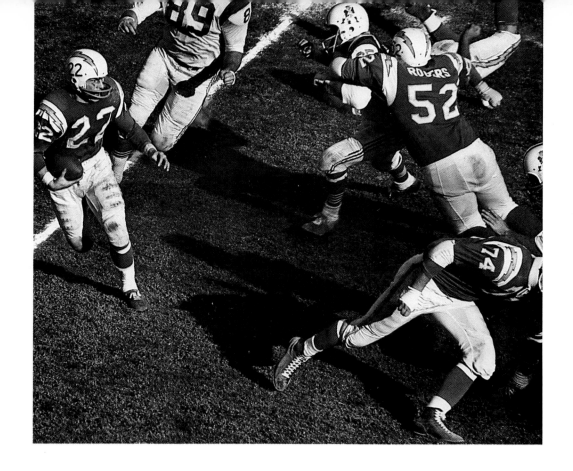

Loyola captain and All-America Jerry Harkness goes up over Cincinnati's Ron Bonham for the jump shot that pulls the Ramblers within two points with less than three minutes left in the NCAA title game. Harkness will later hit the tying basket to send the game into overtime, when Vic Rouse will grab an offensive rebound and lay it in at the buzzer for a 60–58 victory.

San Diego's Keith Lincoln follows the block of teammate Ron Mix (74) for a few of his 206 yards rushing in the Chargers' 51–10 rout of the Boston Patriots in the AFL title game. Lincoln has a career day, also catching seven passes for 123 yards as the Chargers show the nation how entertaining the air-it-out AFL can be, rolling up 601 yards in total offense.

Jack Nicklaus becomes the youngest Master ever, at 23, taming the Augusta course with a two-under-par 286 that puts him one stroke ahead of Tony Lema and two ahead of three-time winner Sam Snead. Many observers write him off after his opening round of 74, but Nicklaus charges back with a 66 in the second round to get back in contention.

1963

The Dodgers have moved to Los Angeles, but the excellence continues as Sandy Koufax is simply unhittable. His numbers: a record of 25–5, an ERA of 1.88, 11 shutouts, 306 strikeouts, a pair of wins with an ERA of 1.50 in the Dodgers' World Series sweep of the Yankees, a no-hitter and, of course, the first of his three Cy Young awards.

Kodak introduces the Instamatic   JFK is assassinated in Dallas

1 9 6 4
The Winner's Circle

Baseball: St. Louis Cardinals
NFL/AFL: Cleveland Browns/Buffalo Bills
College Football: Alabama
NHL: Toronto Maple Leafs
NBA: Boston Celtics
College Basketball: UCLA
Masters: Arnold Palmer
U.S. Open (golf): Ken Venturi
British Open: Tony Lema
PGA: Bobby Nichols
Australian Open: Roy Emerson
French Open: Manuel Santana
Wimbledon: Roy Emerson
U.S. Open (tennis): Roy Emerson
Australian Open: Margaret Smith Court
French Open: Margaret Smith Court
Wimbledon: Maria Bueno
U.S. Open (tennis): Maria Bueno
Kentucky Derby: Northern Dancer
Preakness: Northern Dancer
Belmont: Quadrangle
Indianapolis 500: A.J. Foyt

Ken Venturi keeps his cool as temperatures soar into triple digits during U.S. Open play at the Congressional Country Club in Washington. A once promising pro, Venturi's earnings had dropped to $3,848 in 1963, and he came to the Open as a man in search of his game. But he finds it in the heat, firing a 66–70 on the 36-hole final day, good enough to win the tournament by four strokes over Tommy Jacobs.

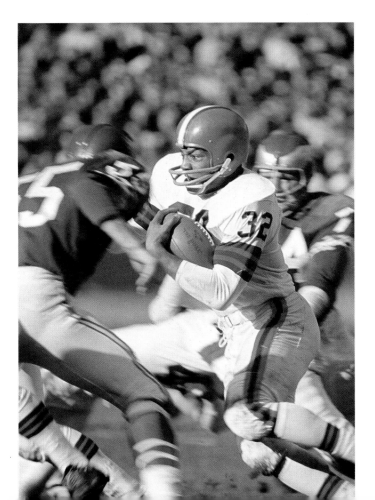

The incomparable Jim Brown (left against the Eagles) becomes the first man to run for 10,000 yards in a career as he leads the Browns to an NFL title. In the championship game against Baltimore, Cleveland keeps the Colts off-balance with a surprising passing attack, but Brown still rushes for 114 yards on 27 carries, most of them punishing out-side sweeps.

The first game of the World Series is a tough one for Yankee pitcher Whitey Ford, who gets tagged out at the plate by Cardinals catcher Tim McCarver (above) and then gets ripped for five runs in just over five innings to take the loss. He won't pitch again in the series as St. Louis, led by McCarver's 11 hits and five RBIs, goes on to win in seven games.

81

1964

It is a scene that will be repeated in boxing rings throughout the world over the next 15 years: Muhammad Ali clowning, taunting, exultant in victory, and his trainer Angelo Dundee, the smiling attendant. The loser this time is the heavily favored Sonny Liston, unable to answer the bell for the seventh round. It is the last time the boxing world will take the newly crowned champion so lightly.

Richard Petty wins the Daytona 500 by a full lap and breaks the event's speed record by almost two mph. Most shocking of all, he does it in a Plymouth (below, left), long considered a patsy in distance races. But Plymouth's new engine turns the tide and sends its competitors scurrying.

LBJ signs the Civil Rights Act   Republicans nominate Barry Goldwatwer for president

With a ladder of Japanese officials looking on, the great Bob Hayes streaks to a gold medal in the 100-meter Olympic final in Tokyo (below). The margin of victory is an incredible seven feet as Hayes pulls away in the final 40 meters to bury the field. Hayes will later become a three-time All-Pro receiver for the Dallas Cowboys.

A virtual unknown when he won the 800-meter gold in 1960, Peter Snell of New Zealand comes to Tokyo as the favorite. He doesn't disappoint his fans, winning the gold medal in both the 800- and 1,500-meter events. One month later, in New Zealand, he will break the world record in the mile for the second time, with a run of 3:54.1.

Khrushchev is ousted in the USSR, Brezhnev takes over   Douglas MacArthur dies

1964

Don Schollander becomes the first swimmer to win four Olympic gold medals, with individual victories in the 100-meter freestyle (53.4) and the 400-meter freestyle (4:12.2, a world record) and team wins in the 4x100 and 4x200-meter relays. Schollander, just 18, will go on to win a silver and a gold medal at the '68 Olympics in Mexico City.

The Gulf of Tonkin Resolution is passed   India's Jawaharlal Nehru dies

1965

The Winner's Circle

Baseball: Los Angeles Dodgers
NFL/AFL: Green Bay Packers/Buffalo Bills
College Football: Alabama/Michigan State
NHL: Montreal Canadiens
NBA: Boston Celtics
College Basketball: UCLA
Masters: Jack Nicklaus
U.S. Open (golf): Gary Player
British Open: Peter Thomson
PGA: Dave Marr
Australian Open: Roy Emerson
French Open: Fred Stolle
Wimbledon: Roy Emerson
U.S. Open (tennis): Manuel Santana
Australian Open: Margaret Smith Court
French Open: Lesley Turner
Wimbledon: Margaret Smith Court
U.S. Open (tennis): Margaret Smith Court
Kentucky Derby: Lucky Debonair
Preakness: Tom Rolfe
Belmont: Hail to All
Indianapolis 500: Jim Clark

Jack Nicklaus is all smiles after yet another birdie during his historic third-round 64 at the Masters. Nicklaus will go on to shoot a final-round 69 to finish with a 17-under-par 271, the lowest total in Masters' history and nine strokes ahead of Arnold Palmer and Gary Player. Once an unpopular player, Nicklaus hears more and more applause as galleries begin to recognize his greatness.

Wilt Chamberlain is traded from the San Francisco Warriors to the Philadelphia 76ers, but his rivalry with Bill Russell continues as the two knock heads in the playoffs with Russell and the Celtics winning once again, this time in seven games. Chamberlain's teams will beat Russell's Celtics only once in eight playoff series, but Chamberlain backers will point to Russell's superior supporting cast.

Bill Bradley leads Princeton to the Final Four, averaging 29.5 ppg during the regular season and 35.4 during the NCAA tournament. The Cinderella story will end when the Tigers fall to Michigan but Bradley finishes with a flourish when he pours in 58 points in the consolation game against Wichita State. Oxford, the New York Knicks and the U.S. Senate lie in store.

Maury Wills (30) signals slide. Ron Fairly (6) signals to stay standing. Jim Lefebvre (5) is confused and ends up stumbling across the plate and injuring his heel. His run helps L.A. win Game 3 of the World Series against the Twins, but his injury prevents him from playing again in the Dodgers' seven-game victory.

1965

Unable to lift his right arm without pain, Bart Starr is a doubtful starter almost until kickoff, but once the NFL title game gets going, he is as cool and efficient as ever, completing 10 of 18 passes for 147 yards in Green Bay's convincing 23–12 win over the Cleveland Browns. Jim Taylor and Paul Hornung share the rushing load as usual, combining for 201 yards.

Malcolm X is assassinated   Watts erupts in race riots

1966

The Winner's Circle

Baseball: Baltimore Orioles
Pro Football: Green Bay Packers
College Football: Notre Dame
NHL: Montreal Canadiens
NBA: Boston Celtics
College Basketball: UTEP
Masters: Jack Nicklaus
U.S. Open (golf): Billy Casper
British Open: Jack Nicklaus
PGA: Al Geiberger
Australian Open: Roy Emerson
French Open: Tony Roche
Wimbledon: Manuel Santana
U.S. Open (tennis): Fred Stolle
Australian Open: Margaret Smith Court
French Open: Ann Haydon Jones
Wimbledon: Billie Jean King
U.S. Open (tennis): Maria Bueno
Kentucky Derby: Kauai King
Preakness: Kauai King
Belmont: Amberoid
Indianapolis 500: Graham Hill
World Cup: England

An injury to his hoof puts Buckpasser out of the Triple Crown races, but he comes charging back under the driving ride of Braulio Baeza to win the Arlington Classic and smash the world mile record by three-fifths of a second with a time of 1:32 ⅗. Among the field of fine colts that he defeats is the winner of the Kentucky Derby and the Preakness, Kauai King.

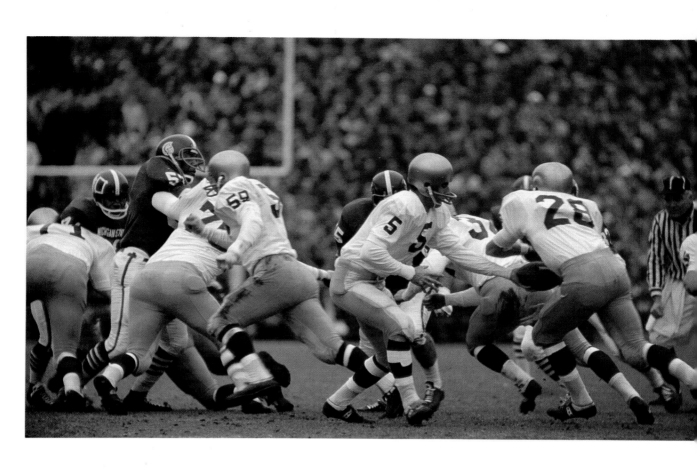

Three weeks after Buckpasser's equine mile, Jim Ryun breaks the human version even more authoritatively with a clocking of 3:51.3 in Edwards Stadium in Berkeley, to better the old record by a full 2.3 seconds. Ryun, just 19, surges to the lead with 700 yards to go and simply runs away from the field to become the first American in 29 years to hold the record.

Notre Dame quarterback Terry Hanratty hands off to Rocky Bleier in the first quarter of the much ballyhooed matchup between No. 1 Notre Dame and No. 2 Michigan State. Few could guess that Hanratty would get hurt and the Irish would go conservative, choosing to run out the clock and settle for a 10–10 tie to preserve their top national ranking.

1966

Bobby Hull, he of the curved stick and the mighty slap shot, lets fly with the blast that will net his record 51st goal in the season's 61st game. His mark will be surpassed many times in the expansion era, but Hull's 610 career goals still place him fifth on the alltime list.

Great move: Baltimore trades Milt Pappas and a pair of nobodies to Cincinnati for Frank Robinson, who proceeds to win the Triple Crown with 49 homers, 122 RBIs and a .316 batting average. He also hits two homers in the Orioles' four-game Series sweep of the Dodgers.

Star Trek premiers on TV   Ronald Reagan is elected governor of California

1967

The Winner's Circle

Baseball: St. Louis Cardinals
Pro Football: Green Bay Packers
College Football: USC
NHL: Toronto Maple Leafs
NBA: Philadelphia 76ers
College Basketball: UCLA
Masters: Gay Brewer Jr.
U.S. Open (golf): Jack Nicklaus
British Open: Roberto De Vicenzo
PGA: Don January
Australian Open: Roy Emerson
French Open: Roy Emerson
Wimbledon: John Newcombe
U.S. Open (tennis): John Newcombe
Australian Open: Nancy Richey
French Open: Francoise Durr
Wimbledon: Billie Jean King
U.S. Open (tennis): Billie Jean King
Kentucky Derby: Proud Clarion
Preakness: Damascus
Belmont: Damascus
Indianapolis 500: A.J. Foyt

Bob Seagren, the all-American USC student, vaults 17' 7" for the world record at the San Diego Invitational in Balboa Stadium. Seagren will go on to break the record again, in 1968, with a vault of 17' 9" in the Olympic trials, then win the gold medal in Mexico City before raising the world record to 18' 5 ¾" in '72. In all, he broke the world mark four times.

Guard Jerry Kramer hoists coach Vince Lombardi aloft after the Packers' 33–14 triumph over the Oakland Raiders in Super Bowl II in Miami. It is a jubilant moment for Lombardi, who will retire as Packer coach after the game, and also for an aging Packer team that looked extremely vulnerable after dropping its last two regular-season contests.

The world of college basketball waited in terror for a young man named Lew Alcindor to finish his freshman season and become eligible for varsity play. Their fears prove justified in '67 as Alcindor dominates the opposition, leading the Bruins to a 30–0 season, scoring 20 points and grabbing 18 rebounds in a 79–64 rout of Dayton for the national title.

1967

O.J. Simpson bursts through for a few of the 128 yards he will gain against Indiana in a 14–3 Rose Bowl victory. The game confirms the Trojans' national title, earned primarily in a late-season showdown between Simpson and UCLA quarterback Gary Beban; both performed brilliantly, but it was Simpson's 64-yard touchdown gallop that gave USC the 21–20 win.

Muhammad Ali, now a fervent Black Muslim, refuses induction into the armed services, declaring himself a conscientious objector. In May he will be convicted of draft evasion and eventually stripped of his title. Howard Cosell (to Ali's right) remains among his staunchest supporters throughout the ordeal. In 1971, the Supreme Court overturns his conviction.

Elvis and Priscilla are married   Thurgood Marshall is appointed to the Supreme Court

1968

The Winner's Circle

Baseball: Detroit Tigers
Pro Football: New York Jets
College Football: Ohio State
NHL: Montreal Canadiens
NBA: Boston Celtics
College Basketball: UCLA
Masters: Bob Goalby
U.S. Open (golf): Lee Trevino
British Open: Gary Player
PGA: Julius Boros
Australian Open: Bill Bowrey
French Open: Ken Rosewall
Wimbledon: Rod Laver
U.S. Open (tennis): Arthur Ashe
Australian Open: Billie Jean King
Wimbledon: Billie Jean King
French Open: Nancy Richey
U.S. Open (tennis): Virginia Wade
Kentucky Derby: Forward Pass
Preakness: Forward Pass
Belmont: Stage Door Johnny
Indianapolis 500: Bobby Unser

He brashly predicts victory before the game; he backs it up on the field. Joe Namath of the Jets throws for 206 yards in New York's shocking 16–7 defeat of the heavily favored Baltimore Colts in Super Bowl III. The biggest surprise is the ease with which the Jets are able to run, as Matt Snell plows ahead for 121 yards. It is a game that will establish the AFL's credibility once and for all.

Detroit's Denny McLain charges from the dugout in joy after the Tigers come from behind for the 5–4 victory that makes him the first man since Dizzy Dean in 1934 to win 30 games. McLain will win one more game before the season is through to finish with 31; his mark has not been equaled since. After winning 24 games in '69, McLain will win only 17 more over the next three seasons.

Dancer's Image wins the Kentucky Derby by 1 ½ lengths, then is disqualified after a postrace urinalysis reveals traces of butazolidin, an analgesic used to reduce inflammation. Forward Pass is declared the winner, and a full-scale investigation is launched to discover who is responsible. The results are inconclusive, and the matter remains a mystery to this day.

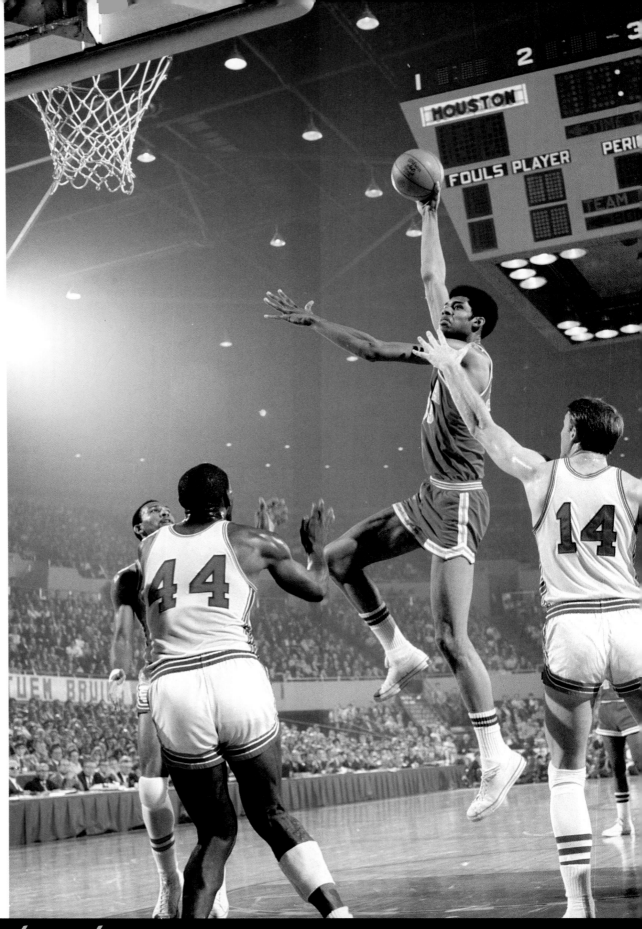

1968

Houston stops UCLA's 47-game winning streak with a 71–69 victory in January, but the Bruins turn the tables in the NCAA tournament, employing a diamond-shaped zone to limit Elvin Hayes (44) to 10 points and hold the Cougars to a 28% shooting night in a 101–69 UCLA rout. Lew Alcindor (left) hooks his way to 19 points and 18 rebounds as the Bruins win their fourth title in five years.

Arthur Ashe's booming serve defeats Tom Okker of Holland in a marathon five-set U.S. Open final 14–12, 5–7, 6–3, 3–6, 6–3. Ashe becomes the first, and still the only, black man to win the event, but the press, convinced that his victory is a fluke, pays more attention to the upsets in the earlier rounds. Ashe will prove his tennis mettle by winning the Australian Open two years later and Wimbledon in 1975.

North Vietnam launches the Tet offensive   Jackie Kennedy marries Aristotle Onassis

Dashing Jean-Claude Killy of France flies down windy Mount Casserousse to win the gold medal in the downhill at the Winter Olympics in Grenoble. He will navigate his way through a nearly impenetrable fog to win the slalom and giant slalom as well, becoming the first man since Austria's Toni Sailer in '56 to capture all three events. His reward: a hero's status at home and a mountain of endorsements.

An unforgettable Olympic moment: Tommie Smith (center) and John Carlos raise black-gloved fists on the victory stand after their 1–3 finish in the 200-meter finals in Mexico City. Their intent is to protest racism in the U.S., but Olympic officials are outraged and ban the two Americans from the Olympic village. Few remember that Smith ran a 19.83 to set a 200-meter world record that will stand for three years.

Demonstrators are beaten and arrested at the Democratic convention in Chicago

102

1 9 6 8

It may be the most amazing athletic feat in history. Bob Beamon, in his first attempt in the Olympic finals, soars nearly six feet into the air, landing with a world-record long jump of 29' 2 ½" The world mark, which had increased only 8 ¼" since 1935, had just been bettered by an astonishing 21 ¾". Beamon was so over-come with emotion after the announce-ment of the record that he nearly fainted.

1969

The Winner's Circle

Baseball: New York Mets
Pro Football: Kansas City Chiefs
College Football: University of Texas
NHL: Montreal Canadiens
NBA: Boston Celtics
College Basketball: UCLA
Masters: George Archer
U.S. Open (golf): Orville Moody
British Open: Tony Jacklin
PGA: Ray Floyd
Australian Open: Rod Laver
French Open: Rod Laver
Wimbledon: Rod Laver
U.S. Open (tennis): Rod Laver
Australian Open: Margaret Smith Court
French Open: Margaret Smith Court
Wimbledon: Ann Haydon Jones
U.S. Open (tennis): Margaret Smith Court
Kentucky Derby: Majestic Prince
Preakness: Majestic Prince
Belmont: Arts and Letters
Indianapolis 500: Mario Andretti

The bookies overrate the NFL once again, and the upstart AFL comes away with another Super Bowl as Len Dawson (right) leads the Kansas City Chiefs to a convincing 23–7 win over the Minnesota Vikings. Facing the awesome rush of Minnesota's Purple People Eaters, Dawson stands coolly in the pocket and completes 12 of 17 passes for 142 yards and a TD. The two leagues will merge before the '70 season.

Bill Russell (left), having replaced Red Auerbach in 1966, performs as Boston's player-coach in his farewell season, leading the Celtics to their 11th title in 13 years. The Lakers are favored in the finals, but the Celtics come through in the clutch as usual, winning the seventh game in L.A. 108–106. Russell's scoring is down in the playoffs, but he still averages over 20 rebounds per game.

Tom Seaver wins 25 games and a Cy Young award as he pitches the Miracle Mets to the World Series in perhaps the most improbable story in sports history. Made prohibitive underdogs at season's start, the Mets win 25 of 34 games in September to overtake the Chicago Cubs, then sweep Atlanta in the playoffs and defeat the favored Baltimore Orioles in five games in the Series.

Mario Andretti and crew chief Andy Granatelli are all smiles as Andretti, plagued by bad luck in past Indy 500s, finally gets the winner's laurels, averaging 156.867 over the 200 laps at the Indianapolis Motor Speedway. Andretti will have the fastest qualifying times in '76 and '87 but will never win the race again.

Bill Hartack, aboard Majestic Prince, enjoys the victor's spoils for his record-tying fifth win in the Run for the Roses. A stretch duel between Majestic Prince and Arts and Letters sets the stage for a rivalry that will continue into the Preakness, won by Majestic Prince, and the Belmont, won by Arts and Letters.

Benchmarks Neil Armstrong walks on the moon   Sesame Street debuts

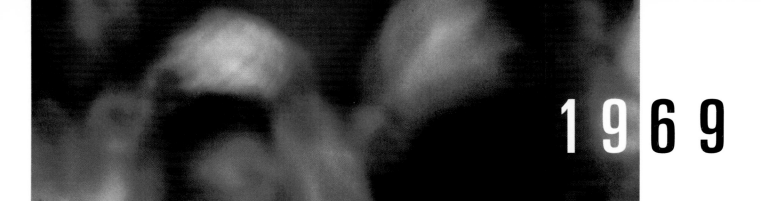

1969

Rod Laver becomes the only player in history to win two Grand Slams as he dominates men's tennis, winning 31 matches in a row and losing only two sets in the finals of the four major tournaments. The following year he will win 14 tournaments and earn more than $200,000. Painful tennis elbow will force him to retire from the pro circuit in 1976.

Woodstock embodies a generation   Golda Meir becomes the Israeli prime minister

1970

The Winner's Circle

Baseball: Baltimore Orioles
NFL: Baltimore Colts
College Football: Nebraska/Texas
NHL: Boston Bruins
NBA: New York Knicks
College Basketball: UCLA
Masters: Billy Casper
U.S. Open (golf): Tony Jacklin
British Open: Jack Nicklaus
PGA: Dave Stockton
Australian Open: Arthur Ashe
French Open: Jan Kodes
Wimbledon: John Newcombe
U.S. Open (tennis): Ken Rosewall
Australian Open: Margaret Smith Court
French Open: Margaret Smith Court
Wimbledon: Margaret Smith Court
U.S. Open (tennis): Margaret Smith Court
Kentucky Derby: Dust Commander
Preakness: Personality
Belmont: High Echelon
Indianapolis 500: Al Unser
World Cup: Brazil

The Intrepid, with John Ficker at the helm, defeats Australia's Gretel II 4–1 to retain the America's Cup. Gretel appears to have the second race won by more than a minute, but the win is given to Intrepid when the judges rule that Gretel illegally bumped Intrepid at the start of the race. The boats will split their next two meetings before Intrepid sails to a solid 1:44 victory in the fifth and deciding contest.

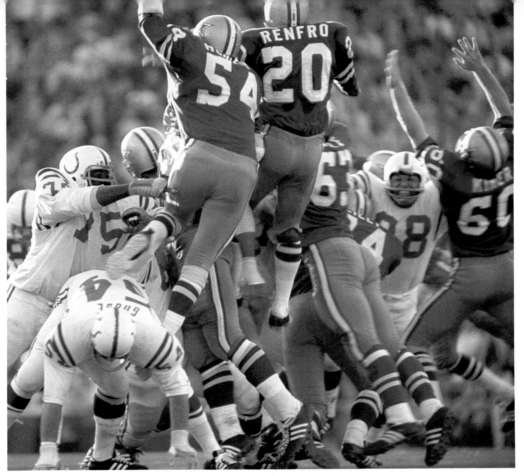

The Super Bowl finally has a dramatic finish as the Dallas defenders are unable to block this 32-yard field goal by Baltimore kicker Jim O'Brien with :05 left that gives the Colts a 16–13 win. The game is marred by errors—the teams combine for 10 turnovers, including the key interception thrown by Cowboy quarterback Craig Morton with 1:09 left in the game.

Baltimore's Brooks Robinson snares a drive down the third-base line off the bat of Cincinnati's Lee May and throws him out to complete just one in a series of sparkling plays in the World Series. He also has nine hits, two homers and a team-leading six RBIs as the Orioles beat Cincinnati and the Big Red Machine in just five games.

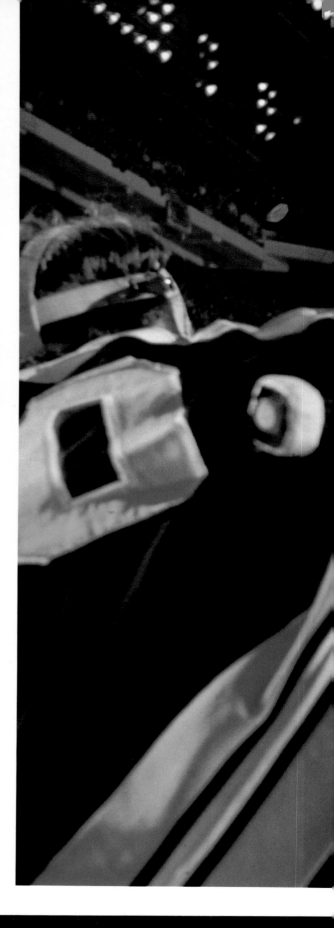

Margaret Smith Court, long a dominant figure in women's tennis, finally wins the Grand Slam. Court sprains her ankle against Billie Jean King in the Wimbledon finals but perseveres anyway, winning in 2½ hours 14–12, 11–9. With King absent from the U.S. Open, Court breezes to an easy win over Rosie Casals to complete the Slam.

The amazing Bobby Orr leads the Boston Bruins to their first Stanley Cup title since 1941. He also revolutionizes his sport by becoming the first defenseman to lead the league in scoring, with 120 points. Five years later, he will lead again, with 46 goals and 89 assists for 135 points, still the most ever for a player at his position.

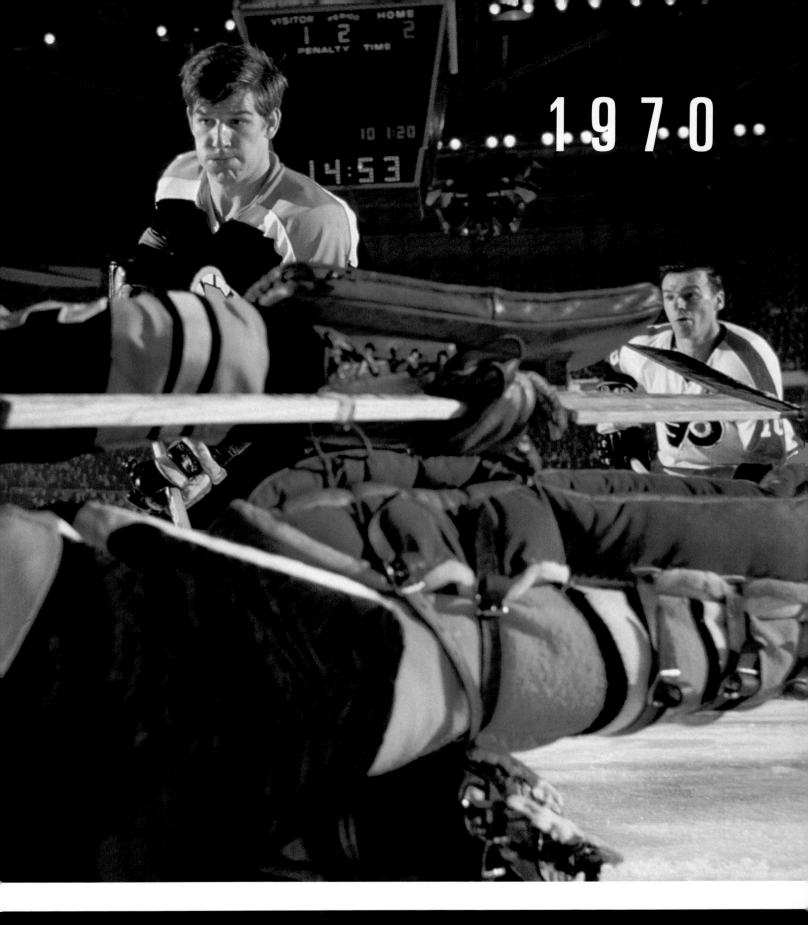

1970

The Nerf ball bounces onto the market   Four students are killed at Kent State

1971

The Winner's Circle

Baseball: Pittsburgh Pirates
NFL: Dallas Cowboys
College Football: Nebraska
NHL: Montreal Canadiens
NBA: Milwaukee Bucks
College Basketball: UCLA
Masters: Charles Coody
U.S. Open (golf): Lee Trevino
British Open: Lee Trevino
PGA: Jack Nicklaus
Australian Open: Ken Rosewall
French Open: Jan Kodes
Wimbledon: John Newcombe
U.S. Open (tennis): Ilie Nastase
Australian Open: Margaret Smith Court
French Open: Evonne Goolagong Cawley
Wimbledon: Evonne Goolagong Cawley
U.S. Open (tennis): Billie Jean King
Kentucky Derby: Canonero II
Preakness: Canonero II
Belmont: Pass Catcher
Indianapolis 500: Al Unser

It is a great year for the flamboyant Lee Trevino and his horde of followers, known as Lee's Fleas. Trevino's greatest triumph comes at the U.S. Open, where he battles Jack Nicklaus to a tie in regulation, then goes on to beat him by three strokes in a playoff—this after breaking the tension on the first playoff tee by tossing a rubber snake at a surprised Nicklaus. When has the game of golf been more entertaining?

The gangly giraffe in the nets is rookie Ken Dryden, who shocks the NHL by joining the Montreal Canadiens in March and leading them to their 16th Cup. He allows only three goals per game against the Bruins and Blackhawks and is named the playoff MVP. He will lead Montreal to five more Stanley Cups and win five Vezina trophies as the league's outstanding goaltender before retiring to pursue a career in law.

Al Unser speeds to his second straight win in the Indy 500, making him the fourth man to accomplish the feat. Driving his Johnny Lightning Special, Unser sets a new speed record of 157.735 mph in defeating Peter Revson by a full 20 seconds. Twenty people are injured at the beginning of the race when the pace car goes out of control and plows into the photographers' bleachers.

Roger Staubach (above) looks for a receiver during the Cowboys' 24–3 rout of the Miami Dolphins in Super Bowl VI. Staubach wins the MVP award, but Dallas's Doomsday Defense is the real star, holding the Dolphins to just 185 net yards. Duane Thomas, the eccentric Cowboy who refused to talk to the press all season long, runs for 95 yards and a touchdown.

Ali goes to the canvas in the 15th round, the victim of a vicious left hook from Joe Frazier, and the myth of his invincibility tumbles with him. He will get to his feet and finish the fight but will lose the decision, his first. Many think it signals the end for Ali, but as ever, he defies expectation; in two memorable fights he will avenge the loss, and in a third, against George Foreman, he will become champ once more.

1971

Oscar Robertson's traveling magic show goes to Milwaukee as the master is traded to the Bucks in his 11th season, but now he has an assistant in the person of Lew Alcindor, soon to change his name to Kareem Abdul-Jabbar. Together they conjure an NBA title as the Bucks go 12–2 in the playoffs, including a four-game sweep of the Baltimore Bullets in the finals.

Alan Shepard hits a golf ball on the moon   The Pentagon Papers are published

1972

The Winner's Circle

Baseball: Oakland Athletics
NFL: Miami Dolphins
College Football: USC
NHL: Boston Bruins
NBA: Los Angeles Lakers
College Basketball: UCLA
Masters: Jack Nicklaus
U.S. Open (golf): Jack Nicklaus
British Open: Lee Trevino
PGA: Gary Player
Australian Open: Ken Rosewall
French Open: Andres Gimeno
Wimbledon: Stan Smith
U.S. Open (tennis): John Newcombe
Australian Open: Virginia Wade
French Open: Billie Jean King
Wimbledon: Billie Jean King
U.S. Open (tennis): Billie Jean King
Kentucky Derby: Riva Ridge
Preakness: Bee Bee Bee
Belmont: Riva Ridge
Indianapolis 500: Mark Donohue

Rollie Fingers's waxed moustache may make him look 19th century, but unfortunately for the Cincinnati Reds, his wicked stuff is very much present in the World Series as Fingers saves two games and wins another in Oakland's seven-game triumph. With Reggie Jackson nursing a pulled hamstring, Gene Tenace takes up the slack on offense, hitting four homers and driving in nine of Oakland's 16 runs.

The new man in the middle for UCLA is a giant redhead named Bill Walton. With help from a supporting cast that includes forward Keith—later Jamaal—Wilkes (foreground), Walton leads the Bruins to two straight NCAA championships and averages 20.3 points and 15.7 rebounds per game in his varsity career.

Jim Kiick dives across from the one with the decisive score in Miami's 14–7 Super Bowl win over Washington. The victory will up the Dolphins' record to 17–0, making them the only undefeated and untied team in NFL history. Only Garo Yepremian's fumble on a botched passing try allows the Redskins to score at all.

117

New York's Walter Tkaczuk (18) and Boston's Phil Esposito battle for the puck while Ranger goalie Eddie Giacomin looks on. Esposito is held scoreless in the Bruins' six-game Stanley Cup win, but he passes off for eight assists. He also leads the NHL in scoring, with 133 points on 66 goals and 67 assists.

His Celtics nemesis is long retired, but Wilt Chamberlain keeps on going, here laying in two points during the Lakers' five-game rout of the New York Knicks in the NBA Finals. Chamberlain's domination of the boards against New York's front line is the key to the series as the Dipper averages 23.2 rebounds per game.

Benchmarks Five men are caught breaking into the Watergate

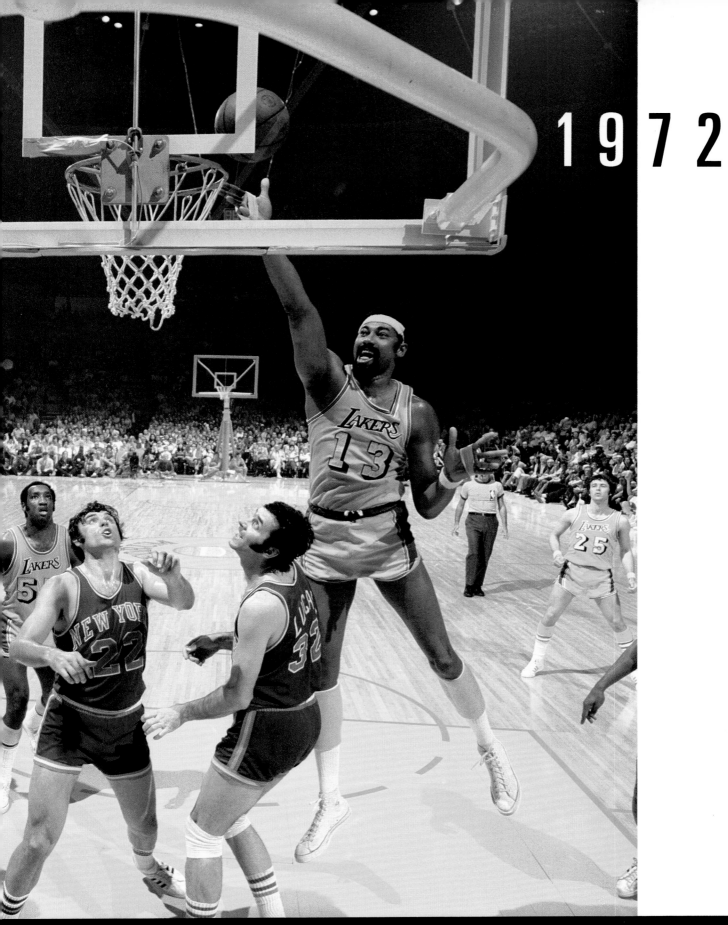

1972

Nixon visits China   Bobby Fischer beats Boris Spassky in chess

The world watches in horror as eight Palestinian terrorists invade the Summer Games in Munich, taking over the Israeli dorm in the Olympic village (above), and leaving 11 Israeli athletes dead in their wake. After a hiatus of 34 hours, the Games go on, but who can think about sports?

The tragedy in Munich obscures an amazing feat: swimmer Mark Spitz's seven gold medals, the most ever won in a single Olympics. Spitz sets world records in all four individual events in which he competes: the 100- and 200-meter freestyles; and the 100- and 200-meter butterflies.

Roberto Clemente is killed in a plane crash   Title IX is signed into law

Frank Shorter of the U.S. cruises to victory in the Olympic marathon (2:12:19.8) but is surprised to hear boos as he enters Munich's Olympic Stadium for the finish. In fact, the spectators were booing a prankster who had run on the track just before him. It is a sweet victory for the Munich-born Shorter, who becomes the first American to win the marathon since 1908.

Nixon defeats George McGovern in a landslide   Jackie Robinson dies

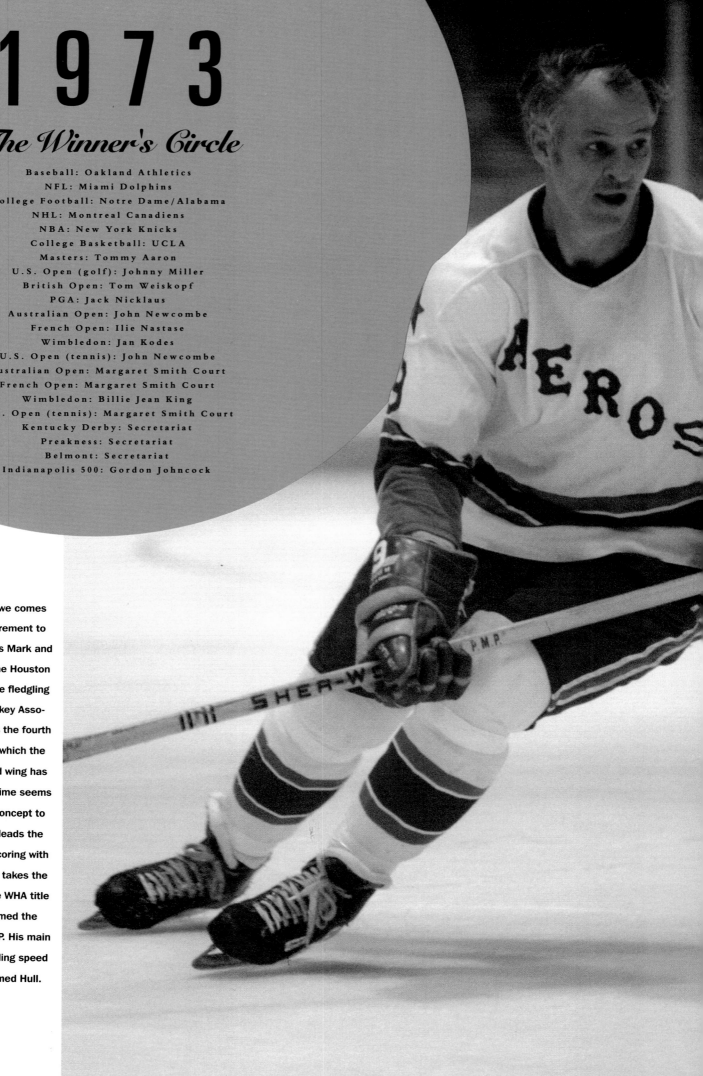

1973

The Winner's Circle

Baseball: Oakland Athletics
NFL: Miami Dolphins
College Football: Notre Dame/Alabama
NHL: Montreal Canadiens
NBA: New York Knicks
College Basketball: UCLA
Masters: Tommy Aaron
U.S. Open (golf): Johnny Miller
British Open: Tom Weiskopf
PGA: Jack Nicklaus
Australian Open: John Newcombe
French Open: Ilie Nastase
Wimbledon: Jan Kodes
U.S. Open (tennis): John Newcombe
Australian Open: Margaret Smith Court
French Open: Margaret Smith Court
Wimbledon: Billie Jean King
U.S. Open (tennis): Margaret Smith Court
Kentucky Derby: Secretariat
Preakness: Secretariat
Belmont: Secretariat
Indianapolis 500: Gordon Johncock

Gordie Howe comes out of retirement to join his sons Mark and Marty on the Houston Aeros of the fledgling World Hockey Association. It is the fourth decade in which the 45-year-old wing has played but time seems a foreign concept to Howe. He leads the league in scoring with 100 points, takes the Aeros to the WHA title and is named the league's MVP. His main rival? A balding speed demon named Hull.

O.J. Simpson slashes his way across the snowy turf in Shea Stadium to become the first NFL running back to gain over 2,000 yards in a single season. With his 200-yard day against the Jets, Simpson will end the year with 2,003. No one will come close until the season is expanded to 16 games in 1978.

The thundering hands of George Foreman produce one of the most humiliating beatings in heavyweight history as Joe Frazier is knocked down three times in the first round and three more in the second, the final knockdown coming after two lefts to the head and a devastating right cross that knocks Frazier in the air and to the canvas.

Chris Evert, already America's favorite teenager in ponytails, makes her pro debut in March, then goes on to the semi-finals of the U.S. Open for the third straight year since losing to Billie Jean King in the semis at age 16. She will win the French Open and Wimbledon in 1974 and go on to dominate women's tennis for more than a decade.

First comes a record time at the Kentucky Derby, then a solid win at the Preakness. But it is the third leg of the Triple Crown that finally convinces the skeptics of the greatness possessed by the stocky 3-year-old named Secretariat, who wins the Belmont (right) by 31 lengths and runs the 1½ miles in 2:24, still the fastest ever.

1973

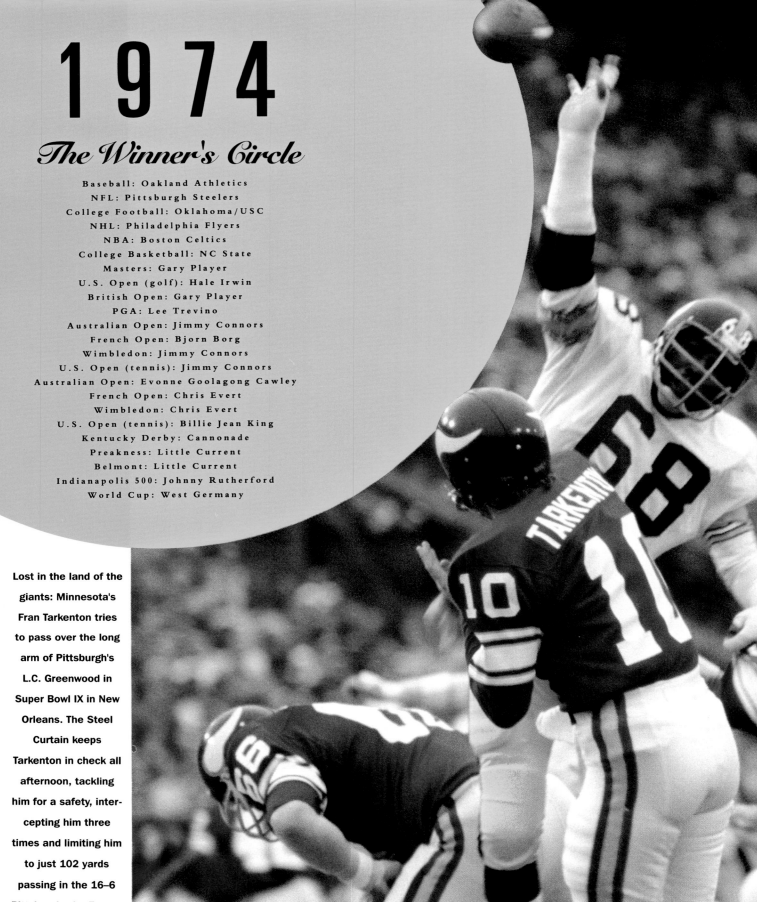

1974

The Winner's Circle

Baseball: Oakland Athletics
NFL: Pittsburgh Steelers
College Football: Oklahoma/USC
NHL: Philadelphia Flyers
NBA: Boston Celtics
College Basketball: NC State
Masters: Gary Player
U.S. Open (golf): Hale Irwin
British Open: Gary Player
PGA: Lee Trevino
Australian Open: Jimmy Connors
French Open: Bjorn Borg
Wimbledon: Jimmy Connors
U.S. Open (tennis): Jimmy Connors
Australian Open: Evonne Goolagong Cawley
French Open: Chris Evert
Wimbledon: Chris Evert
U.S. Open (tennis): Billie Jean King
Kentucky Derby: Cannonade
Preakness: Little Current
Belmont: Little Current
Indianapolis 500: Johnny Rutherford
World Cup: West Germany

Lost in the land of the giants: Minnesota's Fran Tarkenton tries to pass over the long arm of Pittsburgh's L.C. Greenwood in Super Bowl IX in New Orleans. The Steel Curtain keeps Tarkenton in check all afternoon, tackling him for a safety, intercepting him three times and limiting him to just 102 yards passing in the 16–6 Pittsburgh win. Franco Harris is the Steeler workhorse on offense, rushing for 158 yards on 34 carries.

The relief is evident on the face of Henry Aaron after he hits his 715th home run, off the Dodgers' Al Downing in Atlanta, to propel him past Babe Ruth into first place on the alltime career home run list. For months he has had to endure media scrutiny, a stream of racist hate mail and a barrage of criticism intended to demean his accomplishment. Through it all, he maintains the quiet dignity for which he is known.

Johnny Rutherford, driving his McLaren (14), wins the first of his three Indy 500s, charging from the 25th pole position into fourth place in the first 10 laps of the race, then moving into second and drafting behind A.J. Foyt, who is trying for his fourth Indy win. With 150 laps to go, Foyt experiences engine trouble and is forced to retire from the race, leaving Rutherford with the lead that he never relinquishes.

1974

All eyes are on George Foreman as he struggles to get to his feet after a flurry of punches from Muhammad Ali drops him to the canvas in the eighth round of their title bout in Zaire. Foreman fails to beat the count, and the amazing Ali, thanks to a bizarre tactic he later dubs the rope-a-dope, is the heavyweight champ once again.

The gap-toothed Bobby Clarke (16) leads the Philadelphia Flyers to their first Stanley Cup title, collecting six points and shadowing Bobby Orr to distraction in the six-game final series win over the Boston Bruins. Clarke, who must take regular insulin injections for his diabetes, will lead the Flyers to a second title in '75 and be named the league's MVP.

Nixon resigns   Mikhail Baryshnikov defects to the U.S.

1 9 7 5
The Winner's Circle

Baseball: Cincinnati Reds
NFL: Pittsburgh Steelers
College Football: Oklahoma
NHL: Philadelphia Flyers
NBA: Golden State Warriors
College Basketball: UCLA
Masters: Jack Nicklaus
U.S. Open (golf): Lou Graham
British Open: Tom Watson
PGA: Jack Nicklaus
Australian Open: John Newcombe
French Open: Bjorn Borg
Wimbledon: Arthur Ashe
U.S. Open (tennis): Manuel Orantes
Australian Open: Evonne Goolagong Cawley
French Open: Chris Evert
Wimbledon: Billie Jean King
U.S. Open (tennis): Chris Evert
Kentucky Derby: Foolish Pleasure
Preakness: Master Derby
Belmont: Avatar
Indianapolis 500: Bobby Unser

Pete Rose, feisty as ever, leads the Reds in their seven-game World Series triumph over the Boston Red Sox. Rose is a ubiquitous presence in the Series, leading all regulars with a .370 batting average and an on-base percentage of .469. With the Reds trailing 3–2 in the seventh inning of the seventh game, Rose singles in the game-tying run to set the stage for Joe Morgan's game-winning bloop single in the ninth.

Soccer legend Pele is wooed from retirement to play for the New York Cosmos of the North American Soccer League and to proselytize for his beloved sport among the unenlightened. He is a success on both counts, leading the Cosmos to an NASL title and setting attendance records all around the league. But when Pele retires for good in 1977, the crowds leave with him.

Pittsburgh's Lynn Swann is elegance incarnate in the Steelers' 21–17 Super Bowl defeat of the Dallas Cowboys, making four acrobatic catches for a Super Bowl-record 161 yards and a touchdown to account for all but 48 of Pittsburgh's passing yards. For his efforts, he is named the game's Most Valuable Player.

John Wooden, the wizard of Westwood, calls it quits after guiding UCLA to its 10th NCAA title in 12 years with a 92–85 win over Kentucky. His last title may be his most impressive as he fashions a championship team without the dominant presence of Alcindor or Walton, relying instead on a revolving cast of stars led by forward Marques Johnson. UCLA has yet to win another NCAA title.

On a torturously hot night in Manila, a pair of warriors named Ali and Frazier stage a battle of epic proportions as each fighter seems beaten, then finds some inner source of courage to sustain him. But it is Ali who has the final surge, battering Frazier with chilling consistency in the late going. When Eddie Futch, Frazier's kindly trainer, tosses in the towel after the 14th round, it is an act of mercy.

Billie Jean King relaxes on her throne as she awaits her much-ballyhooed match with Bobby Riggs in 1973. She will defeat Riggs handily and usher in a new era of pride in women's sports.

SI Favorites

GOING FISHING WITH THE KID
John Underwood visits Ted Williams

HE'S BURNING TO BE A SUCCESS
Underwood profiles the astonishing Tim Rossovich

THE BEST AT EVERYTHING
William Oscar Johnson visits weightlifter Vasili Alexeyev

THE GLORY GAME AT GOAT HILLS
Dan Jenkins recalls the golf of his youth

WOULD YOU LET THIS MAN INTERVIEW YOU?
Myron Cope spends some time with the voluble Howard Cosell

SHOOTINGS IN THE NIGHT
Kenny Moore reports on the tragedy in Munich

BEAUTY AND THE BEAST
Frank Deford examines the enigmatic Robyn Smith

SUPERMEX AND THE GRINGOS
Jenkins records Lee Trevino's U.S. Open win in 1972

SWINGING JOE
Jenkins hangs out with Joe Willie Namath

BAD IS BEAUTIFUL
Curry Kirkpatrick takes a look at Ilie Nastase

THE CRUEL DECEPTION
Jack Olsen offers a startling progress report on the black athlete

'LAWDY, LAWDY, HE'S GREAT'
Mark Kram reports from Ali-Frazier III in Manila

THE GLORIOUS ORDEAL
Ron Fimrite covers Henry Aaron's 715th home run

GOING FISHING WITH THE KID

BY JOHN UNDERWOOD

There has probably never been a better pure hitter than the amazing Ted Williams. He retired from baseball in 1960, at the age of 42, having hit .316 in his final season. Three years earlier, back from a stint in Korea, he hit .388. He remains the last man to break the magical .400 mark; he did it in 1941. John Underwood paid him a visit in Florida in 1967 and described the essential Wiliams' life-style, one that he pursues to this day.

The Kid said it was about time we showed up. It was 5:15 in the morning. The sun had not yet begun its assault on the Florida Keys. By 10 o'clock it would be 85 degrees, and Charley Trainor, the photographer, would have his freckles double-coated with a petroleum compound made for World War II aviators marooned at sea. The Kid had bacon—a good two pounds of bacon—bubbling and spitting in twin skillets on the stove, and the coffee was hot. "All right," he said, "get the hell out of the road."

We were standing there like children who have awakened to strange events. "Just sit your behinds down and stay out of the road. We're making history here. How do you like your eggs?"

There was some ponderous shuffling as the three of us who were now his subjects found seats at the large dinette table. There were Charley the photographer and Edwin Pope, the writer from Miami, and myself, and however improbable our status as fishermen, we were there to go for tarpon with The Kid, who is an expert at it, who may be, in fact, the best at it, the way he used to be the best at putting a bat on a ball. He had invited us to an early breakfast, because he said he did not trust us to find our own at that hour and he wanted to be at the fishing spot no later than 7. He had it scouted.

The Kid said his cooking would not win prizes, but as a man alone after two aborted marriages he knew some of the mysteries of steaks, chops, broiled chicken and roast beef. "I do a pretty fair job with them," he said. "I do not make pies," he said, raising his eyebrows and the side of his mouth.

He had on the red Bermuda shorts I have come to think of as his home uniform in Islamorada, and a faded red shirt that had a few character holes in it. He wore Sears, Roebuck tennis shoes without socks, and his copper-brown calves stuck out prominently from the tails of the Bermudas. In 1938, when he was 19 years old and a pitcher-outfielder in San Diego, just starting as a professional ballplayer, he was 6'3" and weighed 168 pounds. Eventually, when he had been exposed to major league regimens, he got up to 200 pounds, but it was still appropriate to call him The Splinter. The Splendid Splinter, to be sure, because there was more to him than attenuation. His own particular preference for a nickname was always The Kid. Occasionally in conversation he still refers to himself as The Kid. It is a pleasing way of taking the edge off the first person singular.

The exposed calves were a giveaway to his enormous natural power. He had never appeared terribly strong in a baseball uniform, but baseball players do not audition in Bermuda shorts. The power had to be there somewhere. There were always the wrists and hands, of course, and the eyes. Everybody talks about the wrists and eyes. People used to say he could read the label on a revolving record with those eyes, but he says that was fiction. The wrists and eyes look ordinary enough. His legs give him away....

To fish with Williams and emerge with your sensitivities intact is to undertake the voyage between Scylla and Charybdis. It is delicate work, but it can be done, and it can be enjoyable. It most certainly will be educational. An open boat with The Kid just does not happen to be the place for one with the heart of a fawn or the ear of a rabbit. There are four things to remember: 1) he is a perfectionist; 2) he is better at it than you are; 3) he is a consummate needler; and 4) he is in charge. He brings to fishing the same hard-eyed intensity, the same unbounded capacity for scientific inquiry he brought to hitting a baseball.

Williams encourages a constant ebb and flow of ideas, theories, critiques, digs, approvals and opprobriums. His favorite appellation is "Bush" short for bush-leaguer, but with Williams a mark of accreditation. If he calls you Bush, you're in. Often he confers it on the guides....

The Kid put a shapeless white hat on his head and an extra layer of grease on his lips and assumed his waiting stance on top of a tackle box, looking out across the water, his left hand on his hip, his right holding a weapon: a Ted Williams reel with 15-pound monofilament line and a Ted Williams seven-foot rod. Sears puts the Williams name on its top line of equipment, after himself approves it. He grants Sears about 60 days a year of his time, attending clinics, making films, doing promotional work. It takes another 45 days to fulfill his obligation as a Red Sox vice-president, which consists mainly of trying, in the spring, to pound into the heads of young hitters the recipe for becoming the greatest hitter who ever lived. Another 60 days are spent at his boys' camp in Lakeville, Mass. From August to October he retires to a little cabin on the Miramichi River in New Brunswick and fishes for Atlantic salmon.

From the tackle box Williams could make conversation and watch for the coming of the tarpon. In this stance The Kid allowed his stomach to take its course uninhibited, letting it stick out. Sometimes he rolled on the sides of his feet as he kibitzed with the rest of us. His stomach is no longer a splinter's stomach, but otherwise he appears in excellent condition. He is 48 now but looks 35. As a young man he had been shocked to see the hair on his chest turning silver, but only a little of the silver ever got to his head....

It was just after 11 o'clock when the tarpon hit. Actually, it hit The Kid's second cast; it passed by his first, spooking slightly, and he had to put the second one out 80 feet. The tarpon jumped, exposing its great body, the scales jingling like castanets. It was obviously bigger than the one he had lost the day before. Swiftly Williams joined the battle, planting the hook with those three quick bursts. He moved with the action, leaning, sitting down, knees bent, knees straight, talking, checking the drag, getting Jack to maneuver the boat. A mixture of suntan oil and sweat got into his eyes, and he wiped at it with his left hand. We were a quarter of a mile from the spot where the tarpon hit when he got it up to the boat....

They hoisted the fish up in the air. "Ninety-five pounds," said Brothers. It had taken 35 minutes....

"Here, look at this," said Ted, displaying the broken head of the red-and-yellow bucktail lure that he took from the fish's mouth. "Isn't that something? He split it in half." They lowered the stricken tarpon into the water, and Jack began to work it around, washing water through the gills, and gradually it began to revive. "He's going to make it," said Ted. "He's all right, he'll make it. He'll make it unless some shark comes along and bites his tail."

"All right," he said. "Lunchtime."

Excerpted from an original story published in
SPORTS ILLUSTRATED, *August 21, 1967*

HE'S BURNING TO BE A SUCCESS

BY JOHN UNDERWOOD

Few athletes embodied the Age of Audacity more fully than Eagle linebacker Tim Rossovich, one of sport's most celebrated flakes. Since his retirement from football, Rossovich has continued his flamboyant ways, becoming a Hollywood stuntman and making an apearance in 1985 on The Love Boat. John Underwood visited with him in 1971.

He had the aerosol can in his hand, and the shaving lather billowed out, and when he began to apply it to his face, a familiar, fundamental impulse stirred within him—the possibilities seemed enormous—and he began to spray the lather around, sprsssssshhh, over his forehead and around his chest, and then down his arms and over the length and breadth of his 6'4", 245-pound naked body. And before the Earth had turned much farther, he had made of himself a pillar of white frosting, awesome to behold. And he looked in the mirror and saw that it was good. And because this was not something he would want to keep to himself, he ran outside the Sigma Chi house, at the University of Southern California, and down the street. And the

cars on Figueroa Avenue bucked and jerked at the sight of him gliding among them. And as he turned and ran back, molting froth, Tim Rossovich chuckled inside, and he knew that he had done it again, and he was pleased....

The party was in an apartment at the Penn Towers in Philadelphia.... The doorbell rang, and when the door was opened a man with a Fu Manchu mustache and an immense hedge of curly hair the texture of pork rinds stood in the doorway, not in shaving cream this time but in flames. Ablaze. On fire. Guests cried out in horror. "Oh, God, he's..." "Somebody do something!" The flaming man walked into the room, where [Steve] Sabol and a guest knocked him to the floor and began beating him with blankets. The flames extinguished, Tim Rossovich got to his feet, looked casually around the room, said, "Sorry, I must have the wrong apartment," and walked out....

The lounge is on the Philadelphia Main Line, and he has become well known there.... This night he had a cast on his arm, and he explained that he had broken the arm at the Philadelphia Eagles' practice that afternoon. The regulars commiserated with him, and soon they were discussing some minor point of football. Apparently incensed by what was being said, Rossovich began shouting and pounding on the bar again. The cast splintered and began to disintegrate. Pieces of plaster fluttered silently down like snowflakes. The lounge grew quiet. Everybody was looking, stunned, at the exposed arm. Rossovich held it up, his face expressive of an epiphany. "I'm cured!" he yelled.

The stories are told—in locker rooms, at bowling lanes, over long-distance phones—by almost anyone who knows or has ever met Tim Rossovich and by Rossovich himself. Only those who feel insecure around him, like coaches who think his life-style is a threat to the Republic, try to keep his wondrous light under a bushel. Tim Rossovich eats light bulbs. He wears tie-dyed shirts and shower-of-hail suits, Dracula capes and frontier buckskins and stands on his head in hotel lobbies. Sometimes when he stands on his head his head is in a bucket of water....

Excerpted from an original story published in
SPORTS ILLUSTRATED*, September 20, 1971*

THE BEST AT EVERYTHING

BY WILLIAM OSCAR JOHNSON

Between 1970 and 1978, Vasili Alexeyev was unbeaten in weightlifting competition, setting 80 world records and dominating his sport as none before. In 1975, William Oscar Johnson traveled to Alexeyev's native Russia and came back with a vivid portrait of this supremely confident athlete.

Vasili Alexeyev, the premier sports hero of the Union of Soviet Socialist Republics, stood in his garden amid his strawberry plants, his red peppers and his roses. The autumn sun shone on the south of Russia as if it were the south of France. Alexeyev's arms, thick as tree trunks, were akimbo, the vast muscles at rest in the sun. His kingly chest and belly, broader than any barrel, bass drum or office safe in common use today, expanded surrealistically when he inhaled. His torso glittered when he moved, for he was draped from right shoulder to left hip—a distance of perhaps four feet—with a brilliant vermilion silk sash adorned with row upon row of small medallions; the sash was so laden it looked like a swath of golden mail. It weighed seven or eight pounds, but was no burden for Vasili Alexeyev. At 33, Alexeyev weighs 324 pounds, stands 6' 1½" and is the strongest man in the world....

On this occasion Alexeyev was posing for formal portraits in his garden, wearing a heavy black suit and beginning to perspire. He glowered at the photographer from beneath furry black eyebrows. "Smile?" said the photographer meekly. Alexeyev's face became thoughtful. He scowled and then bellowed, "Schmile!" The sound rose from the deep caverns of his chest like the thunder and turbulence within a volcano. "Schmile!" Then he smiled. And the camera clicked. Smile. Click. And so it went. Alexeyev's brow dripped as the noon sun beat upon his black wool suit. At last the formal shooting was done, but Alexeyev held up a huge hand and spoke urgently in Russian. His two sons, Sergei, 12, and Dmitri, 9, hurried to his side. Alexeyev removed the glorious sash and arranged his sons in front of him. Then he gently hung the silk across both their chests. "Schmile!" he roared and beamed at the camera. The photographer took many pictures of the proud father and his sons before Vasili Alexeyev pronounced the session over....

[Later, Johnson observed Alexeyev in training.]

Suddenly the door of Alexeyev's house banged open and the great man stepped [out to the courtyard]. He was dressed in electric-blue sweat pants, Adidas sneakers, a thin apple-green T-shirt. In his right hand he carried a bulging Adidas bag and looked not unlike a gigantic commuter bound for his train. And Vasili Alexeyev was indeed on his way to work. He strode about 25 mighty paces, and there he was at his office, chairman of the board, to say nothing of king of the mountain.

In those 25 paces from his back door to the bar, the weights and the rubber mats laid by the brick wall, everything in Alexeyev's existence as premier sports hero of the Soviet Union and strongest man in the world was on display. He moved with a powerful swagger across the courtyard bricks.... His face was composed in the benign, even saintly, self-confident expression of an old-fashioned king absolutely certain of his divine right to reign. There might have been music, *The Hallelujah Chorus* perhaps, but it was not necessary.

Excerpted from an original story published in Sports Illustrated, *April 14, 1975*

THE GLORY GAME
AT GOAT HILLS

BY DAN JENKINS

Dan Jenkins, author of the popular novels SEMI-TOUGH and DEAD SOLID PERFECT, first revealed his comic talents as a writer for SI. In this story, written in 1965, he described the unusual brand of golf favored by his hardscrabble group of Texas pals. The course where they played had ceased to exist, "swallowed up by the bulldozers of progress," as Jenkins put it, but he felt compelled to recount the tales anyway, hoping perhaps that the telling might explain why he didn't play as much golf as he used to.

We called him Cecil the Parachute, because he fell down a lot. He would attack the golf ball with a whining, leaping half-turn—more of a calisthenic than a swing, really—and occasionally, in his spectacular struggles for extra distance, he would soar right off the end of elevated tees.

He was a slim, bony, red-faced little man, who wore crepe-soled shoes and heavily starched shirts that crackled like crunched glass. When he was earthbound Cecil drove a delivery truck for a cooky factory, Grandma's Cookies, and he always parked it—hid it, rather—behind a tall hedge near the clubhouse. When the truck was there, out of sight of passing cars (or of cooky-company dispatchers snooping on cooky-truck drivers), you could be pretty sure that not only was Cecil out on the course but so were Tiny, Easy Reid, Magoo, Foot the Free, Grease Repellent, Ernie, Matty, Rush, Little Joe, Weldon the Oath, Jerry, John the Band-Aid and Moron Tom.

There was also the very good chance that all of us would be in one hollering, protesting, club-slinging fifteensome. Anyhow, when Cecil the Parachute had the truck hidden you knew for sure that the game was on.

The game was not the kind of golf that Gene Sarazen or any of his stodgy friends ever would have approved of. But it was, nevertheless, the kind we played for about 15 years, from the mid-'40s to the late '50s, at a windy, dusty, indifferently mowed, stone-hard, broomstick-flagged, practically treeless, residentially surrounded public course named Worth Hills in Fort Worth, Texas. Goat Hills, we called it, not too originally.

[Jenkins immortalizes the "Great Scooter Wreck."]

We were lounging. Matty, who had a crew cut and wore glasses and looked collegiate (and grew up to be a doctor), was resting against a rock pillar on the porch, playing tunes on his front teeth with his fingernails. He could do that. Learned it in study hall. For money he could even play Sixty Minute Man, or Rocket 88 or whatever happened to be No. 1 on the jukebox at Jack's Place on the Mansfield Highway, where most of us went at night to "hustle the pretties," as Moron Tom phrased it, and watch truck drivers fight to see who bought the beer. I was reading either *The Best of S.J. Perelman* or *The Brothers Karamazov*. Any kind of book would prompt needling whoops from Tiny, who was a railroad conductor, or Weldon the Oath, who was a postman, or Grease Repellent, who worked at the Texaco station three blocks away. ("Hey, Jenkins! What you gonna do with all them facts clangin' around in yer head?") Foot the Free, which was short for Big Foot the Freeloader, was there, practice-putting at a small, chipped-out crevice in the concrete of the porch.... Magoo was around. And Little Joe. Presently John the Band-Aid showed up, striding grimly from the parking lot, clubs over his shoulder, ready to go. He had beaten a Turf King pinball machine somewhere on University Drive—had found the A, B and C lit, had lit the D, then hit the feature—and he had some money....

[After choosing teams, the match begins.]

Little Joe and I took a scooter, one of those two-seaters with three wheels, and John and Magoo took one. The rest walked. We were an eightsome. If others came later they would join up along the way, as always, and there would be some action for them, too. Plenty.

With only eight players it was a fairly simple game to book keep. You played each of the other seven individually on the front nine, on the back and on the 18—three bets each to start. Without any presses—new bets—that was a sizable investment right there. But new bets came quickly, because of an automatic one-down press rule and big, get-even bets on 9 and 18. It was certainly nice to birdie the 9th and 18th holes sometimes. Like maybe $100 nice.

Naturally, there was always a long pause at both the 9th and 18th tees to figure out how everybody stood. Like this particular day. John the

Band-Aid, I recall, had shot even par but was down to everyone.

"I got to be the alltime world's champion unlucky," he said, beating his driver against the tee marker. "Magoo can't play and he's beatin' me, and Matty can't play and he's beatin' me, and my young partner's dead as an old woman and...."

John the Band-Aid, who wore glasses and a straw hat and kept a handkerchief tied around his neck for protection against sunburn, rarely observed honors on the tee. In fact, the game sort of worked in reverse etiquette. The players who were losing teed off first.

"I'm gonna hit this one right into young Stadium Drive," said John, impatiently. The 9th at the Hills was a long par-4. The tee was on a bluff, above a desperate drop-off into a cluster of under-nourished hackberry tres, a creek, rocks and weeds. Ideally, the drive had to carry over the trees and creek and into the uphill fairway, leaving about a seven-iron to the green. Stadium Drive was behind the green.

As John the Band-Aid went into his backswing, Little Joe said, "Hit it, Daddy."

John said, "Mother, I'm hittin' hard as I can." He curved a wondrous slice into the right rough, and coming off of his follow-through slung the club in the general direction of Eagle Mountain Lake, just missing Little Joe. The Band-Aid's shot irritated Little Joe, and so did the flying club. "Man, man," said Joe. "They ought to put me in a box and take me to the state fair for bein' in this game."

I was fairly mad, too. One under par and no money ahead. Maybe that's why I pointed the scooter straight down the hill and let it run. We were almost instantly out of control. "Son of a young...," said Joe, holding on. The scooter zoomed, but the front wheel struck a boulder and, like a plane taking off, we were in the air. I sailed straight over the front, and Joe went out the

right side. The scooter, flipping and spewing clubs, landed on both of us, mostly on my left leg.

I think I was out for about 10 seconds before I heard all of the laughter behind me and felt the clubs and rocks underneath. They pulled the scooter off, and off Joe's white canvas bag—or what was left of it. Battery acid had been jolted out of the scooter and was already beginning to eat away at the bag.

"I got two says Joe don't have a bag before we get to 18," said Magoo. Foot called it. Although my left ankle was so swollen I had to play the rest of the way with only one shoe, we continued. It was on the 14th green that we noticed Magoo was a winner. When Joe went to pick up his bag after putting out, the only things left were the top metal ring, the bottom, the wooden stick and the shoulder strap. Not only that, Joe's left pants leg was going fast....

Excerpted from an original story published in Sports Illustrated, *August 16, 1965*

WOULD YOU LET THIS MAN INTERVIEW YOU?

BY MYRON COPE

Myron Cope visited with Howard Cosell in 1967. Cosell's distinctive broadcasting style had already transformed him into the man that America loved to hate, but the bright spotlight of MONDAY NIGHT FOOTBALL was still to come.

"Oh, this horizontal ladder of mediocrity," sighs Howard Cosell, ruminating on the people who make up the radio-television industry, which pays him roughly $175,000 a year. "There's one thing about this business: there is no place in it for talent. That's why I don't belong. I lack sufficient mediocrity."

Cosell fondles a martini at a table in the Warwick bar, across the street from American Broadcasting Company headquarters. Anguish clouds his homely face. His long nose and pointed ears loom over his gin in the fashion of a dive bomber swooping in with fighter escort. "This is a terrible business," he says. It being the cocktail hour, the darkened room is packed with theatrical and Madison Avenue types. A big blonde, made up like Harlow the day after a bender, dominates a nearby table, encircled by spindly, effete little men. Gentlemen in blue suits, with vests, jam the

bar. A stocky young network man pauses at Cosell's table and cheerfully asks if he might drop by Cosell's office some day soon. Cosell says certainly, whereupon the network man joins a jovial crowd at the bar. "He just got fired," Cosell whispers. "He doesn't know I already know." The man, he is positive, wants his help, but what is Cosell to do when there are men getting fired every week?

"This is the roughest, toughest, cruelest jungle in the world," Cosell grieves. A waiter brings him a phone, and he orders a limousine and chauffeur from a rental agency. He cannot wait to retreat to his rustic fireside in Pound Ridge up in Westchester County. It is Monday evening, barely the beginning of another long week in which he, Howard W. Cosell, middle-aged and tiring, must stand against the tidal wave of mediocrity, armed only with his brilliance and integrity.

It has been only 11 years since Cosell quit a New York law practice to become a sportscaster. Yet here he is, the most controversial figure in the business, an opinionated lone wolf in a profession populated by pretty-faced ex-athletes and fence-straddling play-by-play announcers who see angry sponsors under their beds. Teen-agers and adult athletes and men in neighborhood saloons do imitations of his nasally acerbic voice, which assaults millions on 30 radio and TV shows a week. His interviews with Muhammad Ali are the Hope Diamond in ABC's *Wide World of Sports,* television's most successful sports series. (To the disgust or titillation of viewers, Cosell meticulously addresses the heavyweight champion by his Muslim name....

Yet, most of all, Cosell's forward progress stems from the fact that, alone among sportscasters of national stature, he works at his trade. He goes out and looks for news and personalities, instead of waiting for gossip at Toots Shor's.

Excerpted from an original story published in SPORTS ILLUSTRATED, *March 13, 1967*

SHOOTINGS IN THE NIGHT

BY KENNY MOORE

In 1972, two years before he began writing regularly for SI, Kenny Moore was a competitor in the Olympic Marathon in Munich. Five days before his fourth-place finish, the tragedy unfolded that left 11 Israeli athletes dead and a world in shock. At SI's request, Moore recorded his firsthand account of the terrible day.

I was torpid, just out of bed, ready to jog on a humid, glaring day. The Olympic Village gate was locked. A guard, dressed in silly turquoise, said, "There have been shootings in the night. You cannot leave."

I started back to my room. On the way I met my teammate, hammer thrower George Frenn, whose parents were born in Lebanon. He told me Arab terrorists had broken into the Israeli quarters, shot two people and taken others hostage. George was seething. "I hate lunatics," he said.

I lived in an apartment on the fifth floor of the U.S. building with Frank Shorter, Steve Savage, Jon Anderson and Dave Wottle, all middle- or long-distance runners. Frank was on our terrace, staring at police lines, ambulances and newsmen assembled under cover near the Israeli dorm, 150 yards away....

We took turns on the terrace, plucking seeds from a fennel plant there and grinding them in our palms. Below, people played chess or Ping-Pong. The trading of Olympic pins continued. Athletes sunbathed by the reflecting pool. It seemed inappropriate, but what was one supposed to do? The scratchy, singsong notes of European police sirens sounded incessantly. Rumors leaped and died. There were 26 hostages. There were seven. The terrorists were killing a man every two hours. They were on the verge of surrender.

At 3:30 p.m. I phoned a friend in the press village.

"Have you heard?" he asked. "The Games have stopped."

"Stopped? You mean postponed or canceled?"

"Postponed for now. But they say it may be impossible to start them again."

I went back to the room, where my wife Bobbie was waiting, and I wept. I experienced level after level of grief: for my own event, the marathon, those years of preparation now useless; for the dead and doomed Israelis; and for the violated sanctuary of the Games.

In Mexico and here the village had been a refuge, admittedly imperfect, from a larger, seedier world in which individuals and governments refused to adhere to any humane code. For two weeks every four years we direct our kind of fanaticism into the essentially absurd activities of running and swimming and being beautiful on a balance beam. Yet even in the rage of competition we keep from hurting each other, and thereby demonstrate the meaning of civilization. I shook and cried as that illusion, the strongest of my life, was shattered.

[The evening was filled with yet more rumors, including a late, erroneous report that the Israelis had been rescued.]

We awoke to the final horror. The first newspapers said, "Sixteen Dead."

I walked to the memorial service. Russian soccer players were practicing on a field beside the stadium. Concession stands were open, smelling of sauerkraut. The program was long-winded in four languages. The crowd applauded when [Avery] Brundage said the Games would go on.

Excerpted from an original story published in
SPORTS ILLUSTRATED, *September 18, 1972*

BEAUTY AND THE BEAST

BY FRANK DEFORD

By 1972, women were a force to be reckoned with in sports, even in the macho world of horse racing, where an enigmatic character named Robyn Smith was making her mark. Frank Deford, now the editor in chief of THE NATIONAL, was dispatched to get the story, the result being just one of the many memorable pieces he would contribute to the magazine over the next 17 years.

Robyn Smith, the jockey, invented herself a few years ago so that she could succeed in that role. Few athletes have forfeited more than she has to chase after a dream, to try to live out a little girl's fantasy, for she gave up a good and glamorous life in the pursuit. She changed her style and her habits, she traded in a knockout face and figure for a jockey's stark image, and she discarded her past, pretending almost that she never had one, that she just materialized, walking out of the mist at dawn one morning late in 1968 at Santa Anita. Even her closest friends have no firm idea who she is or where she came from or even, for sure, what her name is. Nor, as she protests, is any of that really important. She has constructed this whole other person, forming her out of perseverance and independence and ambition and talent—and because she likes the new person much more than whoever Robyn Smith was before.

And it has worked. There is nothing there anymore but Robyn Smith, the jockey.

Once she was good looking enough to work seriously toward a Hollywood career, but by now the transformation is so complete that Robyn Smith actually looks her prettiest in racing silks. She is 5'7", standing on long, lovely legs, the kind so fine that women envy them; not just the things that men whistle at when a skirt rides high. She has dimples, chestnut hair and eyes the color of twilight that alternately doubt and challenge. Yet seldom does she flatter herself. Usually she wears pants and baggy cardigans, and after them racing silks look positively feminine on her.

She claims her natural weight is around 110, but that is preposterous. A high-fashion model of her height would hardly be that light. Probably Robyn weighed 125 before she became a jockey.

She strips at no more than 105 now, is flat-chested and her riding breeches hang down, flapping, off her hips. "Her little rear end is like a couple of ham hocks," says a friend who worries about her. Her face is gaunt and drawn, and life comes to it only from the sun and the freckles on her nose....

A cat came to the door of the barn. One of Robyn's stories is that she was once allergic to cats and dogs and horses and stable dust. This is why she never rode as a child. Robyn Smith, the jockey, doesn't have this allergy, although it is never clear exactly why. She took the cat in her lap and petted it devotedly and was lost, absolutely lost, for a while. Montaigne wrote, "When I play with my cat, who knows if I am not a pastime to her more than she is to me?" and one thinks that of Robyn with cats and horses alike. She has broken down and cried, hopelessly, just because a time conflict has robbed her of the chance to breeze a horse. For animals she has patience, and with them she never wears that look of suspicion she reserves for all the prying people.

The fact is, though, that obscured by all the forced *National Velvet* business, in barely four years this young woman has risen from learning how to stay on a horse to a position among the elite in a vary hard, dangerous profession. That she has managed this ascent despite the strong bias against women in her field makes the success story all the more remarkable. Miss Smith is no *National Velvet*; she is pure and simple Horatio Alger, an old-fashioned all-American melting-pot hero who just happens to be a heroine. Her natural instincts and a large talent were requisite, but what kept her afloat were the corny storybook values: determination, confidence, stick-to-it-iveness, sacrifice and all the rest. She has never let up....

"I'm thin, but I'm strong," Robyn explains clinically, getting set to flex again. "I always had good muscles. I'm a rare physical individual—and I'm not trying to be narcissistic about it. It's just that I'm very unusual in that way."

Yet Robyn has taken off so much weight that she appears to have no emotional reservoir to sustain her. Her system is littered with the residu-

effects of weight pills, water pills, hormone pills, big pills, little pills, pill pills that she gobbles indiscriminately. Even when she was a world-beater at the spring meeting, she was constantly at a temperamental flood tide. She breaks into tears regularly, not only over losing a race, but say, while watching some banal TV drama. The least aggravation unnerves her. People fall out of her favor upon the smallest alleged slight, only to return just as whimsically to her good graces. Her fetish for freedom borders now on mania; it is easier to schedule an appointment with the Dalai Lama than Robyn Smith. She has become less receptive to criticism, and woe to the most well-intentioned innocent who forgets and idly tells her the same thing twice....

Thus, while the criticism of Robyn is often cruel and unfounded, she hurts her reputation with her temper and her vague, devious, even fictional responses.... The bald facts are that there is no record of any Robyn Caroline Smith (or anyone like that) born in San Francisco when she claims—Aug. 14, 1944, nor for several years on either side of that date. Nor does any person with that name seem to have attended school in Hawaii, where Robyn says she grew up. Clearly, either the rest of her authorized life history is as bogus as the college-Hollywood malarkey, or she has adopted a new name.

The irony in all this mystery is that no one who knows Robyn well thinks she is hiding anything deep and dark in her past. The feeling is that she probably is just making a harmless retreat from a life that was sad or drab or both.... Some friends suspect that she came from a broken home or possibly was an orphan. Others think she may have endured a bad marriage during that blank period when she was supposed to have been an English major at Palo Alto. Robyn says she has no living relatives. By her spare account, her parents both died of natural causes a couple of years ago.

Nonetheless, the one constant, if vague, reference point in her allusions to her childhood is a strong, magnanimous father whom Robyn reluctantly identifies (this time) as a wealthy lumberman. Robyn's father pops up in her rare off-guard recollections only to give her things or to take her places, such as on hunting trips or on wonderful boats. Sometimes the father is referred to as a stepfather or uncle. He never has a name.

Asked about the "y" in her name, she declares without equivocation that it is "the girl's way" of spelling Robin. Oh. The birth date on her jockey's license makes her 28 in two weeks, though it is possible that she cheated a little when she first applied for a license, claiming her age was 24. Vanity aside, there could be a good reason for that, since no one over 25 can ride as an apprentice. Anything is possible. Maybe she is 16. Maybe she is Anastasia. Who really knows anything about Robyn Caroline Smith's past except that somehow it pains her?

Excerpted from an original story published in SPORTS ILLUSTRATED, *July 31, 1972*

SUPERMEX AND THE GRINGOS

BY DAN JENKINS

Dan Jenkins was known as a writer who could routinely turn in brilliant news stories that read as if he had been given weeks, instead of hours, to prepare them. Lee Trevino's first major championship—the U.S. Open in 1968—offered Jenkins yet another opportunity to confirm that reputation.

Super Mex is what he called himself. Super Mexkin. And there he was out there in the midst of all of that U.S. Open dignity with his spread-out caddie-hustler stance and his short, choppy public-course swing, a stumpy little guy, tan as the inside of a tamale, pretty lippy for a nobody, and, yeah, wearing those red socks. And here were all of these yells coming from the trees and the knolls of the Oak Hill Country Club in Rochester, coming from all of the other Lee Trevinos of the world. "Whip the gringo," hollered Lee's Fleas, a band of instant Mexicans enthusiastic enough to rival anybody's army, some of them $30-a-week guys like Trevino himself was just a little more than a year ago.

Lee Trevino whipped all of the gringos last week. He mainly whipped a gringo named Bert

Yancey, the tournament leader for the first three days, in a head-to-head, you-and-me thing on the final day, the kind of match a hustler really likes; but in so doing, he knocked off everything else in Rochester, including a good golf course, a strong field, a couple of USGA records that looked untouchable, and a $30,000 check.

What Lee Trevino really did, when he won the Open championship last Sunday, however, was shoot more life into the game of golf than it has had since Arnold Palmer, whoever that is, came along. Trevino will not only go out and fight a course for you in the most colorful of ways, he'll say most anything to most anybody. He'll hot dog it. He'll gagline it. And he'll respond. In a gang-some of 30 or 40 visor-gripping Bert Yanceys, most of whom seem to have graduated from the yep-and-nope school of public relations, Lee Trevino had already made himself known to a degree.

He had received more pretournament press than anyone simply because he talked a lot and said things like, "I used to be a Mexkin, but I'm makin' money now so I'm gonna be a Spaniard." Well, now, you take this kind of fellow and give him a major championship and what you've got is instant celebrity.

It all happened in one day, actually, but that is all it ever takes. It happened on Sunday, the last day of the Open, when Trevino went out and did what no one thought he could do—turn Bert Yancey's game into a shambles, one on one, and totally ignore the near presence of Jack Nicklaus. Trevino did it although he had not won an event on the PGA tour, and, in fact, had only been on the tour for a short while—a couple of months last summer and all this season. Which is not so long, especially for a man who has not had a life-long acquaintance with money. In winning, Trevino further had the audacity to tie Nicklaus' 72-hole 1967 Open record of 275 and set a record of his own by becoming the first player ever to shoot four straight rounds under par in an Open: 69, 68, 69 and 69.

Excerpted from an original story published in
SPORTS ILLUSTRATED, *June 24, 1968*

SWINGING JOE

BY DAN JENKINS

Jenkins, in addition to covering golf, wrote frequently on pro football for the magazine. Here he meets a subject perfectly suited to his talents: Joe Namath in the early stages of his career—bold, brash, expressive of his time. Were we ever that young?

Stoop-shouldered and sinisterly handsome, he slouches against the wall of the saloon, a filter cigarette in his teeth, collar open, perfectly happy and self-assured, gazing through the uneven darkness to sort out the winners from the losers. As the girls come by wearing their miniskirts, net stockings, big false eyelashes, long pressed hair and soulless expressions, he grins approvingly and says, "Hey, hold it, man—foxes." It is Joe Willie Namath at play. Relaxing. Nighttiming. The boss mover studying the defensive tendencies of New York's off-duty secretaries, stewardesses, dancers, nurses, bunnies, actresses, shopgirls—all of the people who make life stimulating for a bachelor who can throw one of the best passes in pro football. He poses a question for us all:

Would you rather be young, single, rich, famous, talented, energetic and happy—or President?

Joe Willie Namath is not to be fully understood by most of us, of course. We are ancient, being over 23, and perhaps a bit arthritic, seeing as how we can't do the Duck. We aren't comfortably tuned in to the Mamas and the Uncles—or whatever their names are. We have cuffs on our trousers and, freakiest of all, we have pockets we can get our hands into. But Joe is not pleading to be understood. He is youth, success, the clothes, the car, the penthouse, the big town, the girls, the autographs and the games on Sundays. He simply is, man....

Right now, this moment, whatever Joe means to himself behind his wisecracks, his dark, rugged good looks, and his flashy tailoring, he is mostly one thing—a big celebrity in a celebrity-conscious town. This adds up to a lot of things, some desirable, some not. It means a stack of autographs everywhere he goes ("Hey, Joe, for a friend of mine who's a priest, a little somethin' on the napkin, huh?"), a lot of TV and radio stuff, a lot of photography stills for ads and news and continual interviews with the press. Such things he handles with beautiful nonchalance, friendliness—and lip.

Then comes the good part. It means he gets to sit at one of those key tables in Toots Shor's—1 and 1A, the joke goes—the ones just beyond the partition from the big circular bar where everyone from Des Moines can watch him eat his prime rib. It means that when he hits P.J. Clarke's the maitre d' in the crowded back room, Frankie Ribando, will always find a place for him, while, out front, Waiter Tommy Joyce, one of New York's best celebrity spotters, will tell everyone, "Joe's inside." It means he can crawl into the Pussy Cat during the late hours when the Copa girls and the bunnies are there having their after-work snacks, even though the line at the door may stretch from Second Avenue to the Triborough Bridge....

Excerpted from an original story published in
SPORTS ILLUSTRATED, *October 17, 1966*

BAD IS BEAUTIFUL

BY CURRY KIRKPATRICK

When Curry Kirkpatrick caught up with Ilie Nastase in 1972, the flamboyant Rumanian had just won the U.S. Open, amazing courtside observers in the process with his combination of unorthodox play and outrageous behavior. Kirkpatrick, ever a lover of the offbeat, captured his subject perfectly.

It is a basic matter of record that bad has always been better than good. Bad has more substance, more technique, more style, more noise, color and taste, more imagination, more passion, more variety and more of whatever there remains to sink one's teeth into. It seems only appropriate that commentators from Walt Whitman to Longfellow to John the Apostle have spoken of the condition as inherent in our species. "All men are bad and in their badness reign," is what Shakespeare wrote in a sonnet. It comes as no particular surprise, then, that bad currently seems to be in a lot more demand than good. And reigning, too.

Among recent fun people who have ingrained themselves in American pop culture just by hanging around being bad are Clifford Irving, Jane Fonda, Mick Jagger, Ben the movie-star rat and a whole flock of sports boys who talk a lot, don't talk at all, fight in bars, refuse to fight in wars, kiss girls, pop pills, smoke weed, drink alcohol, change their name, demand money, jump teams, flay the citizenry and boogaloo to Francis Scott Key. Now we're really talking bad.

All the same, men such as Muhammad Ali, Joe Namath, Dick Allen, Duane Thomas, Bobby Fischer and Derek Sanderson make the world of sport seem somewhat more logical and realistic when they descend from their false pedestals and are shown, as they have been, to share the discipline lacks, hangups and crazies that burden us all in one way or another.

The game of tennis has always been a haven of gentility in this world, a place where customs die slowly and manners are as important as physical skill. Bad takes different configurations in tennis. Bad is a momentary glance, an offhand remark, a kick of the foot, a wave of the arm, a delay, a stance, a stare. As a result, most of tennis' historical bad boys never would have been able to cut the mustard as evil characters in our other vicious, insensitive games. Bad in tennis was always only semibad. Which is why the game's newest, baddest star is such a refreshing personality.

Ilie Nastase, a 26-year-old, 6', 175-pound Rumanian, is a man for tennis' time. He is just the person needed to crush old molds, outsmart hoary conventions and even break the austere rules that have held the game back from that one crucial, giant step to total public acceptance and the big time.

He is a nonpareil showman, an utterly exasperating gamesman, a pouting, crying genius with a racket in his hand and a curse on his lips. He is a magnificent enfant terrible any self-respecting sport would be glad to call its own. At a given moment Nastase will out-charisma Ali, out-sex Namath, out-temperament Fischer and out-bad anybody you care to suit up. He is the first Iron Curtain athlete ever to make this kind of an impact on world sport, and his potential is unmatched anywhere. He is the Wimbledon runner-up, the U.S. Open champion, the Grant Prix point leader and the winner of over $100,000 for the season. This weekend in his hometown of Bucharest only a minor miracle can stop him from leading his team and a worshipful country to victory over the U.S. in the Davis Cup. At the top of the tennis world, bad looks to be reigning once again. This fall Ilie has it all....

If Nastase were Br'er Rabbit, controversy would be his briar patch. If you're looking for trouble, you've come to the right place, he seems to be saying. In reality, trouble is a piece of the game for him; it is a vital part of life. "Why they talk me all the time, babee?" he asks in happy, lilting English, a speech pattern that is broken into the pleasing Latinate sounds of his Rumanian accent. His use of the English language is devoid of almost all prepositions and articles as well as many forms of the verb "to be." His slang—"babee," "shuddup"—is impeccable. "Why they listen me and nobody else and ask me behave? What is behave? Every player like this, not only me, babee. We all nervous, all temperament, all crazy."

Generally speaking, this slump-shouldered, sloe-eyed, handsome man has dominated the international circuit for the past few years mainly through outrageous histrionics rather than by his natural racket flair or any degree of consistent winning. He has filled tournaments on four continents with bizarre, funny and sometimes unfortunate moments better suited to something out of *opera bouffe* than to tennis competition. Here is Nastase disputing line calls. There, arguing with umpires and spectators. Here, engaging in sit-down delays. Nastase glares and makes notorious gestures. He mimics opponents' styles and mistakes. He imitates all manner of jungle noises and animal habits in explanation of how and what the man across the net is doing. At the same time that he is taunting and infuriating everyone, Nastase is joking and laughing it up much like the cute and horrid little boy who spoils the birthday party even as he blows out the candles....

In Paris, Nastase persuaded the umpire to address him as "Mr. Nastase" in a match with Cliff Richey. He proceeded to grunt barnyard sounds in an impersonation of Richey's efforts. He called Richey "an-ee-mal, an-ee-mal" and then said to him, "Richey, you wonder why they not call you mister like me? Because you not gentleman, Richey. You an-ee-mal." The two have barely spoken since.

At the Royal Albert Hall in London, Nastase's mimicry angered Clark Graebner to such an extent that the American climbed across the net, grabbed Nastase by the shirtfront and threatened to crack open his head with the racket. Nastase later defaulted, claiming he was "physically terrified." Graebner was silently acclaimed as a saviour by touring pros everywhere.

In Nice during a mixed doubles match Nastase blasted two volleys that knifed into the back of Gail Chanfreau, who was trying to escape on the other side. The first one was a mistake, he said. So was the second one. Trembling and in tears, Chanfreau hurled her racket at Nastase's modishly clipped bangs...

The success of the past few years seems to have affected Nastase only in his relations with [Ion] Tiriac, who broke off their tour doubles partnership prior to Wimbledon this June....

Still Tiriac, like everyone else Nastase touches, cannot help but be charmed by him most of the time. Nastase has never mourned a defeat for more than a few minutes—even at Wimbledon, where he laughingly swept his way through adoring crowds who mobbed him an hour after he had lost the biggest tournament in the world. Tennis is a fancy with him, life a whirl; and even if he is enjoying such a fairy-tale existence to excess, as one cynic points out, "because he knows what the alternative is back behind the Curtain," that is his privilege.

So Ilie Nastase is just some country Communist hot dog lucky enough to have Dominique, money, soul, all that fun and all those marvelous shots. So tennis is just some sport lucky enough to have him.

Excerpted from an original story published in
SPORTS ILLUSTRATED, *October 16, 1972*

THE CRUEL DECEPTION

BY JACK OLSEN

In 1968, SI 's Jack Olsen wrote a ground-breaking five-part series on the status of the black—then called negro—athlete. In the course of the story, he cited voluminous evidence in rebuttal to the popular image of sport as an enlightened haven of opportunity for black athletes. It is a work that remains as relevant today as it was on the day that it was written.

Every morning the world of sports wakes up and congratulates itself on its contributions to race relations. The litany has been repeated so many times that it is believed almost universally. It goes: "Look what sports has done for the Negro."

To be sure, there are a few fair-minded men who are willing to suggest that perhaps the Negro has done something for sports in return. Says George McCarty, athletic director of the University of Texas at El Paso, "In general, the nigger athlete is a little hungrier, and we have been blessed with having some real outstanding ones. We think they've done a lot for us, and we think we've done a lot for them."

The McCarty attitude is echoed on many campuses. Says a university president: "Sure, the Negroes helped our image, but don't forget, they got built up, too. Every one of them that's been here got out of the ghetto. Four of our colored alumni are playing pro basketball right now, and seven are in pro football, and you can't just say that we got a bunch of cattle in here and milked them. It was profitable both ways."

Some argue that anyone with two eyes can see what sports have done for the Negro, and offer Willie Mays as exhibit A. Where would Willie be without baseball? Chopping cotton? Firing a smelter in Birmingham? Or take Bill Russell, player-coach of the Boston Celtics. He goes around making antiwhite remarks and collecting a six-figure check for taking part in a game. Without sports, the argument runs, he would be lucky to be working as a janitor in his hometown of Oakland. Jim Brown is another one. He retires from pro football with a fortune in his sock and becomes an overnight success as a movie actor, all because of sports, and then founds an organization aimed at getting black men jobs, all the while talking out of the side of his mouth about the whites. Why, sports *created* Jim Brown, gave him a free education at Syracuse University, catapulted him to national fame as a star fullback for the Cleveland Browns....

You can hear these arguments any night of the week in the saloon of your choice, even in the *Negro* saloon of your choice. The cliche that sports has been good to the Negro has been accepted by black and white, liberal and conservative, intellectual and red-neck. And the Negro athlete who has the nerve to suggest that all is not perfect is branded as ungrateful, a cur that bites the hand. "If only we could achieve in housing, in education, in economic opportunity, all the things we have achieved in sports," says a typically grateful Negro leader, "the race problem in the United States would disappear."

But Negro athletes do not agree. Almost to a man, they are dissatisfied, disgruntled and disillusioned.

Black collegiate athletes say they are dehumanized, exploited and discarded, and some even say they were happier back in the ghetto.

Black professional athletes say they are underpaid, shunted into certain stereotyped positions and treated like subhumans by Paleolithic coaches who regard them as watermelon-eating idiots.

A member of the University of Houston's coaching staff once made the mistake of telling Halfback Warren McVea, "I think this university's athletic program has been pretty damn good to you." McVea, a short, black artillery shell of a man, snapped back, "I think I've been pretty damn good to this university. I want you to remember one thing: you came to me, I didn't come to you."

"People say, 'Wasn't football good to you?'" recalls Jim Parker, retired All-Pro lineman of the Baltimore Colts. "I say, 'Hell, no, I've been good to it.' Football did no better for me than what I put into it."

Someone asked Percy Harris, line football coach at all-black Du Sable High School in Chicago, what he got out of four years of scholarship athletics at various institutions in the Southwest. "Well, let's see," the 28-year-old Negro mused. "At the University of New Mexico I got a sweater. At Cameron State College in Oklahoma I got a blan-

ket. At Southwestern State I got a jacket and a blanket."

"Black students aren't given athletic scholarships for the purpose of education," says [sociologist] Harry Edwards. "Blacks are brought in to perform. Any education they get is incidental to their main job, which is playing sports. In most cases, their college lives are educational blanks." And like it or not, face up to it or not, condemn it or not, Harry Edwards is right.

With rare exceptions, the American college coach expects his Negro athletes to concentrate on the job for which they were hired. The aim is neither graduation nor education. The *sine qua non* for the Negro athlete is maintaining his eligibility. At the end of the last second of the last minute of the last hour of a Negro athlete's eligibility, he is likely to find himself dumped unceremoniously into the harsh academic world. Tutors who wrote his themes disappear; professors who gave him superior grades for inferior work rigidize their marking standards; counselors who advised courses in basket-weaving and fly casting suddenly point out that certain postponed courses in English and mathematics and history must be passed before graduation....

James Baldwin wrote: "Every Negro boy ... realizes, at once, profoundly, because he wants to live, that he stands in great peril and must find, with speed, a thing, a gimmick, to lift him out, to start him on his way. *And it does not matter what the gimmick is.*" For some it is narcotics. For others it is crime. For more than a few the only gimmick that seems feasible is sports.

Melvin Rogers, 45 years old, gym teacher and basketball coach at all-Negro Eula D. Britton High school, in Rayville, La., sits at a table in the jerry-built "separate-but-equal" school and speaks softly. "If people only knew what we have to go through to produce that one boy out of hundreds who makes it. People say, 'My, my, aren't you proud? You coached Elvin Hayes, and now he's got a $440,000 contract in pro basketball.' Well, I'm proud of Elvin, sure I am, but look out that window over there. See that big fellow playing baseball? He went to school here, had a high IQ, too, but for him it was sport or nothing.... He went up to

the majors for a tryout and didn't make it. Now age has caught up with him, and he's a nothing. He fell for a dream. He could have been just about anything he wanted—except a major league catcher."

The Negro who overemphasizes sports has become the caricature of his race. He turns it into a system of esthetics, his own private art. Sport becomes his *raison d'etre*, and all too often it is a savagely misleading one. The black athlete who fails to become a Wilt Chamberlain or an Elgin Baylor or an Oscar Robertson finds himself competing for employment in an economic market that has little use for the breakaway dribble and the fadeaway jump....

Nor is it true that the successful Negro high school athlete steps automatically into a paradise of fair play and equal opportunity. Most often he picks up his college scholarship and enters a schizophrenic world where he is lionized on the field and ignored off it. "I don't want to be known as the fastest nigger on campus," says Tommie Smith of San Jose State College—but he is. Most famous Negro Athletes try to become accustomed to this double standard, but few succeed. Other black athletes twist and squirm and fight to become accepted, suffer losses, lick their wounds and return to fight again and wind up embittered and discouraged.

Excerpted from an original story published in SPORTS ILLUSTRATED*, July 1, 1968*

'LAWDY, LAWDY, HE'S GREAT'

BY MARK KRAM

The third fight between Muhammad Ali and Joe Frazier took place in 1975, in Manila. It was an unforgettable battle, dominated first by Ali, then by Frazier, and finally by Ali again. Frazier had "taken the child of the gods to hell and back," was how Mark Kram summed up the bout in one of the most lyrical news stories ever run in SI.

It was only a moment, sliding past the eyes like the sudden shifting of light and shadow, but long years from now it will remain a pure and moving glimpse of hard reality, and if Muhammad Ali could have turned his eyes upon himself, what first and final truth would he have seen? He had been led up the winding red-carpeted staircase by Imelda Marcos, the First Lady of the Philippines, as the guest of honor at the Malacanang Palace. Soft music drifted in from the terrace as the beautiful Imelda guided the massive and still heavyweight champion of the world to the long buffet ornamented by huge candelabra. The two whispered, and then she stopped and filled his plate, and as he waited the candles threw an eerie light across the face of a man who only a few hours before had survived the ultimate inquisition of himself and his art.

The maddest of existentialists, one of the great surrealists of our time, the king of all he sees, Ali had never before appeared so vulnerable and fragile, so pitiably unmajestic, so far from the universe he claims as his alone. He could barely hold his fork, and he lifted the food slowly up to his bottom lip, which had been scraped pink. The skin on his face was dull and blotched, his eyes drained of that familiar childlike wonder. His right eye was a deep purple, beginning to close, a dark blind being drawn against a harsh light. He chewed his food painfully, and then he suddenly moved away from the candles as if he had become aware of the mask he was wearing, as if an inner voice were laughing at him. He shrugged, and the moment was gone.

A couple of miles away in the bedroom of a villa, the man who has always demanded answers of Ali, has trailed the champion like a timber wolf, lay in semidarkness. Only his heavy breathing disturbed the quiet as an old friend walked to within two feet of him, "Who is it?" asked Joe Frazier, lifting himself to look around. "Who is it? I can't see! I can't see! Turn the lights on!" Another light was turned on but Frazier still could not see. The scene cannot be forgotten; this good and gallant man lying there, embodying the remains of a will never before seen in a ring, a will that had carried him so far—and now surely too far. His eyes were only slits, his face looked as if it had been painted by Goya. "Man, I hit him with punches that'd bring down the walls of a city," said Frazier. "Lawdy, Lawdy, he's a great champion." Then he put his head back down on the pillow, and soon there was only the heavy breathing of a deep sleep slapping like big waves against the silence.

Time may well erode that long morning of drama in Manila, but for anyone who was there those faces will return again and again to evoke what it was like when two of the greatest heavyweights of any era met for a third time, and left millions limp around the world. Muhammad Ali caught the way it was: "It was like death. Closest thing to dyin' that I know of."

Excerpted from an original story published in
SPORTS ILLUSTRATED, *October 13, 1975*

THE GLORIOUS ORDEAL

BY RON FIMRITE

Ron Fimrite was in Atlanta when Henry Aaron finally surpassed Babe Ruth as baseball's alltime home run leader. Like Roger Maris before him, Aaron had been forced to endure a torturous ordeal for daring to challenge the beloved Babe.

Henry Aaron's ordeal ended at 9:07 p.m. Monday.

It ended in a carnival atmosphere that would have been more congenial to the man he surpassed as baseball's alltime home-run champion. But it ended. And for that, as Aaron advised the 53,775 Atlanta fans who came to enshrine him in the game's pantheon, "Thank God."

Aaron's 715th home run came in the fourth inning of the Braves' home opener with Los Angeles, off the Dodgers' Al Downing, a left-hander who had insisted doggedly before the game that for him this night would be "no different from any other." He was wrong, for now he joins a company of victims that includes Tom Zachary (Babe Ruth's 60th home run in 1927), Tracy Stallard (Roger Maris' 61st in 1961), and Guy Bush (Ruth's 714th in 1935). They are destined to ride in tandem through history with their assailants.

Downing's momentous mistake was a high fastball into Aaron's considerable strike zone. Aaron's whip of a bat lashed out at it and snapped it in a high arc toward the 385-foot sign in left centerfield. Dodger Centerfielder Jimmy Wynn and Leftfielder Bill Buckner gave futile chase, Buckner going all the way to the six-foot fence for it. But the ball dropped over the fence in the midst of a clutch of Braves' relief pitchers who scrambled out of the bullpen in pursuit. Buckner started to go over the fence after the ball himself, but gave up after he realized he was outnumbered. It was finally retrieved by reliever Tom House, who even as Aaron triumphantly rounded the bases ran hysterically toward home plate holding the ball aloft. It was, after all, one more ball than Babe Ruth ever hit over a fence, and House is a man with a sense of history....

It rained in Atlanta during the day, violently on occasion, but it was warm and cloudy by game time. It began raining again just before Aaron's first inconsequential time at bat, as if Ruth's phantom were up there puncturing the drifting clouds. Brightly colored umbrellas sprouted throughout the ball park, a brilliant display that seemed to be merely part of the show. The rain had subsided by Aaron's next time up, the air filled now only with tension. Henry wasted little time relieving that tension. It is his way. Throughout his long career Aaron had been faulted for lacking a sense of drama, for failing to rise to critical occasions, as [Willie] Mays, say, or Ted Williams had. He quietly endured such spurious criticism, then in two memorable games dispelled it for all time. And yet, after it was over, he was Henry Aaron again....

"I feel I can relax now. I feel my teammates can relax. I feel I can have a great season."

It is not that he had ever behaved like anyone but Henry Aaron. For this generation of baseball fans and now for generations to come, that will be quite enough.

Excerpted from an original story published in
SPORTS ILLUSTRATED, *April 15, 1974*

1976-1983

The Era of

FRE

DOM

THE ERA OF FREEDOM

BY STEVE WULF

et's rewind the tape back to 1976, and while we're waiting, I have a little story to tell. Actually, it's more of a confession, and since the truth will set you free, what better way to start talking about the Era of Freedom? In January of 1976, I was 25 and working for *The Fort Lauderdale News*. Super Bowl X, between the Pittsburgh Steelers and Dallas Cowboys, was being played in Miami, and I was told to do the game story. The paper had only three working credentials to the game, though, so it was decided that I would write the story from my television at home and from notes provided to me by sports editor Bernie Lincicome and the two reporters assigned to the locker rooms.

Everything would have gone off without a hitch except for one thing. I fell asleep in the third quarter. No excuse. I hadn't worked or partied particularly late the night before. It's just that, to this day, I have a hard time lounging through an entire football game without nodding off. Anyway, I woke up deep in the fourth quarter, just in time to see Roger Staubach throw a too-little, too-late touchdown pass to wide receiver Percy Howard. I remember it was Percy Howard because 1) Percy Howard was from Fort Lauderdale and 2) it was the only pass Percy Howard ever caught in the NFL.

I, however, had dropped the ball. How could I write the definitive account of the ultimate game when 15 minutes of it were missing from my consciousness? Remember, children, this was back in the old days before the VCR, and we pioneers didn't have videotape to help us. Which reminds me, the tape is almost rewound, so let's cut to the chase.

Thanks to excellent notes provided by my colleagues and the mimeographed play-by-play handed out in the press box of the Orange Bowl, I was able to reconstruct what I had slept through, and I wrote a good story about the Steelers' upset victory. If I recall correctly, my lead went something like, "Cinderella wore black...." (Hey, I was young then.) The punch line to this tale is that 12 months later, my Super Bowl X story was awarded third place in the news category of the Florida Sportswriters Association contest. This says more about the nature of such contests than it does about my writing, but still, I've always wondered where I would have finished had I actually seen the whole game.

Ah, here we are, 1976. If you experienced a sense of deja vu in 1990, that's because in '76 the baseball owners pulled a lockout in spring training and Raymond Floyd won the Masters. (He nearly won it 14 years later.) Dorothy Hamill skated and Bruce Jenner ran, jumped and heaved their ways into our hearts. It was nice to meetcha, Nadia Comaneci. Chris Evert dominated women's tennis, winning Wimbledon and the U.S.

Open. Detroit rookie pitcher Mark Fidrych told the ball, "Flow, gotta flow now, gotta flow," and America went with the flow, making the 19-game winner the hottest name in the game.

The most far-reaching news in baseball that year was the free agency granted to pitchers Dave McNally and Andy Messersmith. The decision by arbitrator Peter Seitz broke the bank, so to speak, and in November of '76 free-agent Reggie Jackson signed a contract with the Yankees for a then-unheard-of $3 million. Some teams got their money's worth. Messersmith signed with the Braves, owned by Ted Turner, and when the pitcher, whose number was 17, came out on the field one day, the name on his back was Channel, which made him a walking billboard for Turner's SuperStation. The Age of Freedom was under way.

Other remarkable stars emerged in '77. Jockey Steve Cauthen, 17, won more than $6 million in purses to set an alltime, single-season record and captivate the racing public. Seattle Slew won the Triple Crown. Janet Guthrie became the first woman to start her engines at the Indianapolis. Reggie Jackson hit three home runs in the sixth and decisive game of the World Series to lay claim to the title of Mr. October.

This was also the year I joined SPORTS ILLUSTRATED as a reporter. Like Reggie, I was a free agent, although I signed for somewhat less than $3 million. I came to New York by way of Boston, where I had been free-lancing (read starving) for several months. My first assignment for SI was to check the facts in a section of what was then known as FOOTBALL'S WEEK, a compendium of happenings in college football. At one juncture, I had to call the sports information director—SID for short— at Brigham Young to verify that the backup for quarterback Gifford Nielsen had saved the day for the Cougars. At SI, when the writer doesn't know a name or a fact, he or she uses the word *Koming* or the notation *tk*. The passage I had to check contained the following sentence: "Nielsen's backup, Koming Koming, threw for tk yards." In my innocence, I asked the SID, "Now, your backup quarterback is named Koming Koming?" I figured he must be one of those Samoan football players. The SID said, "No, but we do have someone named Marc Wilson." I replied, "Oh, yes, of course, that's who I meant." I neglected to ask him how to spell Marc, however, so the name in the magazine read, incorrectly, "Mark Wilson." Thus began my education at SI.

The year 1978 brought another Triple Crown winner, Affirmed, with Cauthen aboard and Alydar chasing him. Leon Spinks upset Muhammad Ali to set boxing, dentistry and-driving schools on their ears. Billy Martin and Woody Hayes both made pugnacious exits. Under the kinder, gentler managing of Bob Lemon, the Yankees made a ferocious late-season charge to overtake the Red Sox.

We're up to 1979 now. Magic State beat Bird State to win the NCAA basketball title. Within a 42-day span, Sebastian Coe set world records in the 800 meters, the mile and the 1,500 meters. Willie Stargell's Pirates, whose theme song was *We Are Fam-i-lee*, delivered a stirring message that with love and brotherhood, you can oversome obstacles as daunting as a 3-1 deficit to Baltimore in the World Series.

On the eve of a new decade, the order seemed to be changing.

O.J. Simpson carried the ball for the last time, while O.J. Anderson ran for 1,605 yards in his rookie year. Billie Jean King, 35, won a record 20th Wimbledon title, in women's doubles, and 16-year-old Tracy Austin beat Evert in the U.S. Open finals. Most important of all, as far as I was concerned, SI began to send me out to write stories.

Nineteen-hundred eighty was the most bittersweet year in memory. The Winter Olympics in Lake Placid were joyous, thanks to the U.S. hockey team and Eric Heiden, but the Summer Olympics in Moscow seemed empty because of the American boycott in protest of the invasion of Afghanistan. Roberto Duran and Sugar Ray Leonard engaged in one of the great welterweight fights of all time, which Duran won, but in the rematch, Duran cried, "*No mas.*" There were wunderkind—21-year-old John McEnroe, 22-year-old Masters champion Seve Ballesteros, 19-year-old NHL MVP Wayne Gretzky and 20-year-old Laker rookie Magic Johnson—and wun-

der-elders like Jack Nicklaus, who won the U.S. Open and PGA at the age of 40. But there was also the sight of Muhammad Ali throwing in the towel after 10 rounds of his fight with Larry Holmes. It was an especially bittersweet year for Philadelphia, which saw the Flyers go to the Stanley Cup finals, the 76ers go to the NBA Finals, the Phillies go to the World Series and the Eagles go to the Super Bowl. Unfortunately, only the Phillies emerged victorious.

It was the 150th anniversary of Lewis Carroll's birth in 1981, and to borrow a theme from *Alice in Wonderland*, the sports year got curiouser and curiouser. Nicklaus shot an 83 in the British Open, a tournament he had won or finished second in 10 times. A Mexican of Mayan descent cast a spell called Fernandomania over hitters and fans alike. But the most bizarre aspect of '81 was the baseball strike that cost the game approximately a third of the season. Four teams that had no idea they had won anything were declared champions of the first half of the year. The team with the best record in baseball at the end, the Cincinnati Reds, did not receive a postseason invitation, while the Kansas City Royals, who had the 17th best record, did.

One of the biggest and most far-reaching stories of 1982 was actually an SI cover story. It began, "Cocaine arrived in my life with my first-round draft into the National Football League," and it detailed the harrowing downfall of former NFL defensive lineman Don Reese. The piece opened a great many eyes to the pervasiveness and danger of drugs in sports.

It was also in '82 that St. Louis Cardinals pitcher Joaquin Andujar delivered his now-famous quote, "My favorite word in the English language is youneverknow." Youneverknow about some people—Joaquin first and foremost—but it's true of less flighty types as well. Take Baltimore manager Earl Weaver, for example. One day in 1982 I discovered he was a Shakespearean scholar.

This was back in spring training, and ex-umpire Ron Luciano was at the ballpark in Miami to promote his new book. Weaver spotted his old adversary and told him that his book was factually inaccurate. Luciano answered the charge by citing poetic license. To which Weaver replied, "Ron, as it says in *Hamlet*, 'To thine own self be true.'" Edwin Pope, the eminent columnist for *The Miami Herald*, recorded the conversation in his paper the next day, but an overzealous desk man altered Weaver's quote to read, "as Horatio says in Hamlet...."

Well, the next time Weaver saw Pope, he lit into him. "Edwin," said Weaver, "if Polonius didn't bloody say it, I've lived the last 35 years of my life backwards." Weaver didn't actually use the word "bloody"—that's a bowdlerization. Chances are it was the first time that Polonius and the word Weaver *did* use were ever uttered in the same breath. It turns out that Earl had a good English teacher in high school in St. Louis, and her Shakespearean lessons had never been forgotten.

The United States always won the America's Cup, and the National League always won the All-Star Game, right? Wrong in 1983. *Australia II*, with its secret keel, sped past *Liberty* to wrest the 132-year-old Cup from the U.S. for the first time. Fred Lynn's grand slam helped the AL break the NL's 11-game winning streak in the 50th All-Star Game, in Chicago.

A major drug scandal hit the Kansas City Royals, who went through a substance-abuse problem of a different sort later that summer. George Brett's go-ahead, two-out ninth inning homer on July 24 off the Yankees' Rich Gossage was disallowed because Brett had too much pine tar on his bat. AL president Lee MacPhail overturned the umpires' decision and ordered that the game be continued in Yankee Stadium on August 18.

That tiny, four-out game, which was finally played after a month of protests, lawsuits and George Steinbrenner tirades, remains one of the more memorable games I've ever covered. To close out the top of the ninth, Yankee manager Billy Martin positioned pitcher Ron Guidry in centerfield and rookie first baseman Don Mattingly at second base. Then in the bottom of the ninth, relief pitcher Dan Quisenberry retired the Yankees in order for one of his record 45 saves that year. The game took all of 12 minutes. Or three weeks, four days, four hours and 14 minutes, depending on how you looked at it.

And so the Era of Freedom went from a pitcher who talked to a ball to an owner who squawked over a bat. We're at the end of the tape now. We saw a lot in those eight years. The onset of free agency helped bring about parity and the ends of dynasties. The NBA was lifted out of its prolonged economic slump by Larry Bird, Magic Johnson and finally, Michael Jordan. Women gained increasing visibility in the sports arena. It was an era that gave us great stars, like George Brett and Walter Payton and Dr. J, but it was also an era of promises unkept: Mark Fidrych, Joe Charboneau, Houston McTear, Ralph Sampson, Jim Craig, Tracy Austin, Art Schlichter, and, let us not forget, Percy Howard.

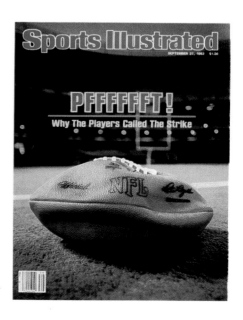

It was a time when big-time college sports were corrupted big time, when individual athletes succumbed to drugs in ever-increasing numbers, but those are the growing pains that come with any period of sudden development, and there can be no argument that there was a world of change in these years. Let's put it this way: this was not an era that you could sleep through.

I'll remember the time fondly, partly because of the richness of the events I witnessed, but also because it brought me to SPORTS ILLUSTRATED, a magazine that I loved when I was just one of its readers and love still as one of its writers. As the '79 Pirates were to Willie Stargell, SI is to me. Hey, I grew up here. I woke up here too.

1 9 7 6

The Winner's Circle

Baseball: Cincinnati Reds
NFL: Oakland Raiders
College Football: University of Pittsburgh
NHL: Montreal Canadiens
NBA: Boston Celtics
College Basketball: Indiana
Masters: Ray Floyd
U.S. Open (golf): Jerry Pate
British Open: Johnny Miller
PGA: Dave Stockton
Australian Open: Mark Edmondson
French Open: Adriano Panatta
Wimbledon: Bjorn Borg
U.S. Open (tennis): Jimmy Connors
Australian Open: Evonne Goolagong Cawley
French Open: Sue Barker
Wimbledon: Chris Evert
U.S. Open (tennis): Chris Evert
Kentucky Derby: Bold Forbes
Preakness: Elocutionist
Belmont: Bold Forbes
Indianapolis 500: Johnny Rutherford

Franz Klammer has the world at his feet as he begins his downhill run at the Winter Olympics in Innsbruck. As a native Austrian and the winner of eight of nine World Cup downhill races in '75, the pressure on Klammer for an Olympic victory is intense. Bernhard Russi of Switzerland makes a torrid run ahead of him, but Klammer attacks the last 1,000 meters of the course to win by one-third of a second.

Demure Dorothy Hamill allows herself a shy smile on the victory stand after her gold medal win in women's figure skating. Her success will spawn a wave of Dorothy wannabes as women all over the U.S. have their hair cut in the Hamill style. After several highly publicized romances and a failed marriage to Dean Paul Martin, she will marry Dr. Ken Forsythe in 1987 and give birth to daughter Alexandra in '88.

John Naber looks up at the clock to discover that he has broken the world record in the 100-meter backstroke for the second time in 24 hours at the Olympics—the first record came in the semifinals—with a time of 55.49 seconds. Five days later, Naber will win another gold with a time of 1:59.19 in the 200-meter back-stroke, becoming the first man to break the two-minute mark in the event.

1976

Kent Benson comes down with one of his 45 rebounds in five games during the NCAA tournament, while Scott May seems to cower in awe. The Hoosiers will go on to beat Michigan 86–68 in the title game to finish the season at a perfect 32–0.

Bjorn Borg may look awkward on this shot, but his play at Wimbledon is pure efficiency as he trounces Ilie Nastase in straight sets to begin his string of five straight Wimbledon titles. Only the French Open, which he wins six times, is kinder to the placid Swede.

Sylvester Stallone takes the ring as Rocky   Chairman Mao dies

Dwight Stones breaks his own world record—set at the NCAA championships two months earlier—with a high jump of 7' 7¼" at the Bicentennial Meet of Champions in Philadelphia in August. In between the two meets comes Stones's troubled Olympics in Montreal where his negative comments about the French-Canadian organizers earn him the enmity of the crowd.

Johnny Bench looks skyward as his two-run shot in the fourth inning puts the Reds in front 3–1 in Game 4 of Cincinnati's World Series sweep of the Yankees. Bench will hit a second homer in the ninth—a three-run blast—and is the engine that drives the Big Red Machine throughout the Series, pounding out a team-leading eight hits in 15 at bats, four of them going for extra bases.

An Israeli raid frees 105 hostages at Entebbe Airport in Uganda

1976

Oakland's Ken Stabler looks to deliver one of the precision darts that will help the Raiders to an easy 32–14 win over the Minnesota Vikings in Super Bowl XI. Stabler will complete 12 of 19 passes for 180 yards and a touchdown, including four tosses to the elusive Freddie Biletnikoff for 79 yards as the Raiders run up 429 yards in total offense. The Vikings fall to 0–4 in Super Bowl play.

The U.S. celebrates its bicentennial   Philadelphia is struck by Legionnaire's Disease

1977

The Winner's Circle

Baseball: New York Yankees
NFL: Dallas Cowboys
College Football: Notre Dame
NHL: Montreal Canadiens
NBA: Portland Trail Blazers
College Basketball: Marquette
Masters: Tom Watson
U.S. Open (golf): Hubert Green
British Open: Tom Watson
PGA: Lanny Wadkins
Australian Open: Roscoe Tanner/Vitas Gerulaitis
French Open: Guillermo Vilas
Wimbledon: Bjorn Borg
U.S. Open (tennis): Guillermo Vilas
Australian Open: Kerry Melville Reid/Evonne
Goolagong Cawley
French Open: Mima Jausovec
Wimbledon: Virginia Wade
U.S. Open (tennis): Chris Evert
Kentucky Derby: Seattle Slew
Preakness: Seattle Slew
Belmont: Seattle Slew
Indianapolis 500: A.J. Foyt

It is a matchup of ex-Bruins as Portland's Bill Walton and L.A.'s Kareem Abdul-Jabbar, with five NCAA titles between them, meet in the NBA Western Conference finals. Although the numbers favor Jabbar (27.8 points and 16.0 rebounds per game to Walton's 19.3 and 15.3), it is Walton's Blazers who win in four games and go on to the NBA finals where they defeat the 76ers in six games.

Ted Turner's Courageous (US 26) defeats Ted Hood's Independent in the America's Cup Trials to earn the right to defend the Cup against the challenger from down under, Australia. Courageous will go on to an easy 4–0 victory, as Australia's lighter weight is no advantage in the moderate winds off Newport Harbor. The win runs the U.S.'s record in Cup competition to 73–7.

Steve Shutt (22) celebrates as his shot slides past prone Bruin goalie Gerry Cheevers to put Montreal in front 3–0 in Game 2 of the Canadiens' four-game sweep of the Boston Bruins in the Stanley Cup finals. Guy Lafleur is the sparkplug for Montreal, collecting two goals and seven assists to lead all scorers and win the Conn Smythe Trophy as series MVP.

167

The mighty swing of Reggie Jackson produces a record five home runs in New York's six-game World Series defeat of Los Angeles. His apotheosis as Mr. October is assured in Game 6, when he hits three consecutive homers to drive in five runs in the 8–4 victory that clinches the Series for the Yanks.

As Jean Cruguet thunders down the stretch aboard Seattle Slew, he sneaks a peek behind him to find Iron Constitution as his only rival in the waning moments of the Preakness Stakes. Slew will finish 1 ½ lengths in front, then go on to win the Belmont and become the first undefeated Triple Crown winner.

1977

1978

The Winner's Circle

Baseball: New York Yankees
NFL: Pittsburgh Steelers
College Football: Alabama/USC
NHL: Montreal Canadiens
NBA: Washington Bullets
College Basketball: Kentucky
Masters: Gary Player
U.S. Open (golf): Andy North
British Open: Jack Nicklaus
PGA: John Mahaffey
Australian Open: Guillermo Vilas
French Open: Bjorn Borg
Wimbledon: Bjorn Borg
U.S. Open (tennis): Jimmy Connors
Australian Open: Chris O'Neil
French Open: Virginia Ruzici
Wimbledon: Martina Navratilova
U.S. Open (tennis): Chris Evert
Kentucky Derby: Affirmed
Preakness: Affirmed
Belmont: Affirmed
Indianapolis 500: Al Unser
World Cup: Argentina

A pudgy 18-year-old Czech named Martina Navratilova defects to the U.S. in 1975. Three years later she is in the Wimbledon finals against the reigning queen of tennis, Chris Evert. The experts wait for the ingenue to wilt beneath Evert's steady barrage of ground strokes, but it is Navratilova who proves the more durable, outlasting her rival for a 2–6, 6–4, 7–5 win and her first major title. The two will meet again.

Pete Rose breaks out of a 5-for-44 batting slump with two hits against the Cubs on June 14, then goes on to hit in 44 straight games to tie Wee Willie Keeler for the National League's longest batting streak, leaving only Joe DiMaggio's wondrous 56 straight beyond his reach. Rose has some hairy moments: four times his only hit is a bunt; six times he gets a hit in his last at bat.

Steve Cauthen and Affirmed finish a neck in front of Alydar and Jorge Velasquez in the Preakness, a scenario that is repeated with only minor variation in all three Triple Crown races. The electrifying rivalry reaches its climax in the final mile of the Belmont, when the two colts battle neck and neck all the way to the finish line, with Affirmed just barely getting a nose in front at the wire.

171

Volkswagen builds its first car in the U.S.

172

With the partisan home crowd in River Plate Stadium roaring its approval, Daniel Passarella takes a joyride after Argentina's 3–1 overtime win over Holland for the World Cup title. Mario Kempes is the team leader, scoring two of Argentina's goals and leading all World Cup scorers with six.

This Nancy with the laughing face has good reason for merriment: She's Nancy Lopez, the winner of nine LPGA events and $189,813, the most ever won by a woman golfer. She also wins friends—becoming a gallery favorite—and influences people, most notably big-name sponsors for the women's tour.

Karol Wojtyla becomes Pope John Paul II   Carter, Begin and Sadat meet at Camp David

1979

The Winner's Circle

Baseball: Pittsburgh Pirates
NFL: Pittsburgh Steelers
College Football: Alabama
NHL: Montreal Canadiens
NBA: Seattle SuperSonics
College Basketball: Michigan State
Masters: Fuzzy Zoeller
U.S. Open (golf): Hale Irwin
British Open: Seve Ballesteros
PGA: David Graham
Australian Open: Guillermo Vilas
French Open: Bjorn Borg
Wimbledon: Bjorn Borg
U.S. Open (tennis): John McEnroe
Australian Open: Barbara Jordan
French Open: Chris Evert
Wimbledon: Martina Navratilova
U.S. Open (tennis): Tracy Austin
Kentucky Derby: Spectacular Bid
Preakness: Spectacular Bid
Belmont: Coastal
Indianapolis 500: Rick Mears

Eamonn Coghlan of Ireland raises a hand in triumph after running a 3:52.9 mile at a meet in Philadelphia. Seven months earlier, he had set a world record in the indoor mile with a time of 3:52.6 to shatter the old mark by 2.3 seconds. His feat would be overshadowed later in the season by Sebastian Coe, who will run a world-record 3:49 outdoor mile at the Bislett Games in Oslo.

Pittsburgh's John Stallworth makes the catch beyond the outstretched arm of Ram cornerback Rod Perry, then streaks in with the 73-yard touchdown that puts the Steelers in front 24–19 in the fourth quarter of Super Bowl XIV. Two series later, Stallworth will do it again, going 45 yards to set up Franco Harris's one-yard plunge for the 31–19 final score.

The NCAA tournament features the premier showing of what is to become the long-running Larry and Magic Show as Larry Bird's Indiana State meets Magic Johnson's Michigan State in the title game. The much deeper Spartans cruise to an easy 75–64 victory as Bird is held to 19 points and Johnson is named the tournament MVP.

Pittsburgh's Ed Ott slides away from the tag of Baltimore's Rick Dempsey to score the game-winning run in the ninth inning of the Pirates' 3–2 Game 2 World Series victory. Ott was driven home by Manny Sanguillen's pinch single and was aided by first baseman Eddie Murray's curious decision to cut off the throw from rightfield before relaying it to the plate. The Pirates will charge back from a 3–1 deficit to take the Series in seven.

Grete Waitz, the Norwegian schoolteacher who continues to claim she is a track runner and not a marathoner, shatters her own world record by nearly five minutes, winning the New York Marathon in a time of 2:27:33. Waitz, who finishes 11 minutes ahead of any other woman in the race, will go on to win seven of the next nine New York Marathons. Bill Rodgers is the fastest man, with a 2:11:42 for his fourth straight New York win.

Benchmarks   A nuclear accident takes place at Three Mile Isla

1979

A champion is crowned: Sugar Ray Leonard celebrates the 15th-round TKO over Wilfred Benitez that earns him the WBC welterweight title. Leonard, just 23 and in his 26th pro fight, answers all the questions about his inexeperience by battling for 14 rounds with the highly skilled Benitez, then flooring the champion with a left uppercut in the 15th before referee Carlos Padilla stops the fight.

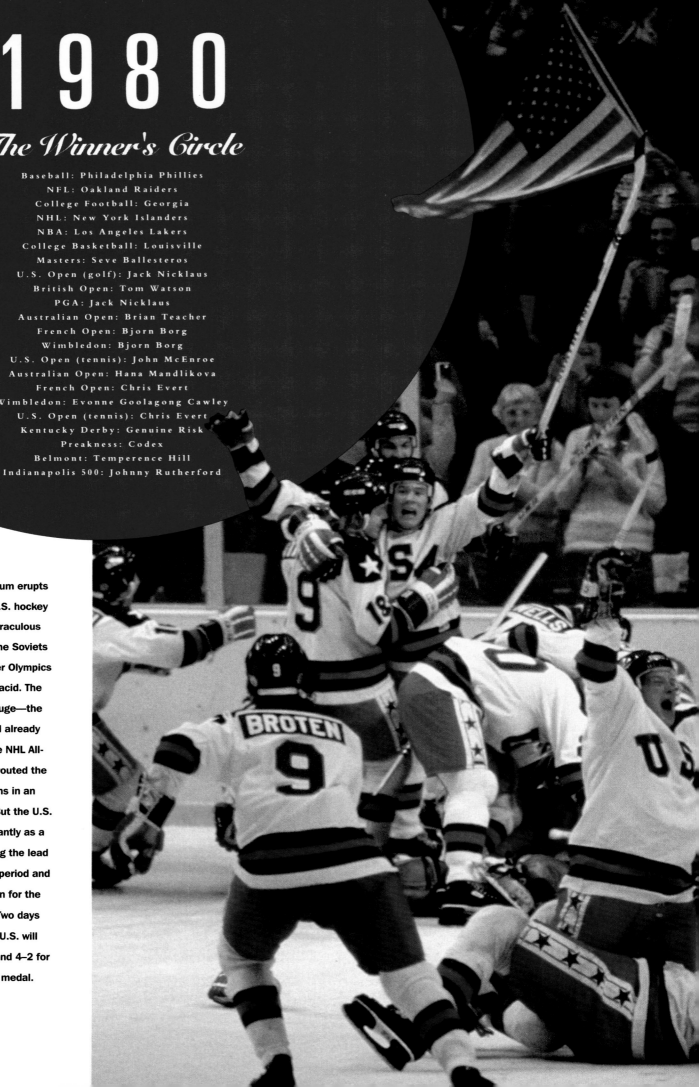

1980

The Winner's Circle

Baseball: Philadelphia Phillies
NFL: Oakland Raiders
College Football: Georgia
NHL: New York Islanders
NBA: Los Angeles Lakers
College Basketball: Louisville
Masters: Seve Ballesteros
U.S. Open (golf): Jack Nicklaus
British Open: Tom Watson
PGA: Jack Nicklaus
Australian Open: Brian Teacher
French Open: Bjorn Borg
Wimbledon: Bjorn Borg
U.S. Open (tennis): John McEnroe
Australian Open: Hana Mandlikova
French Open: Chris Evert
Wimbledon: Evonne Goolagong Cawley
U.S. Open (tennis): Chris Evert
Kentucky Derby: Genuine Risk
Preakness: Codex
Belmont: Temperence Hill
Indianapolis 500: Johnny Rutherford

Pandemonium erupts after the U.S. hockey team's miraculous defeat of the Soviets at the Winter Olympics in Lake Placid. The upset is huge—the USSR had already beaten the NHL All-Stars and routed the Americans in an exhibition. But the U.S. plays brilliantly as a team, taking the lead in the third period and hanging on for the 4–3 win. Two days later the U.S. will defeat Finland 4–2 for the gold medal.

Eric Heiden, with his 27-inch thighs, is America's golden boy in Lake Placid, becoming the first athlete ever to collect five individual gold medals. His toughest race is in the 500 meters against Yevgeny Kulikov of the Soviet Union, the world record-holder. But Kulikov slips coming out of the last turn, and Heiden is able to sprint to victory. He will go on to win the 1,000-, 1,500-, 5,000- and 10,000-meter races.

Sebastian Coe of Great Britian outkicks Steve Ovett (279) to win their 1,500-meter showdown at the Summer Games in Moscow, with a time of 3:38.4, less impressive than his 1:48.5 for the final 800 meters. It is a moment of redemption and release for the mild-mannered Coe, who had finished a disappointing second to Ovett in the 800-meter finals and was under intense pressure to succeed in the 1,500.

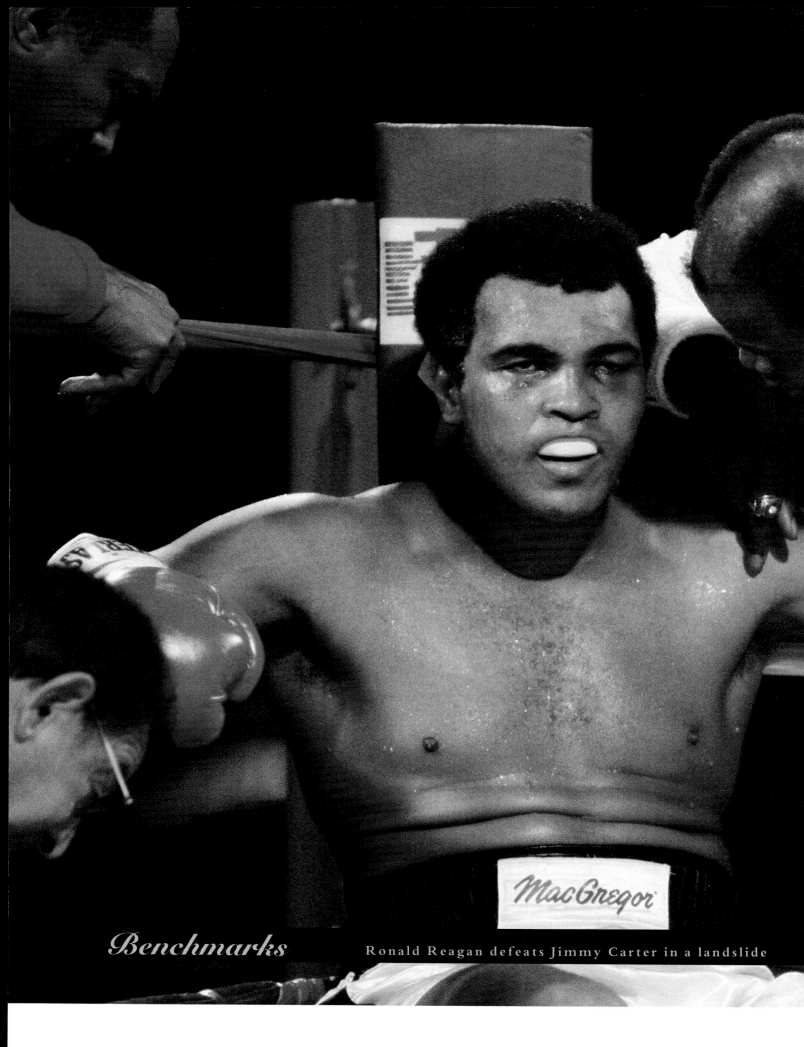

Ronald Reagan defeats Jimmy Carter in a landslide

1980

With his hair dyed black and his weight down to 217, Muhammad Ali seems like the champion of old before his fight with Larry Holmes. But even the masterful Ali at age 38 cannot defy time, and by the 10th round it is clear to the world what Ali himself knew almost from the start: there is no more magic. Trainer Angelo Dundee calls it quits; Ali does not protest.

Mike Schmidt leads the Phillies to a six-game triumph over the Kansas City Royals in the World Series, banging out eight hits, two homers and seven RBIs. He is the key to Philadelphia's pivotal 4–3 victory in Game 5, driving in the first two runs with a homer and scoring the tying run in the ninth. It is the first World Series title for the Phillies.

Solidarity is victorious in Poland   Mount St. Helens erupts

When Kareem Abdul-Jabbar sprains his ankle and is unavailable for duty in the sixth game of the NBA Finals between the Lakers and the 76ers, things look grim for L.A. But rookie point guard Magic Johnson (32) starts at center and leads the Lakers to a 123–107 win with an incandescent performance: 42 points, 15 rebounds, seven assists, three steals and a blocked shot.

Roberto Duran turns his back on Sugar Ray Leonard in the eighth round of their much ballyhooed rematch and speaks the immortal words "no mas" to referee Octavio Meyran, producing perhaps the most bizarre finish in boxing history. Duran will later claim he was bothered by stomach cramps—others say he didn't like being beaten—but the defeat will haunt him for the rest of his career.

The U.S. boycotts the Summer Olympics in Moscow   Alfred Hitchcock dies

1980

With the crowd shouting encouragement, Bill Rodgers lopes toward his third straight victory—his fourth overall—in the Boston Marathon. He will finish with a time of 2:12:11, having run the final six miles on painfully aching legs. It is a gratifying win for the 32-year-old Rodgers, a native New Englander whose first big victory came in Boston in '75 and whose home is in nearby Sherborn.

The TV world wonders: Who shot J.R.?   John Lennon is assassinated in New York

1 9 8 1

The Winner's Circle

Baseball: Los Angeles Dodgers
NFL: San Francisco 49ers
College Football: Clemson
NHL: New York Islanders
NBA: Boston Celtics
College Basketball: Indiana
Masters: Tom Watson
U.S. Open (golf): David Graham
British Open: Bill Rogers
PGA: Larry Nelson
Australian Open: Johan Kriek
French Open: Bjorn Borg
Wimbledon: John McEnroe
U.S. Open (tennis): John McEnroe
Australian Open: Martina Navratilova
French Open: Hana Mandlikova
Wimbledon: Chris Evert
U.S. Open (tennis): Tracy Austin
Kentucky Derby: Pleasant Colony
Preakness: Pleasant Colony
Belmont: Summing
Indianapolis 500: Bobby Unser

The volatile John McEnroe continues to earn the enmity of the British press, berating officials, linesmen and anyone else within earshot and disdainfully referring to Wimbledon as "the pits of the world." But McEnroe's tennis is magnificent, particularly in his 4–6, 7–6, 7–6, 6–4 victory over Bjorn Borg in the finals as he connects on 104 of 167 first serves and wards off 13 of 15 break points.

A rookie pitcher named Fernando Valenzuela emerges from Mexico with a Ruthian physique and an array of baffling stuff that leaves National League hitters gasping. Valenzuela wins his first eight decisions, five of them shutouts, while allowing only four runs in 72 innings for an ERA of .050. He will stumble but still finish at 13–7 with a league-leading 11 complete games.

Phil Mahre charges to victory in the giant slalom at Aspen, a critical win that will help him become the first U.S. skier to earn the overall World Cup title. Taking advice via walkie-talkie from his brother Steve, who has just completed his run, Mahre is able to successfully negotiate an icy patch and fly down the hill with a time that even the great Ingemar Stenmark can't match.

Alberto Salazar leads the pack as he pads along the spongy carpet laid across the Queensboro Bridge between miles 15 and 16 of the New York Marathon. Within the next three miles he will pull away from his pursuers and race only against the clock, finishing in 2:08:13 to fulfill his prerace prediction of a world record time.

San Francisco's Dwight Clark soars through the air to snare Joe Montana's seemingly uncatchable pass in the waning moments of the NFC Championship Game against Dallas. The catch, climaxing a dramatic 89-yard drive, puts the 49ers in front 28–27 and sends them on to the Super Bowl against Cincinnati.

Benchmarks   The American hostages are released in Iran

1981

MTV begins broadcasting   Charles and Diana are royally wed

1982

The Winner's Circle

Baseball: St. Louis Cardinals
NFL: Washington Redskins
College Football: Penn State
NHL: New York Islanders
NBA: Los Angeles Lakers
College Basketball: North Carolina
Masters: Craig Stadler
U.S. Open (golf): Tom Watson
British Open: Tom Watson
PGA: Ray Floyd
Australian Open: Johan Kriek
French Open: Mats Wilander
Wimbledon: Jimmy Connors
U.S. Open (tennis): Jimmy Connors
Australian Open: Chris Evert
French Open: Martina Navratilova
Wimbledon: Martina Navratilova
U.S. Open (tennis): Chris Evert
Kentucky Derby: Gato del Sol
Preakness: Aloma's Ruler
Belmont: Conquistador Cielo
Indianapolis 500: Gordon Johncock
World Cup: Italy

Milwaukee's Doc Medich and Ted Simmons become the unwilling answers to a sports trivia question when Oakland's Rickey Henderson (right) steals his record-breaking 119th base off them in August. Henderson, with his explosive start on the base paths, will go on to steal 130 for the season, a record that has yet to be seriously challenged.

Penn State quarterback Todd Blackledge (left) engineers a 27–24 comeback victory over Nebraska, throwing a low bullet to little-used tight end Kirk Bowman for a 17-yard touchdown with :07 left. The Nittany Lions will go on to defeat Georgia 27–23 in the Sugar Bowl to give Joe Paterno his first national title in 17 years as head coach at Penn State.

Gerry Cooney is trumpeted as a dangerous fighter, capable of taking out champion Larry Holmes with a single punch in their heavily hyped heavyweight bout. But it is Holmes who does almost all the damage, knocking down the game but outclassed Cooney in the 13th round en route to a TKO. Cooney will never challenge for the title again.

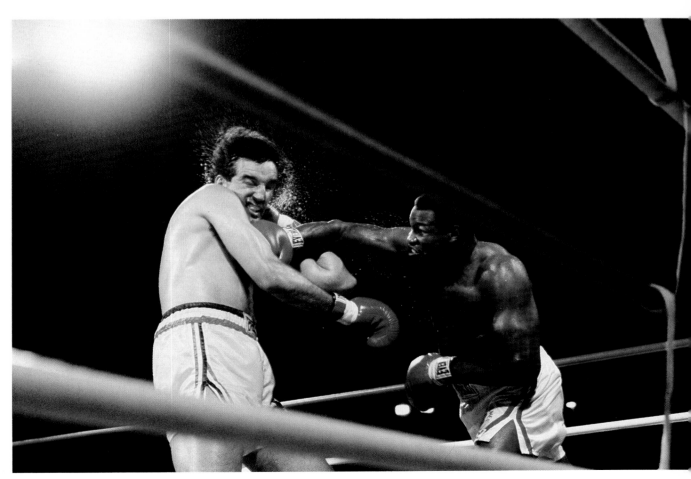

Marco Tardelli lets loose from the edge of the penalty area with the shot that will put Italy in front 2–0 on the way to a 3–1 win over West Germany for its third World Cup title. A header by Paolo Rossi, who scores six goals in Italy's final three games, had put Italy in front 1–0, and Alessandro Altobelli will boot home the insurance goal 12 minutes later.

North Carolina's Michael Jordan goes up for the game-winning jump shot with 17 seconds left in the Tar Heels' 63–62 defeat of Georgetown for the national champion-ship. Nine seconds later, the Hoyas' Freddie Brown, mistaking Carolina's James Worthy for a teammate, will pass the ball to him, thus ending Georgetown's hopes for its first title.

Benchmarks   Tylenol laced with cyanide sets off a national scare

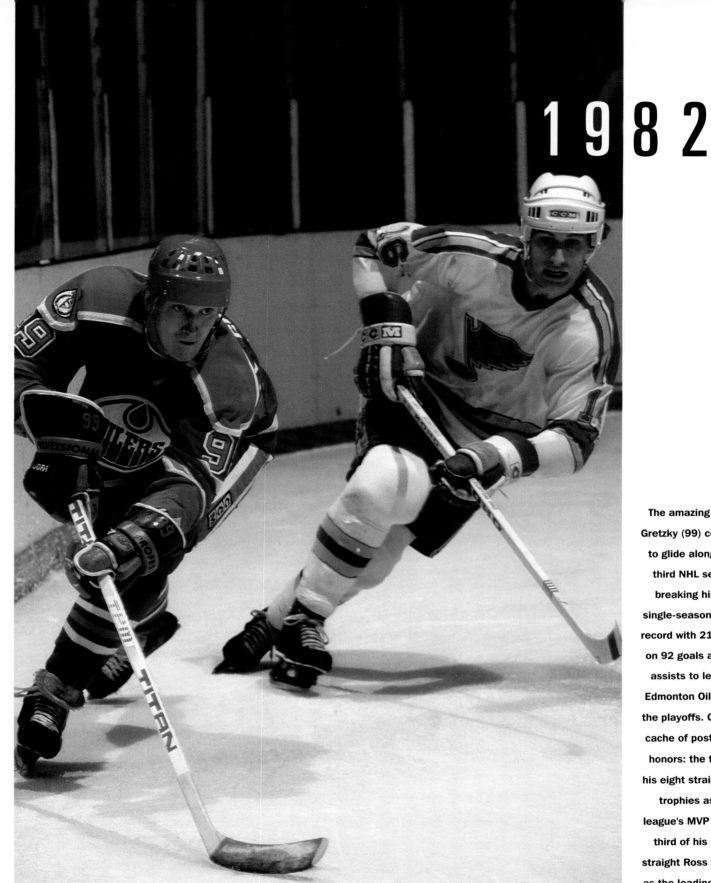

1982

The amazing Wayne Gretzky (99) continues to glide along in his third NHL season, breaking his own single-season scoring record with 212 points on 92 goals and 120 assists to lead the Edmonton Oilers into the playoffs. Gretzky's cache of postseason honors: the third of his eight straight Hart trophies as the league's MVP and the third of his seven straight Ross trophies as the leading scorer.

Argentina invades the Falkland Islands   Brezhnev dies

1983

The Winner's Circle

Baseball: Baltimore Orioles
NFL: Los Angeles Raiders
College Football: University of Miami
NHL: New York Islanders
NBA: Philadelphia 76ers
College Basketball: NC State
Masters: Seve Ballesteros
U.S. Open (golf): Larry Nelson
British Open: Tom Watson
PGA: Hal Sutton
Australian Open: Mats Wilander
French Open: Yannick Noah
Wimbledon: John McEnroe
U.S. Open (tennis): Jimmy Connors
Australian Open: Martina Navratilova
French Open: Chris Evert
Wimbledon: Martina Navratilova
U.S. Open (tennis): Martina Navratilova
Kentucky Derby: Sunny's Halo
Preakness: Deputed Testimony
Belmont: Caveat
Indianapolis 500: Tom Sneva

Jimmy Connors overcomes a painful foot injury, a case of raging diarrhea and temperatures that soar above 100 to defeat Ivan Lendl 6–3, 6–7, 7–5, 6–0 and win his second straight U.S. Open. The key moment comes in the third set when Lendl double-faults on set point, an error that completely unnerves him as he loses the game, the set and then the match, virtually surrendering in the fourth set.

Freshman Cheryl Miller leads USC to the NCAA title in women's basketball, with 27 points, four blocked shots, four steals and nine rebounds in the Women of Troy's 69–67 defeat of Louisiana Tech, the defending champion. Miller will lead USC to another NCAA title the following season and will be named player of the year for 1984, '85 and '86.

Edwin Moses gives himself an impressive birthday present at a meet in Koblenz, breaking the world record in the 400-meter hurdles for the fourth time, with a clocking of 47.02 to chop .11 off his own mark. It is the 85th straight win for Moses, a streak that will yield a gold medal in the '84 Olympics and reach 107 before Moses is beaten by Danny Harris in 1987.

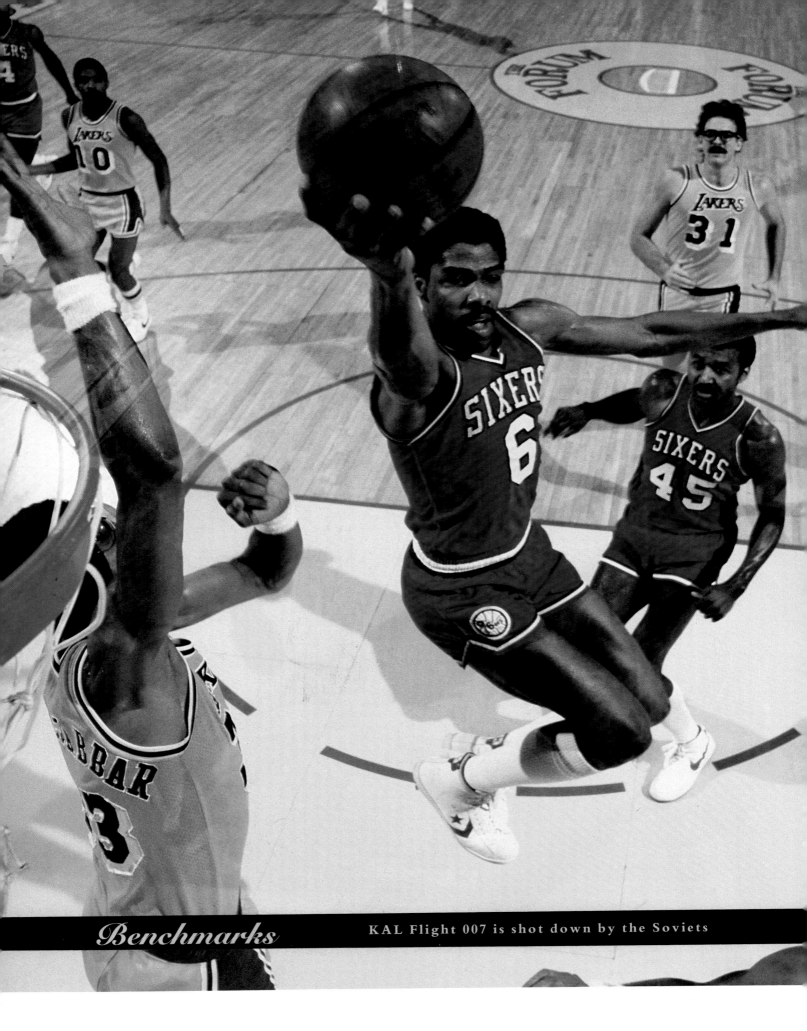

KAL Flight 007 is shot down by the Soviets

1983

Julius Erving leads the Philadelphia 76ers to their first NBA title in 16 years, ending a frustrating run of three failures in the NBA Finals in the previous six seasons. Erving is a force throughout the series sweep against the Lakers, most notably in Game 4 when he scores seven points in a 98-second span to clinch a 115–108 win.

Australia II, skippered by John Bertrand, sails to victory in the America's Cup, marking the first time in 132 years that the trophy has left the U.S. Dennis Conner's Liberty takes a 3–1 lead, but Australia II charges back with three straight wins, including a dramatic comeback in the seventh race for the Cup-clinching victory.

The final episode of M*A*S*H is aired   The U.S. invades Grenada

You don't have to be an elephant to remember the man with the golf club but you don't have to be human, either, as proved by one unusual member of Jack Nicklaus's gallery during a practice round in 1982.

SI *Favorites*

THE RABBIT HUNTER
Frank Deford profiles the inimitable Bobby Knight

AN AMERICAN TRAGEDY
Robert Boyle prsents the chilling facts on acid precipitation

NASTY LITTLE DEVIL
Bil Gilbert introduces the Tasmanian Devil

CLIMBING TO THE TOP AGAIN
John Papanek goes hiking with Bill Walton

RAISED BY WOMEN TO CONQUER MEN
Deford examines Jimmy Connors and the women who made him a champion

YESTERDAY'S CHILD
Kenny Moore spends some time with Mary Decker

IT HAS TO BE A BAD DREAM
Mark Mulvoy helps quadriplegic Darryl Stingley tell his story

A REMINDER OF WHAT WE CAN BE
E.M. Swift recalls the Miracle on Ice at the 1980 Olympics

ARROGANCE AND PANIC
Sarah Ballard assesses the life and times of Martina Navratilova

THE SHOE
William Nack visits the great Bill Shoemaker

THE RABBIT HUNTER

BY FRANK DEFORD

When Frank Deford paid a call on Bobby Knight in 1981, the fiery Indiana basketball coach had already won one national title and succeeded in baffling observers with his unique combination of brilliance and boorishness. Two months after Deford's article, Knight would win his second title, and a third would be his in 1987. Deford's story still stands as the definitive assessment of the essential Knight.

As Bobby Knight is the first to say, a considerable part of his difficulty in the world at large is the simple matter of appearance. "What do we call it?" he wonders. "Countenance. A lot of my problem is just that too many people don't go beyond countenances."

That's astute—Bobby Knight is an astute man—but it's not so much that his appearance is unappealing. No, like so much of him, his looks are merely at odds. Probably, for example, no matter how well you know Coach Knight, you have never been informed—much less noticed yourself—that he's dimpled. Well, he is, and invariably when anyone else has dimples, a great to-do is made about them. But, in Bobby's case, being dimpled just won't fly.

After all: DIMPLED COACH RAGES. No. But then, symbolically, Knight doesn't possess dimples, plural, as one would expect. He has only the prize one, on his left side. Visualize him, standing in line, dressed like the New Year's Baby, when they were handing out dimples. He gets the one on his left side. "What the bleep is this?" says little Bobby, drawing away.

"Wait, wait!" cries the Good Fairy or the Angel Gabriel or whoever's in charge of distributing dimples. But it's too late. Bobby has not time for this extraneous crap with dimples. He's already way down the line, taking extras on bile....

The real issue isn't the countenance anyway. The real issue is the rabbits. And Knight knows that. In the Indiana locker room before a game earlier this season, Knight was telling his players to concentrate on the important things. He said, "How many times I got to tell you? Don't fight the rabbits. Because, boys, if you fight the rabbits, the elephants are going to kill you." But the coach doesn't listen to himself. He's always chasing after the incidental; he's still a prodigy in search of proportion. "There are too many rabbits around," he says. "I know that. But it doesn't do me any good. Instead of fighting the elephants, I just keep going after the rabbits." And it's the rabbits that are doing him in, ruining such a good thing....

What a setup he has. Forty years old, acknowledged to be at the top of his profession. Says the very coach who disparages Knight for being a bully, "Any coach who says Bobby's not the best is just plain jealous." Knight has already won 317 games, and nobody, not even Adolph Rupp, achieved that by his age.

Someday Knight could even surpass Rupp's record 874 wins, a seemingly insurmountable total. Knight has won one NCAA championship, in 1976, and five Big Ten titles in nine seasons; he was twice national coach of the year; he's the only man ever to both play on and coach an NCAA champion. He's the coach at one of America's great basketball schools, one that's also an academic institution of note. The state worships him; Hoosier politicians vie for his benediction. His contemporaries in coaching not only revere him for his professional gifts, but some of his esteemed predecessors—mythic men of basketball lore—see Knight as the very keeper of the game. The torch is in his hands....

In this era of athletic corruption Knight stands four-square for the values of higher education that so many coaches and boot-lickers in the NCAA only pay lip service to. His loyalty is as unquestioned as his integrity. He is the best and brightest ... and the most honorable, too. He has it all, every bit of it. Just lying there on the table. He has only to lean down, pick it up and let the chip fall off. But he can't. For Knight to succeed at basketball—not only to win, you understand, but to succeed because "That's much harder," he says—all the world must be in the game. All the people are players, for or against, to be scouted, tested, broken down, built back up if they matter. Life isn't lived; it's played. And the rabbits are everywhere....

The ultimate contradiction is that Bobby Knight, of all people, profane as he is, seeks after purity. What troubles him is that the game must be muddied by outlanders and apostates—the press, for example. In fact, Knight has studied the subject, and he understands the press better than some writers who cover him understand basketball. He even numbers several writers as friends, and sometimes he will actually offer a grudging admiration beyond his famous institutional assessment: "All of us learn to write by the second grade, then most of us go on to other things."...

Money has never motivated Knight. He has turned down raises, preferring that the money go to his assistants, and he professes not even to know what his salary is—except that, relative to what other teachers at Indiana make, it's too much. This is not to say, of course, that Knight wears a hair shirt. He has a television show, a summer basketball camp, the free use of a car, and, he volunteers, Checkers-like, "I did take a fishing rod once." Also, it's an absolute point of pride with him that he must be paid as much as the Hoosier football coach, Lee Corso. But just as pointedly he has advised alumni and the commercial camp-followers who grubstake coaches on the side to take a wide berth. Recently, however, Knight decided he was a fool to look a gift horse in the mouth, so he solicited bids from shoe companies that were willing to pay him in the hope that his players would wear their sneakers. Adidas won, but instead of sticking this "pimp money," as he calls it, in his own pocket, Knight is turning it over to the university....

And yet, as wary as he is of the hypocritical rabbits all around him, Knight is, in many respects, even more unsparing of himself. The game, we hear so often, has passed so-and-so by. With Knight, it may be the reverse; he may have passed it by. But he loves it so, and therefore he must concoct hurdles so that he can still be challenged by it. He even talks a lot about how nobody is really capable of playing the game well. Ultimately, it may be the final irony that the players themselves must become

interlopers, separating him from the game.

Already he has gone so far that at age 40 winning is no longer the goal. "Look, I know this," he says. "If you're going to play the game, you're going to get more out of it winning. I know that, sure. Now, at West Point I made up my mind to win—gotta win. Not at all costs. Never that. But winning was the hub of everything I was doing....

"But somewhere I decided I was wrong. You could win and still not succeed, not achieve what you should. And you can lose without really failing at all. But it's harder to coach this way, with this, uh, approach. I'm sure I'd be easier on myself and on other people if just winning were my ultimate objective." He pauses; he is in his study at home, amid his books, away from all the basketball regalia. "I never said much about this before."

It was a good secret. Now, Bobby Knight is one step closer to utter control of his game. Now all those dim-witted rabbits cannot touch him. They'll be looking at the scoreboard and the AP poll, judging him by those, but they won't have a clue, not the foggiest. Nobody holds a mortgage on him. Now, you see, now we are talking about definition.

Excerpted from an original story published in SPORTS ILLUSTRATED*, January 26, 1981*

AN AMERICAN TRAGEDY

BY ROBERT H. BOYLE

As SI's readers have come to know, the magazine has long viewed the protection of the environment as an issue of grave concern. In 1981, Robert Boyle wrote this ground-breaking story on acid precipitation.

A chemical leprosy is eating away at the face of the U.S. It's popularly known as acid rain, but rain isn't the only culprit.

The true name for this phenomenon is acid precipitation. In addition to acid rain, it includes acid snow, acid sleet, acid hail, acid frost, acid rime, acid fog, acid mist, acid dew and "dry" deposits of acid particles, aerosols and gases. And it's not only this country's problem. It is, however, the responsibility of the U.S.—as both perpetrator and victim of the ecological crime—to recognize the extreme dangers of acid precipitation and to take steps to remedy it before it becomes so pervasive as to be irreversible.

Acid precipitation is caused by the emission of sulfur dioxide and nitrogen oxides from the combustion of fossil fuels. Natural sources, such as volcanoes and mud flats, can emit sulfur dioxide into the air, but their contribution is small....

Once aloft, the sulfur dioxide and the nitrogen oxides can be transformed into sulfuric and nitric acids by reacting with moisture in the atmosphere, and air currents can carry them hundreds, sometimes thousands, of miles from their source. When these acids precipitate to earth, they can have a devastating impact on lands and waters that have little natural buffering capacity....

Think this kind of stuff is hyperbole? In Canada, where the province of Ontario alone has lost an estimated 4,000 lakes and could lose another 48,000 in the next two decades, there's an urgent need to curb the sources of the pollution, many of them located in the U.S., that have created such devastation and dismal prospects....

In the U.S., acid precipitation falls almost continuously on the ecologically vulnerable lands and waters of West Virginia, Pennsylvania, New Jersey, New York, Rhode Island, Massachusetts, Vermont, New Hampshire and Maine; in short, the 182,496-square-mile northeast quadrant of the U.S. Acid precipitation has destroyed trout streams, trout ponds and bass lakes, which is unsettling if not disastrous; it is also very close to rendering the Quabbin Reservoir, which serves more than two million people in the metropolitan Boston area, an economic disaster....

The next move is up to Congress. Of all those who have addressed the issue, [Dr. Michael] Oppenheimer of EDF [Environmental Defense Fund] says it best: "....Nature operates on a long time scale, but we have been making a host of changes at once, and all the cumulative effects of these changes on this country cannot be understood at once... Acid precipitation is an incipient disaster of the first order, and if we don't do anything, within 10 years we'll start to see seriously significant effects beyond already manifest fishless lakes."

Excerpted from an original story published in
SPORTS ILLUSTRATED, *September 21, 1981*

NASTY LITTLE DEVIL

BY BIL GILBERT

Ever since boyhood, special contributor Bil Gilbert had been fascinated with Tasmania, that isolated outpost off the southern coast of Australia, and with its exotic array of wildlife, most notably the ungainly Tasmanian devil. In 1981, he fulfilled his ambition to travel there and meet this unusual species.

The Hamiltons, we discovered, did have devils, a pair of yearlings that had been trapped by the Tasmanian wildlife service. During the daylight hours they crouched in the far corner of a fenced enclosure, glaring balefully at the cash customers. With a wry chauvinism, Tasmanians often claim that their devil is the ugliest animal in the world. Esthetic judgments are subjective, but it's understandable why this one is commonly held. At a distance—from which devils look their best—they are merely undistinguished, being low-slung, stumpy creatures covered with jet black hair sometimes splashed with white blazes across the chest and rump. In confrontation, they somewhat resemble an ill-formed bear cub or wolverine. Closer examination destroys these and other analogies. A Tasmanian devil doesn't look much like any other single species but rather like bits and pieces of several stuck together without regard for beauty, symmetry or function. My own first flash impression when John Hamilton gingerly presented one for inspection was *mutant!*—of the sort that might proliferate in the aftermath of a nuclear war.

For the devil's size—a large one is three feet long and weighs between 20 and 25 pounds—its head is enormous and would seem to fit better on a wolf or an alligator.... [Its] jaws are studded with teeth that are not only exceptionally large but also numerous; a devil in good working order has 44 choppers, sometimes 46. A dog has 42, a cat 30. It isn't difficult to study this dentation. Somewhat like the python, the devil is so hinged as to be able to open its mouth very wide, and it does this often, being habitually slack-jawed and gapish. Also, it's a steady drooler....

[An actual meeting with a devil in the wild prompted the following speculations.]

C.S. Lewis expressed theological observations ecologically and vice versa. He was of the opinion that we seek other bloods not out of curiosity about their what-hath-God-wrought peculiarities but because we have a desperate need to know and recognize them as our peers and are delighted and comforted by innocent association with other of God's creatures. Lewis thought that since the Fall of Man we have been tempted and seduced by clever but fallacious arguments that we have been set above the rules and rhythms of nature and charged with dominating it. To the extent that we have accepted that proposition—that man is the unnatural animal—we have been made the loneliest of animals, confused about our origins and divorced from the company of our peers. However, our persistent yearning for other bloods is evidence that we haven't completely succumbed to hubris and that we continue to resist dangerous claims about our superiority....

By and by, the battered devil, finding us either unsavory or unfathomable has turned away and satisfied its blood lust by scavenging garbage. Shivering in the midnight cold, we watched until it had finished and departed, feeling, as questing beasts, fulfilled in our blood.

Excerpted from an original story published in SPORTS ILUSTRATED, *October 5, 1981*

CLIMBING TO THE TOP AGAIN

BY JOHN PAPANEK

When John Papanek hiked up a mountain with Bill Walton in 1979—Papanek is the one with the mustache at right—Walton had already had his brilliant career interrupted by serious injury. Sadly for Walton and for basketball, his physical problems would continue, forcing him to miss four entire seasons and significant parts of four others before his retirement in 1988. But Walton never stopped loving the game, and the spirit that Papanek described so vividly persists to this day.

At noon the sky is a brilliant blue, cracked wide open and spilling all over the peaks of Yosemite National Park. The pink-white glaciers and crystal tarns, the rushing streams and slag-gray rocks, the emerald brush and dusty trails are mere handservants to the sun, which is in command. And Bill Walton is walking up a mountain.

Check that. He is *truckin'* up a mountain which, as members of Walton's generation surely know, is quite something else again. Walton is gobbling up yardage like Earl Campbell in the open field, only this field is tilted upward at 60 degrees, and the goal line is way up there about 11,000 feet. His arms, spread like the wings of a giant albatross, flap gently below his russet-haired head. His legs, impossibly long and—although spindly toward the ankles—amazingly strong, eat up great chunks of mountainside with every stride. His feet, gnarled and scarred from the pounding of so many basketball games, feet that have been neglected, inspected and injected, are now resurrected.

Walton is wearing a T-shirt that boldly screams OREGON DEAD on the back. It says so much: that a part of Walton's life—four sometimes happy, sometimes miserable years of living and playing basketball in Portland, Ore.—is dead; and that the wearer of the shirt is part of a legion of young Americans that worships and lives by the funky messages of laid-back California-style life as preached by the Grateful Dead, the original acid-rock band, a vestige of the '60s counterculture that has made it intact almost to the '80s. So, it would seem, has Walton.

Three hours up this mountain, yet it is not work for him; nor would it be for anyone traveling with him. The companion would be pulled along like a smiling water skier on the enormously powerful tendrils of energy that constantly trail Walton. The companion would quickly come to understand why, when Walton is healthy, he is the greatest basketball player alive.

Spend several days with Walton as he is running, no, *truckin'* through his world—playing Frisbee on soft green lawns, buying elegant suits in Beverly Hills, appearing on TV shows, body-surfing in San Diego, playing basketball, doing stand-up comedy at rubber-chicken Rotary luncheons, participating in family sing-alongs, taking grueling bike rides—all of it punctuated by the sounds of the Grateful Dead, and you will begin to understand his energy. And now, *truckin'* up a mountain in the High Sierras, you almost know what is going through his head. Here it comes now....

Truckin' got my chips cashed in
Keep truckin', like the doo-dah man
Together, more or less in line
Just keep truckin' on....

One or another Grateful Dead tune is always running through his head, even when he is triggering fast breaks. Though most of the lyrics seem to have been written just for him. Walton says, "They're for everybody," which is true—at least for the half million "Deadheads" who fully understand the hedonistic messages of the band.

As he hikes, images flicker from Walton's 26 years:

A long, skinny, redheaded kid growing up in a strong Catholic middle-class home in the San Diego suburb of La Mesa. Lots of family activity—music, games, church, books, trips to the mountains, lively discussions. None of the kids—Bill, Bruce, Andy or Cathy—are ever stifled. Ted, a county welfare official, and Gloria, a librarian, encourage their children in their every opinion. But sports are where the kids are headed. At age eight Bill tries basketball, makes his first hoop on his very first shot—a heave from midcourt—and soon he is really playing. Watching, questioning, studying, learning,

practicing. Ted drives him to games all over the area, including ones around the San Diego naval base, where he begins to learn of elbows and broken noses, cracked teeth and bloody lips. At age 14 he is 6'1"; over the ensuing summer he grows to 6'7" and become the 160-pound "Spider Walton" who leads Helix High to 49 straight wins and two district championships. Soon he is 6'11", off to UCLA and those 88 straight victories, two NCAA championships, three College Player of the Year awards.

But suddenly there is all that other stuff, personal things that are getting as much ink and notice as his basketball. The antiwar, anti-Nixon politics. The arrest for protesting the mining of Haiphong Harbor. The long hair, the bike, the strange food he eats, the company he keeps. If one believes the talk, the marijuana he smokes. But, hey, the guy can play basketball.

Then he signs with Portland for big money. What happened to all the socialist talk? And, ugh, the clothes and the hair are worse. And the things he says. Just because he is a vegetarian, does he have to say that his teammates disgust him because they eat "decayed animal flesh"? And what happened to the basketball? He keeps coming up with all sorts of injuries and bone spurs. Some Portland people call them "brain spurs." And he refuses to do what other players do when they are hurting—play anyway. And Jack Scott, the feared "sports activist," moves right into Walton's house, fills his head with more radical ideas, and soon Walton is being hounded all across the country by the FBI because Scott allegedly is hiding Patty Hearst and her Symbionese Liberation Army kidnappers.

The basketball? Even when he does play, the Trail Blazers are awful for two seasons. But that changes in 1976–77 as Walton, quite spectacularly, again becomes the best player on his level, which now happens to be the NBA. The Trail Blazers blow all comers out of the water, and they are even better the next year until Walton goes down with another injury. The team founders, and Walton makes a desperate attempt to play in the playoffs, only to get hurt again. Broken foot.

A volcano erupts. Walton says that the Trail Blazers pressured him into taking painkilling injections, ignoring the risk of serious injury to him, and demands to be traded. The Trail Blazer management become apoplectic, while Walton's injury is so serious he spends seven months in a cast, sees virtually all musculature in his left foot disappear and misses the entire 1978–79 season.

Last spring he signs with a new team, his hometown San Diego Clippers. In the summer more operations—bone spurs are removed from both ankles. And now, one month away from the beginning of training camp, Walton is truckin' up a mountain.

Truckin', I'm a going home
Whoa whoa baby back where I belong
Back home, sit down and patch my bones
And get back truckin' on

Excerpted from an original story published in
Sports Illustrated, *October 15, 1979*

RAISED BY WOMEN TO CONQUER MEN

BY FRANK DEFORD

In 1974, Jimmy Connors won three of four major tournaments and seemed poised to dominate men's tennis for years to come. But while he remained a top player for another decade, he would never again have a transcendent year like '74. In 1978, Frank Deford wrote this feature on Connors. As if in reply, Connors won the U.S. Open the following week. But the story proved prescient: Connors would win only three more major titles over the next 12 years of his career.

A man who has been the indisputable favorite of his mother keeps for life the feeling of conqueror, the confidence of success which often induces real success.
  - SIGMUND FREUD

Jimmy Connors was the indisputable favorite of his grandmother as well, and so, he is most abundantly infused with this magic milk. It surges through his veins, suppressing every doubt and every defeat. And why not? The two women had promised him the world, and, just so, he grasped it in 1974: only 21, but already champion of all he surveyed, Alexander astride Bucephalus astride the globe. He won the Wimbledon final with the loss of but six games. Forest Hills with the loss of but two. Wise men in tennis sat about and seriously contemplated whether he would win every major title for, say, the next decade.

Conqueror was what he was, too, because Connors did not merely win. He assaulted the opposition, laid waste to it, often mocked it, as well, simply by the force of his presence. The other players feared to go against him, because the most awesome legend that can surround any athlete sprang up about Connors: the better any mortal played against him, the better Connors became. So, he became invincible upon the court because no man could beat him, and he was inviolate off the court, because his mother had told him so.

Two months ago, on July 8, Connors lost the 1978 Wimbledon final, winning only seven games against an ascendant Bjorn Borg. Since 1974 Connors has played in seven major finals and lost six....

Gloria Thompson Connors proudly points out that she and her mother are the only women ever to have developed a men's champion. Whatever more Jimmy achieves, theirs was an amazing accomplishment, and no one should be surprised at the obvious—at how much he depends on her. Naturally, if this were not so, it never could have worked....

[Deford examines Connors's childhood]

Soon everything was devoted to Jimmy's tennis potential. It was Gloria's pleasure to become, as she describes it, "a human backboard." No detail was overlooked. On the boys' circuit, free tournament housing would be declined, and the team would spend money it really couldn't afford to spend to stay in a motel, so that Jimbo would not get chummy with the children he had to beat. In St. Louis, Gloria would transport him about to clubs, soliciting good adult players to hit with the child. Those who lacked the zeal for this pastime were dismissed as snobs. At the same time, those pros who took an interest in the boy and sought to help his game were suspected of trying to "steal" him from his mother....

Ah, but off the court he was pampered: bikes and go-carts, a pony. More important, he was spoiled emotionally, always shielded from life's little adversities. This arrangement remains in force to this day. Connors is about as difficult to reach as any public figure in the country; he has been protected for so long that he will go to almost any lengths to avoid personal confrontation off the court; by his own admission he finds it constitutionally impossible to say no. He avoids contention in real life as he seems to seek it on the court.

It is all bizarre and contradictory. Once Connors has been treed, he is not only wonderfully genial, but he also seems to enjoy himself. In paid personal appearances, he is charming, considerate of strangers and supplicants to a fault. He will never refuse an autograph. Children adore him, and he seems happiest of all in the haven of their innocent affection.

But now it seems the price of a lifetime of the Connors insularity must be paid upon the court. Connors seems incapable of making hard decisions—even to honestly assess, much less change, his game or strategy. Out there, on the concrete garden, only the tiger was formed—and his only response is to salivate more tiger juices. That very quality of his mother's that protected him, that let him gain the world championship, now appears to be vitiating him....

But poor Gloria: the existing impression of her derives more from deep-seated biases. People who don't know Mrs. Connors from Mrs. Calabash just plain don't like the idea of her. She is, first of all, dead correct in what she has perceived: that she is viewed as a stage mother, and that Americans do not approve of that species. It is dandy for Mickey Mantle's father to instruct his son to switch-hit, but only a pushy dame like Judy Garland's mother would shove that poor kid onto the stage....

To be sure, it is an unusual relationship. To be sure, Gloria is on guard in private, and Jimmy is obnoxious in public. Guaranteed, they will find a way to louse up public relations. And yet, for all the negative consequences that this unusual relationship might encompass, nobody ever pauses to acknowledge the greater truths: that this relationship contains an extraordinary amount of love, and that this relationship made Jimmy Connors champion of the world....

For power, Connors learned to literally throw himself at the ball. His main source of strength comes from his thighs, it is his secret, a perfect, fluid weight transfer. And then, finally, he grew adept at what is known in tennis as hitting the ball on the rise—meeting the ball as it comes off the court, before it bounces to its apex. That is the ultimate attack, taking it on the rise, a man spitting back bullets. It speeds up the game infinitesimally in time, exponentially in fact, by putting constant pressure upon the other man. To hit on the rise requires three essentials: excellent vision (Connors' is 20–15), superb coordination (he even slugs with a trampoline-like steel racket) and utter confidence....

We should remember that 1974, his year, was swollen with vitriol and tension—and he was near unbeatable. And what of 1978? At the time Borg laid waste to him, it was hard to find a player who did not mention how Connors had mellowed, become friendlier. Bill Norris, a tennis trainer and an old friend, says, "Jimmy's found an inner peace. He's much more aware of other people's feelings."

"Jimmy was brought up to win on hate," says a top player, a contemporary. "How long could anyone keep winning on hate?" If Connors' game is locked into the past, if it remains exactly the same, it may, nonetheless, have diminished in one almost imperceptible way: hitting the ball on the rise. To the keenest eyes, Jimbo does not appear to be taking the ball quite so soon. He has either lost the confidence to perform this feat, or somewhere

deep inside a little bit of the killer instinct has paled, and he is giving the poor guy on the other side a chance, an instant more of breathing room. And the balls are coming back....

It is strange that as powerful as the love is that consumes the Connorses, Jimbo has always depended on hate in order to win. And all along that must have been the hard way. There is no telling how far a man could go who could learn to take love on the rise.

Excerpted from an original story published in SPORTS ILLUSTRATED*, August 28, 1978*

YESTERDAY'S CHILD

BY KENNY MOORE

Long before her collision with Zola Budd in the 1984 Olympics, Mary Decker had been plagued with injuries. When Kenny Moore visited her in 1978, she had just overcome nearly three years of painful shin problems and would soon become a force again in women's track.

On Aug. 4, 1973, Mary Teresa Decker was five feet tall and weighed 89 pounds, counting the braces on her teeth. She was also the best female half-miler in the U.S. On that afternoon she found herself sitting with her teammates at lunch in a hotel dining room in Dakar, Senegal, on the westernmost tip of Africa. The meal was spaghetti; the mood was uneasy, for in the evening the U.S. team would compete against the best African track and field athletes.

Suddenly conversation ceased, except for whispers. A stately file of tall black men had entered the dining room. They wore shining white robes, densely embroidered. As they proceeded between the tables, it was seen that some of them carried roses. They stopped before Mary Decker and stood motionless and solemn. She shrank into her chair.

The leader motioned that she be given the roses. Then he identified himself as an aide to Monsieur Abdou Diouf, the Premier of Senegal, and said that, because it had come to His Excellency's attention that on this day Mary Decker became 15 years old,

he had sent a gift. Whereupon the aide bowed and placed before her a heavy bronze sculpture of an African soldier on a horse. It was, the emissary intoned, from the premier's private collection....

Mary Decker is 19 now, and keeps the statue in her bedroom in Boulder, Colo., along with the medals she won on that 1973 tour of Europe and Africa. She has never discovered the sculpture's history or its age. She has never tried, because for her it is a personal symbol of her exalted and vigorous youth, a youth which, given all that has befallen her since her African adventure, seems dimly of another age....

Decker has always been rewarded for her childlike qualities, so it is natural that she should shed them reluctantly. "She was like Olga Korbut in 1973," says Maren Seidler, America's best woman shot-putter. "Everybody's little darling. The media can cope with little girls. They love 'em because then they don't have to deal with adult women."

Thus Decker today can be characterized as two females, the serious and talented adult runner alternating with yesterday's child....

Decker does not dwell on the somber. If a theme recurs in her conversation, it is reverie. She returns often to the details of that summer when she was 14.... "I got to be a team captain in Russia, but I was too small to carry the big flag, so I got a little flag." Her voice, describing this, is not the child's, but that of a tender older sister....

"I remember a time on the beach in Africa, when all the weight men were seeing how high they could throw me. And body surfing with Mac Wilkins. Afterward the pavement was so hot on my feet that he carried me back to the hotel on his shoulders." Thus delivered from the sea by her great and gentle discus thrower, she received her roses and bronze statue from the premier. "It seems now that I saw all of that through a window," she says. "It would be fun to go back and do it for real."

Excerpted from an original story published in Sports Illustrated, *May 1, 1978*

IT HAS TO BE A BAD DREAM

BY DARRYL STINGLEY
with MARK MULVOY

In August of 1978, in an exhibition game against the Oakland Raiders, New England Patriots receiver Darryl Stingley was struck by a vicious forearm to the neck from defensive back Jack Tatum. The blow fractured Stingley's spine and left him a quadriplegic. In his book, DARRYL STINGLEY: HAPPY TO BE ALIVE, written with current SI managing editor Mark Mulvoy, Stingley told his heartbreaking story.

"Good morning, Mr. Stingley," the voice said.

Good morning? what did she mean, good morning? It was Saturday night in Oakland, and we, the New England Patriots, were playing an exhibition game against the Raiders and about to go in for a touchdown. Good morning? It was night, not morning.

Wait a minute. Where am I? Why am I flat on my back, in bed, staring at a white acoustical ceiling? Why is this lady in a white coat saying, "Good morning, Mr. Stingley"?

It had to be a bad dream.

I tried to move my head, to check out my surroundings. My head wouldn't move. Not an inch. I tried to lift up my right arm. Nothing happened. I tried to move my left arm. Nothing happened. The same thing with my feet; as hard as I tried, I couldn't move them at all. I started to cry and couldn't even wipe the tears that were forming in puddles on my face....

[After realizing his condition, Stingley must overcome near-fatal pneumonia as well as his own bitterness before he can begin his recovery. A high point is his first trip in a new wheelchair designed to take advantage of the fraction of movement in his right arm.]

Slowly, painfully, oh, so painfully, I pushed the control switch on the armrest—and the chair started to move forward. I pulled my right hand back off the button—actually, it was a slow and painful retraction—and the Cadillac came to a halt. Then I slowly worked the switch back toward me, and the chair began to move in reverse. I experimented with the switch for what seemed like an eternity....

And now that end zone—my room—was no obstacle at all. It took me more than an hour to cover the 25 yards from the foyer to my room.

The chair bolted forward, weaved to the right, jumped into reverse, made a U-turn, slammed into a wall, lurched to the left—but I kept making progress.... Finally, I was there, in the end zone, and as I turned the chair ever so slowly to steer it into my room, I heard a lot of commotion behind me....

What a sight! Standing there in the middle of the corridor, about halfway between my room and the lounge where I'd started in the chair, were a whole bunch of doctors, nurses and therapists, and they were clapping. For me! I was getting a standing ovation. My first ovation of any kind since I was taken off the field in Oakland on a stretcher.

"Darryl, you made it, you made it," they all shouted.

"Yep, I made it," I said. "I made it."

After that, nobody at the rehab ever pushed me around in a wheelchair. I drove myself everywhere. And I became a champ with that chair. It became a part of me, a part of my life. In many ways, it is me. I'd like to think that I could make my chair fly if I had to.

Excerpted from Darryl Stingley: Happy To Be Alive, *Beaufort Books, Inc., selection in SI, August 29, 1983*

A REMINDER OF WHAT WE CAN BE

BY E. M. SWIFT

The Olympic year of 1980 was a difficult one for the U.S.—hostages in Iran, a boycott of the upcoming Summer Games in Moscow, tough economic times at home. In the midst of the gloom came the Winter Olympics and the miraculous U.S. hockey team that shocked the world by defeating the Russians and winning a gold medal. Ed Swift was in Lake Placid for its triumph, so it was appropriate that he should write the story naming the team as Sportsmen of the Year.

The impact was the thing. One morning they were 19 fuzzy-cheeked college kids and a tall guy with a beard, and the next.... WE BEAT THE RUSSIANS! In Babbitt, Minn., hometown of Forward Buzzie Schneider, guys went into their backyards and began firing shotguns toward the heavens. Kaboom! Kaboom! WE BEAT THE RUSSIANS! In Santa Monica a photographer heard the outcome of the game and went into his local grocery store, a mom-and-pop operation run by an elderly immigrant couple. "Guess what," he said. "Our boys beat the Russians." The old grocer looked at him. "No kidding?" Then he started to cry. *"No kidding?"*

In Winthrop, Mass., 70 people gathered outside the home of Mike Eruzione, who had scored the winning goal, and croaked out the national anthem. Not *God Bless America*, which is what the players were singing in Lake Placid. *The Star-Spangled Banner.*

One man was listening to the game in his car, driving through a thunderstorm, with the U.S. clinging to a 4–3 lead. He kept pounding his hands on the steering wheel in excitement. Finally he pulled off the highway and listened as the countdown started ... 5 ... 4 ... 3 ... 2 ... 1 ... WE BEAT THE RUSSIANS! He started to honk his horn. He yelled inside his car. It felt absolutely wonderful. He got out and started to scream in the rain. There were 10 other cars pulled off to the side of the road, 10 other drivers yelling their fool heads off in the rain. They made a huddle, and then they hollered together—WE BEAT THE RUSSIANS! Perfect strangers dancing beside the highway with 18-wheelers zooming by and spraying them with grime.

We. The U.S. Olympic hockey team wasn't a bunch of weird, freaky commando types. They were our boys. Clean-cut kids from small towns, well-groomed and good-looking, who loved their folks and liked to drink a little beer. Our boys. Young men molded by a coach who wasn't afraid to preach the values of the good old Protestant work ethic, while ever prepared to stuff a hockey stick down an offending opponent's throat. And don't think that didn't matter, given the political climate at the time—the hostages, Afghanistan, the pending Olympic boycott of the Moscow Games.

But there was more to the story than the moment of victory.

The members of the 1980 U.S. Olympic hockey team weren't named Sportsmen of the Year because of the 60 minutes they played one Friday afternoon in February. The game with the Soviet Union meant nothing to the players politically. Even its impact was largely lost on them until much later, confined as they were to the Olympic Village in Lake Placid, listening to one dinky local radio station and reading no newspapers. "If people want to think that performance was for our country, that's fine," says Mark Pavelich, the small, quiet forward who set up Eruzione's winning goal. "But the truth of the matter is, it was just a hockey game.... We wanted to win it for ourselves."

Not ourselves as in I, me, mine. Ourselves the team. Individually, they were fine, dedicated sportsmen. Some will have excellent pro hockey careers. Others will bust. But collectively, they were a transcendant lot. For seven months they pushed each other on and pulled each other along, from rung to rung, until for two weeks in February they—a bunch of unheralded amateurs—became the best hockey team in the world. The best *team.* The whole was greater than the sum of its parts by a mile. And they were not just a team, they were innovative and exuberant and absolutely unafraid to succeed. They were a perfect reflection of how Americans wanted to perceive themselves. By gum, it's still in us! It was certainly still in *them.*

So for reminding us of some things, and for briefly brightening the days of 220 million people, we doff our caps to them, *in toto.* Sportsmen of the Year....

There was a moment of truth for this team. A

moment when they became one. It was back in September of 1979 when they were playing a game in Norway. It ended in a 4–4 tie and [coach Herb] Brooks, to say the least, was dissatisfied. "We're going to skate some time today," he told them afterward. Then he sent them back onto the ice.

Forward Dave Silk recalls it this way: "There were 30 or 40 people still in the stands. First they thought we were putting on a skating exhibition, and they cheered. After a while they realized the coach was mad at us for not playing hard, and they booed. Then they got bored and left. Then the workers got bored, and they turned off the lights."

Doing Herbies [Brooks's torturous windsprints] in the dark ... it's terrifying. But they did them.... It ended at last, and Brooks had the players coast slowly around the rink so that the lactic acid could work itself out of their muscles. And that was when forward Mark Johnson broke his stick over the boards. Mark Johnson, who made the team go. Mark Johnson, who was its hardest worker, its smartest player. Mark Johnson, whom Brooks never, ever had to yell at. And you know what Brooks said—*screamed*—after skating those kids within an inch of their lives? "If I ever see a kid hit a stick on the boards again, I'll skate you till you *die!*" They believed him. And they would have *died*, just to spite him.... But they weren't an all-star team

anymore. They were together in this, all for one. And Brooks was the enemy. And don't think he didn't know it. It was a lonely year by design, all right.

[Swift recounts the scene after the amazing upset.]

And then it was over. The horn sounded and there was that unforgettable scene of triumph, the rolling and hugging and flinging of sticks. The flags. My God, what a sight. There was the shaking of hands, the staggered, reluctant exit from the ice. But it wasn't until the U.S. players were back in the locker room that the enormity of what they had done hit them. "It was absolutely quiet," recalls Janaszak. "Some guys were crying a little.... No one believed it."

It was then that somebody started a chorus of *God Bless America*, 20 sweaty guys in hockey uniforms chanting, "... from the mountains, to the valleys, na-na-na-na-na, na-na-na ...!" Nobody knew the words. And where was Brooks? Holed up in the men's room, afraid to come out and ruin their celebration. "I almost started to cry," he says. "It was probably the most emotional moment I'd ever seen. Finally I snuck out into the hall, and the state troopers were all standing there crying. Now where do you go? ..."

Excerpted from an original story published in
SPORTS ILLUSTRATED*, December 22–29, 1980*

ARROGANCE
AND PANIC

BY SARAH BALLARD

From the time of her arrival in the U.S. in 1975, Martina Navratilova showed great promise. But her early career was marked by some surprising losses as her temperament seemed to get in the way of her talent. Sarah Ballard visited with her in 1982, just as Navratilova was about to begin her era of dominance in women's tennis.

Like Kareem, Reggie, Billie Jean, O.J., Arnie and Pele, Martina has outlived the need for a surname, which is just as well, because few athletes have suffered such indignities of mispronunciation as she. In spite of almost a decade of practice, tennis umpires on both sides of the Atlantic still have trouble wrapping their tongues around ... Na-*tri*-lova ... Natra-*vi*-lova ... *Nav*-ra-ti-lo-va. Ahh, now you've got it.

But Martina's singularity only begins with her name. She doesn't look like anybody else. Her hooded and slightly melancholy hazel eyes, the flat planes of her face, her straight, baby-fine hair and the extraordinary definition of the muscles of her arms and legs fit no known mold. She doesn't behave like anyone else. At one time or another she overindulged, with the joyous abandon of the newly rich, in almost everything a capitalist

society has to offer, and her not-so-private life has now and then been the talk if not the toast of several continents. She didn't want her life off the court scrutinized, but it happened.

And, when Martina is at her best, she doesn't play like anyone else. She is sublimely gifted in strength, athleticism and talent for tennis. The top of her game beats the top of everybody else's. But. She has the temperament of an operatic diva of the old school. Not since Suzanne Lenglen has such an extravagant personality occupied the center court of women's tennis. Martina is at once warm, generous, passionate, impulsive, paranoid, arrogant, sentimental and naive. At times her mercurial nature inspires her play; at others it gets in the way. Ted Tinling, the majordomo of the women's game, once told *World Tennis*, "She is the greatest serve-and-volleyer women's tennis has ever seen. She has fantastic concept, unbelievable imagination." But. "She has that dramatic Slav temperament that requires the stimulus of a crisis.... She's always going to underassess her own ability to handle it when the storm hits. I've always said she goes from arrogance to panic with nothing in between."

Acceptance has always come slowly to her. She was different. She didn't fit in familiar niches. And she was incapable of calculated charm, of setting out to make people like her. She could only hope that sooner or later tennis fans and the press would take her as she is. Now all that remains to be conquered are the devils on the inside, the ones that have so often grabbed Martina around the heart, just when she most needed to be fearless, and squeezed until even her magnificent talent was no longer equal to the job at hand....

She leaned back in a chair, not her own, in a house, not her own, in a country, not quite her own, and for a moment looked as if she owned the world. "Arrogance to panic," she said with a chuckle "That's a great line. You won't see me go from arrogance to panic with nothing in between anymore. I know there's still a place for me in the history of tennis. It's not too late."

Excerpted from an original story published in
SPORTS ILLUSTRATED, *May 24, 1982*

THE SHOE

BY WILLIAM NACK

Perhaps the greatest jockey of all time, Bill Shoemaker (shown below with his wife, Cindy) had been written about often. But few of his chroniclers had bothered to look up his mother, Ruby, as Bill Nack did when he was preparing this piece in 1980. Nack's visit was fruitful, producing the moving tale of Shoemaker's birth, a story that may account for the remarkable tenacity with which he competed on the racetrack for four decades.

At 3 a.m. on Aug. 19, 1931, in a two-room adobe shack in the West Texas farm town of Fabens, Ruby Shoemaker had already been in labor some six hours. At first she had thought the pains were caused by the cantaloupe she had eaten for dessert the night before. She was only 17, and eight months pregnant. Her husband, B.B., who clerked in the feed store down the street, was out celebrating his birthday. Ruby figured he had gone to Juarez. Brother Phillips of the Fabens Baptist Church had come by to see what he could do, and his wife had come, too, and heated up some water on the four-burner kerosene stove. Brother Phillips had fetched Ruby's mother, Maude Harris, because Ruby had asked for her. Then Doc McClain came by to handle the delivery. The boy, who was born at three, weighed one pound, 13 ounces. He had a full head of black hair, and when Doc McClain held him up, Ruby thought he looked like a drowned rat. The Doc spanked him on the rear but couldn't get a sound from him; he was silent even then. Despairing, the Doc put the baby at the foot of the bed and declared, "That will never live."

"Well, I don't care what you say," said Maudie Harris. "He's cold." She picked up the baby from the foot of the bed and carried him to the sink across the room and got a rag and some soap and washed him off in the water that Brother Phillips' wife had heated. Then she wrapped the baby in a doll's blanket and opened up the oven door and lit the stove. She turned the heat to low and put the baby on a pillow in a shoe box on the oven door. Then she pulled a chair up to the oven and sat there. The baby had his eyes open and he moved now and again but made no sound for two hours. Ruby drowsed on the bed, awoke, drowsed some more. At about five, Ruby heard what she thought was a field mouse crying, a tiny screeching sound. It was the boy. "Ruby, I think he's hungry," Maudie said, and brought him over to the bed. Ruby couldn't get over his hands, how small they were, so small they looked like little claws. The boy was simply too weak to suckle, so they got a breast pump and eyedropper and fed him. Then they tried to fit him with a regular diaper, but he got lost in the huge folds, so they cut the diaper into quarters which fit just right. "He'll live, Ruby, he'll live," Maudie said. "He's a little fighter."

Excerpted from an original story published in
SPORTS ILLUSTRATED, *June 2, 1980*

211

1984-1990

The

SELL

ING
of Sport

THE SELLING OF SPORT

BY CRAIG NEFF

t the dawn of the soon-to-be-roaring 1980s, a former college water polo player named Peter Ueberroth stepped forward with some new ideas on how to market the Olympics. He arrived not a quadrennium too soon: After the financially catastrophic '76 Summer Games in Montreal and the West-boycotted '80 Summer Games in Moscow, the Olympic movement was foundering. Cities were losing interest in hosting the Games.

Ueberroth, a self-made millionaire businessman and president of the 1984 Los Angeles Olympic Organizing Committee (LAOOC), believed that private financing was the solution. He and his LAOOC team persuaded 30 major corporations to ante up cash, goods and services totaling $180 million to be official sponsors of the L.A. Summer Games. Playing up expectations that U.S. viewers would eagerly watch an American-run, Stars-and-Stripes Olympics, Ueberroth extracted three times as much money for television broadcast rights ($225 million from ABC) as any Olympic organizer ever had. He also got some 60,000 volunteers to work for free—the most astonishing labor deal of the decade.

And so the '84 Olympics came off grandly, turning a profit of nearly $250 million and launching an era of widespread corporate sponsorship and staggering television rights fees for all sports. The L.A. Olympics were a watershed. They reversed the course of the Olympic movement and demonstrated how sports could tap into the economic boom of the '80s. This, after all, was the money decade.

Ueberroth benefited from some good fortune, of course. An Eastern-bloc boycott in retaliation for the U.S.-led boycott of '80 diminished the quality of the competition in Los Angeles but also made the Games even more appealing to the American public, clearing a swath to the victory stand for a number of U.S. athletes who probably would not have won gold medals otherwise, among them a 95-pound fireplug of a gymnast named Mary Lou Retton.

But Ueberroth's Olympic success was no fluke. Unlike many past sports executives, he functioned, not as a fan, but as a chief executive officer, who believed that sports had to be ushered into the corporate age. Not everyone cheered this development. In some respects the worst thing to happen to sports in the '80s was the inlux of lawyers and CEO types. Sports seemed too impersonal all of a sudden, too serious, too flush with dollars and with people only interested in getting more of them. Owners, agents, athletes, television executives—they all seemed caught up in the greed.

But a decade is what it is, and the '80s were about big money and bold captains of business.

Ueberroth received Time magazine's 1984 Man of the Year award for his Olympic triumph—think of it: a sports executive the foremost news figure of the year—then moved on to the job of baseball commissioner. When he arrived in 1985, 21 of the 26 major league franchises were in the red, and the sport was being supplanted by football as the national pastime. Detractors said that baseball was too dull for modern America, which was hooked on the dazzle and crunch of NFL action and the fast-cut images of MTV.

Ueberroth responded with another display of business acumen, working to strengthen the game's financial base and taking full marketing advantage of a wave of nostalgia fostered by Ronald Reagan, the ex-baseball announcer residing in the White House. Millions of baby boomers began flocking to ballparks to recapture their childhood memories. Meanwhile, a new generation of stars, including Dwight Gooden, Will Clark and Jose Canseco, enlivened the game. By decade's end, the sport had achieved unprecedented popularity, with nearly every major league team making money and annual attendance leaping by nearly 25% since 1984.

For all that, Ueberroth still may not have been the decade's most successful sports executive. That distinction probably belongs to David Stern, an attorney who took over as NBA commissioner in 1984 and turned his troubled league completely around. At the start of the decade, 17 of 23 NBA teams were losing money and drug use among players was said to be rampant. Stern went to work quickly. With the cooperation of the NBA Players Association, he not only devised the most widely praised drug program in all of sports but also helped initiate a revolutionary revenue-sharing system that linked player salaries to league-wide income and ultimately enriched both players and owners. Both issues—profit-sharing and drug use—continue to plague professional football and baseball, serving as perennial stumbling blocks to an effective collective bargaining agreement. As the '90s arrived, NBA gross revenues had jumped nearly fivefold from 1980, and at least 25 of the 27 franchises were said to be making hefty profits. Attendance was up 41% from 1985. Player salaries were nearing an average of $1 million a year. Stern proved that profits and labor peace need not be incompatible.

Prosperity, it seemed, was the order of the day. By early 1990 the NFL had tapped the rich vein of television money so deeply that every team in the league was guaranteed $32 million per year in TV money through 1993, nearly twice as much as the annual revenue from the previous contract. The league was cashing in too, selling hundreds of millions of dollars' worth of licensed merchandise, ranging from team jerseys to football cards to helmet-shaped doghouses, and was spinning off an international minor league that was scheduled to begin play in the spring of 1991 and generate even more revenue for the NFL and its teams.

Money was everywhere. The NCAA signed a billion-dollar deal for TV rights to its post-season basketball tournament and certain smaller college events. Golf and tennis were paying out so much in prize and appearance money that a player could

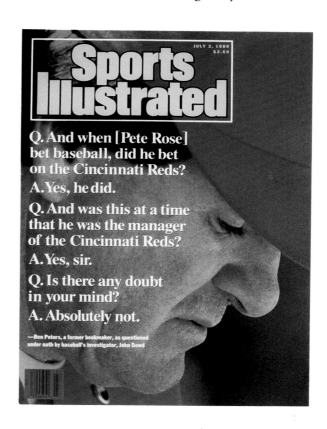

JULY 3, 1989
$2.69

Sports Illustrated

Q. And when [Pete Rose] bet baseball, did he bet on the Cincinnati Reds?
A. Yes, he did.
Q. And was this at a time that he was the manager of the Cincinnati Reds?
A. Yes, sir.
Q. Is there any doubt in your mind?
A. Absolutely not.

—Ron Peters, a former bookmaker, as questioned under oath by baseball's investigator, John Dowd

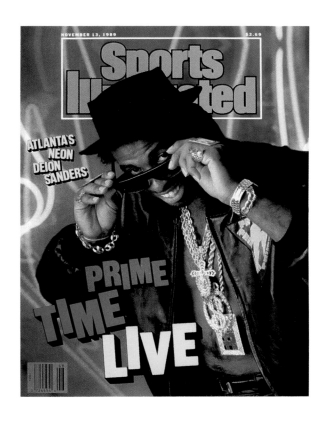

become a millionaire without ever winning a tournament. A weekly sports-business magazine was started called *Sports inc.*, which calculated the "gross national sports product" for 1987 at $50.2 billion. Based on that figure, sports were larger than the auto industry and were responsible for 1.1% of the total U.S. gross national product.

Sports were awash in logos, brand names and marketing gimmicks. No one used the word *sneakers* anymore. Now they were called athletic shoes, and they conferred status the way cars did in the '50s and '60s. Every teen in America had at least one pair of air-pump gel-cushioned waffle-traction rear-stabilized antipronation athletic shoes idling softly in his closet. The desire for the hottest in sports attire and footwear grew out of control; inner-city kids were shooting each other over pairs of Air Jordan basketball shoes, the kind named after and endorsed by Chicago Bulls superstar Michael Jordan, an otherwise exemplary role model.

Speaking of Jordan, he blossomed into a one-man industry. His Air Jordan line, put out by Nike, racked up more than $100 million in annual sales. Jordan was earning $6 million a year in endorsement income alone, and he was turning down more endorsement offers than he accepted. No wonder he could gleefully stick out his tongue at the world every time he soared in for a thunderous dunk.

Corporate sponsorship extended into every sport. A company willing to dole out enough cash could put its John Hancock on any race, game, tournament, bout, match or trash sport it desired. The John Hancock insurance company, in fact, bought the sponsorship rights to the annual Sun Bowl football game, in El Paso, Texas, and renamed it the John Hancock Bowl. Even buildings were stamped with the corporate imprimatur. After taking on the Great Western Bank as a sponsor, The Forum in Los Angeles became The Great Western Forum, which sounds more like a place to discuss Aristotle than to watch the Lakers.

If you didn't have a couple hundred bucks for a courtside seat next to Jack Nicholson at The Forum, there were a multitude of other ways to revel in sports: sports videos, sports video games, all-sports cable-television stations, all-sports radio, 1-900 sports phones, a new daily national newspaper devoted exclusively to sports. Sports books climbed the best-seller lists and flooded the bookstores. Pity the jock so uninteresting that no one had yet ghost-written his autobiography.

Sports had grown out of all proportion to the rest of society. The lowliest rookie in baseball was being paid more per year than the U.S. Secretary of State. Many college football and basketball coaches—some with lucrative shoe contracts—were earning more than the presidents of their schools. Stern, a commissioner, signed a five-year, $27 million contract that included a $10 million signing bonus.

Not surprisingly, with so much money up for grabs, corruption flourished. At times it seemed that Diogenes with his lamp couldn't have found an honest college athletic program. Even after the NCAA created a "death penalty" for schools that repeatedly broke rules, schools still broke them as unscrupulous recruiters couldn't take their eyes off the pot of gold they could claim by winning enough games. Don't ask what education had to do with any of it—the answer was nothing.

Athletes cheated in a variety of ways. They took improper gifts from recruiters, under-the-table money from agents and performance-enhancing drugs—especially anabolic steroids—from teammates and trainers. Steroid use reached epidemic proportions, as was poignantly illustrated by the tragic example of Canadian sprinter Ben Johnson who tested positive at the Olympics. Putting aside the concerns of civil libertarians, sports organizations began instituting drug testing right down to the high school level where some young people were taking steroids for purely cosmetic purposes. To be a powerful, thickly muscled athlete in the '80s was to be suspected of steroid use. Sadly, those suspicions were often well founded.

The professional leagues didn't always display the highest ethics, either. To drive up the value of existing franchises, they let cities do financial backflips to attract new ones. The problem was, virtually no cities *got* new teams; the '80s were the first decade since the '50s in which neither major league baseball nor the NFL expanded. Yet municipalities continued to build expensive stadiums and arenas at taxpayer expense in the hope of someday landing a team, maybe in the 1990s. The city of Oakland even dipped into the public treasury to try to get back an old team: the Raiders.

Blessedly, the rising tide of money washed out the already crumbling sea wall known as amateurism. Certain Olympic sports still tried to maintain the fiction that their athletes weren't out-and-out professionals, requiring them to place their endorsement, appearance and prize money into trust funds from which they could withdraw only training expenses until they retired. But open Olympics were arriving. Pro hockey and soccer players competed in the 1988 Games, and the International Basketball Federation voted to allow NBA players to compete in the Olympics starting in 1992. How far had Olympic sports come? By the early '90s, even swimmers were racing each other for prize money.

Corporate sponsorship and nostalgia for past heroes spawned a new phenomenon: senior sports. The '80s brought us senior golf, senior tennis and senior baseball. Meanwhile, with salaries in big-league sports so astronomically high, more and more athletes were staying fit and competing into their 40s. The glittering names from the '60s and early '70s who were going strong in the '80s included Kareem Abdul-Jabbar, Nolan Ryan, Pete Rose, Jack Nicklaus, Bill Shoemaker and A.J. Foyt.

The '80s didn't lack stars of its own, of course. Basketball had Jordan and Larry Bird and Earvin (Magic) Johnson and hockey had the Great One, Wayne Gretzky. Football was graced with perhaps its most proficient quarterback ever in Joe Montana, as well as its all-time leading rusher in Walter Payton. Boxing had heavyweight Mike Tyson, whose in-the-ring salary at one point was calculated at roughly $50 million an hour.

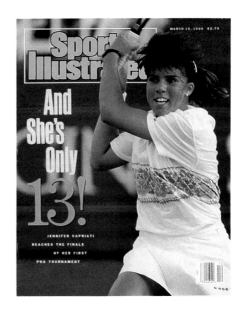

As the 1990s arrived, both Payton and Magic Johnson were talking about someday owning pro teams—what else would a modern player do with his multi-millions?—and sports historians were trying to sort out just what the '80s had given us. It's a relief to report that, as the ensuing pages show, the decade gave us more than the shameless pursuit of money. Sports may have put on a business suit and a Rolex in the '80s, but they didn't lose their ability to surprise, inspire and delight. Let's hope those qualities don't ever get sold off.

1984

The Winner's Circle

Baseball: Detroit Tigers
NFL: San Francisco 49ers
College Football: BYU
NHL: Edmonton Oilers
NBA: Boston Celtics
College Basketball: Georgetown
Masters: Ben Crenshaw
U.S. Open (golf): Fuzzy Zoeller
British Open: Seve Ballesteros
PGA: Lee Trevino
Australian Open: Mats Wilander
French Open: Ivan Lendl
Wimbledon: John McEnroe
U.S. Open (tennis): John McEnroe
Australian Open: Chris Evert
French Open: Martina Navratilova
Wimbledon: Martina Navratilova
U.S. Open (tennis): Martina Navratilova
Kentucky Derby: Swale
Preakness: Gate Dancer
Belmont: Swale
Indianapolis 500: Rick Mears

Joan Benoit takes an emotional victory lap around Memorial Coliseum in Los Angeles after winning the first women's marathon in Olympic history. Unhappy with a slow early pace, Benoit pulls away from the pack and surges to an insurmountable lead, finishing in 2:24:52, the third-fastest marathon ever run by a woman and a time that would have won 13 of the last 20 men's marathons.

Mary Decker wails in pain after a collision with Zola Budd knocks her out of the 3,000-meter Olympic finals. Her pulled gluteus muscle is only a small part of Decker's torment; she weeps too for her troubled Olympic past: too young in '72; injured in '76; stymied by the boycott in '80.

Bill Johnson abandons all caution and simply attacks the downhill course in Sarajevo to become the first American man to win an Olympic gold medal in the event. The cocky Johnson, whose troubled youth included one case of car theft, had brashly predicted his win before the race.

Ben Crenshaw plants a kiss on his cooperative golf ball after hitting out of a bunker and into the hole for a birdie during the third round of the Masters. Crenshaw, a perennial favorite on the Tour, will go on to shoot a final-round 68 to finish two strokes ahead of Tom Watson, thankfully avoiding the calamities that had so often sabotaged his play in the majors.

1984

Detroit's Alan Trammell has a scintillating World Series, collecting nine hits, two homers and six RBIs in the Tigers' five-game defeat of the San Diego Padres. Kirk Gibson, with two homers in the fifth game, and Jack Morris, with a pair of complete-game victories, were the other heroes for Detroit, which became the first AL team since the 1927 Yankees to go wire to wire in the regular season and win the World Series.

Indira Ghandi is assassinated   Michael Jackson wins eight Grammy awards

Wendell Tyler runs for 65 yards on 13 carries in San Francisco's 38–16 rout of the Miami Dolphins in Super Bowl XIX. He also is a tenacious pass blocker, providing invaluable protection for the brilliant Joe Montana, who dominates the game, completing 24 of 35 passes for 331 yards and three touchdowns. Montana also scrambles for 59 yards and a touchdown on the ground.

Martina Navratilova cruises to her second straight U.S. Open title, defeating Chris Evert 4–6, 6–4, 6–4. Although Evert uses an array of skidding returns and passing shots to win the first set, Navratilova wears her down once again, winning her 13th straight match over Evert. The two remain the unchallenged elite of women's tennis until Steffi Graf wins her first major in '87.

Vanessa Williams, the first black Miss America, is stripped of her crown

222

1984

Freshman supersub Michael Graham slams for two of his 14 points in Georgetown's 84–75 win over Houston for its first-ever NCAA title. With Houston's Akeem Olajuwon and Georgetown's Patrick Ewing battling one another to a standoff, it is Graham and the much deeper Hoya bench that make the difference as wave after wave of replacements execute John Thompson's aggressive defensive scheme to perfection.

The Vietnam Memorial is unveiled in Washington   Trivial Pursuit hits it big

1985

The Winner's Circle

Baseball: Kansas City Royals
NFL: Chicago Bears
College Football: Oklahoma
NHL: Edmonton Oilers
NBA: Los Angeles Lakers
College Basketball: Villanova
Masters: Bernhard Langer
U.S. Open (golf): Andy North
British Open: Sandy Lyle
PGA: Hubert Green
Australian Open: Stefan Edberg
French Open: Mats Wilander
Wimbledon: Boris Becker
U.S. Open (tennis): Ivan Lendl
Australian Open: Martina Navratilova
French Open: Chris Evert
Wimbledon: Martina Navratilova
U.S. Open (tennis): Hana Mandlikova
Kentucky Derby: Spend A Buck
Preakness: Tank's Prospect
Belmont: Creme Fraiche
Indianapolis 500: Danny Sullivan

Boris Becker, only 17, dives, slides and skids his way to a 6–3, 6–7, 7–6, 6–4 victory over Kevin Curren in the Wimbledon finals, making him the youngest man ever to win the event. His victory transforms him into an instant national hero in his native West Germany where he will soon become a corporation unto himself, commanding huge fees for interviews and commercial endorsements.

With a crowd of 28,269 looking on in Chicago's Wrigley Field, Pete Rose rips a line drive to right field against the Cubs' Reggie Patterson for his 4,191st hit, tying him with his idol Ty Cobb for first place on the major league career-hits list. He will break the record three days later off San Diego's Eric Show and retire in '86 with a seemingly unreachable total of 4,256 hits.

Another career mark is set three weeks after Rose's as Grambling coach Eddie Robinson gets his 324th win (27–7 over Prairie View A&M) to surpass Alabama's Bear Bryant as the winningest college football coach in history. Working on a limited budget during his 44 years at all-black Grambling, Robinson was able to recruit some 200 future NFL players, more than any other school in the nation.

225

Danny Sullivan goes into a 360-degree spin on his first attempt to pass Mario Andretti during the Indy 500 but he succeeds on his second, diving low and shooting by Andretti on Lap 140, then going on to finish 2.5 seconds in front. Shunning cautious tactics, Sullivan has his fastest lap—at a zippy 205 mph—on his next-to-last.

Libby Riddles is the only competitor to brave a blinding blizzard on the 15th day of the 1,135-mile Iditarod Sled Dog Race from Anchorage to Nome, a decision her rivals consider foolish. But Riddles's gamble pays off as she finishes in front two days later to become the first woman to win the grueling event.

1985

Ed Pinckney (54) powers Villanova to the NCAA title with 16 points, six rebounds and five assists in the Wildcats' 66–64 win over supposedly invincible Georgetown. Villanova plays a near-perfect game, hitting nine of its 10 shots in the second half and playing superb defense against the talented Hoyas. Guard Gary (Gizmo) McLain makes just two turn-overs in 40 minutes against the relentless Georgetown pressure.

Gorbachev comes to power   Coca-Cola introduces the new Coke

1986

The Winner's Circle

Baseball: New York Mets
NFL: New York Giants
College Football: Penn State
NHL: Montreal Canadiens
NBA: Boston Celtics
College Basketball: Louisville
Masters: Jack Nicklaus
U.S. Open (golf): Ray Floyd
British Open: Greg Norman
PGA: Bob Tway
French Open: Ivan Lendl
Wimbledon: Boris Becker
U.S. Open (tennis): Ivan Lendl
French Open: Chris Evert
Wimbledon: Martina Navratilova
U.S. Open (tennis): Martina Navratilova
Kentucky Derby: Ferdinand
Preakness: Snow Chief
Belmont: Danzig Connection
Indianapolis 500: Bobby Rahal
World Cup: Argentina

Jesse Orosco is a portrait in jubilation after the last out is recorded in the Mets' World Series triumph over the Boston Red Sox. His joy is understandable: New York was within one strike of losing the Series in Game 6 before a series of clutch hits and Bill Buckner's error at first gives the Mets a 6–5 win. The final game is almost anti-climactic as home runs by Ray Knight and Darryl Strawberry power the Mets to an 8–5 victory.

Cocaine claims a life at its peak when Maryland's Len Bias dies of an overdose within 40 hours of his first round draft selection by the Boston Celtics. Apparently convinced of his invulnerability, Bias had snorted too much cocaine for even his strong athlete's heart. Terps coach Lefty Driesell will be forced to resign four months later after intense criticism of Maryland's athletic program.

The 54-year-old Bill Shoemaker guides Ferdinand to victory in the Kentucky Derby, finessing his way from dead-last around and through a field of 15 other horses, finally darting through an opening at the top of the stretch and driving his colt home to win by 2 ¼ lengths over the English colt Bold Arrangement. It is the fourth Derby win for Shoe but the first for 73-year-old trainer Charlie Whittingham.

Win one for the geezer: Jack Nicklaus, at 46, takes his sixth and most dramatic Masters with a final-round 65 that has all of America rooting. Nicklaus had not won a Tour event in two years, but the years seem to roll back as the Golden Bear makes his charge with six birdies and an eagle on the last 10 holes to roar past eight other golfers and finish with a Masters-record 30 on the final nine holes of play.

Benchmarks   The Statue of Liberty celebrates her 100th birthday

After losing one-shot last-day margins at both the Masters and the U.S. Open, Greg Norman overcomes howling winds and impenetrable rough to win the British Open by a comfortable five strokes for his first major tournament victory.

Phil Simms plays a near-perfect game to lead the Giants to a stunning 39–20 rout of the Denver Broncos in the Super Bowl. Simms is a metronome of consistency, completing 22 of 25 passes for 268 yards and three touchdowns as New York charges back from a 10–9 halftime deficit with 17 points in the third quarter to take the lead for good.

The Challenger explodes after takeoff   Ferdinand Marcos flees the Philippines

1987

The Winner's Circle

Baseball: Minnesota Twins
NFL: Washington Redskins
College Football: University of Miami
NHL: Edmonton Oilers
NBA: Los Angeles Lakers
College Basketball: Indiana
Masters: Larry Mize
U.S. Open (golf): Scott Simpson
British Open: Nick Faldo
PGA: Larry Nelson
Australian Open: Stefan Edberg
French Open: Ivan Lendl
Wimbledon: Pat Cash
U.S. Open (tennis): Ivan Lendl
Australian Open: Hana Mandlikova
French Open: Steffi Graf
Wimbledon: Martina Navratilova
U.S. Open (tennis): Martina Navratilova
Kentucky Derby: Alysheba
Preakness: Alysheba
Belmont: Bet Twice
Indianapolis 500: Al Unser

The Redskins fall behind 10–0 in the first quarter but storm back with a 35-point 356-yard second quarter to swamp the hapless Broncos in Super Bowl XXII. Washington's Doug Williams begins the day as the first black quarterback in Super Bowl history but ends it as one of the top performers in Super Bowl history, period, completing 18 of 29 passes for 340 yards and four touchdowns as the Skins cruise to the 42–10 win.

The fans are the losers as usual when NFL players go on strike for three weeks of the regular season, owners hire replacement teams to continue play and the notion of "scab football" is born. Average attendance dips to 24,697 until the players return to the field in late October, still without a collective-bargaining agreement.

Dennis Conner skippers the Stars & Stripes to a sweep of Australia's Kookaburra III in the waters off Fremantle, leading around every mark in every race of the America's Cup Series to avenge his loss in '83 and return the Cup to the U.S. Even the Australian fans seem warmed by Conner's stirring moment of redemption.

Martina Navratilova uses a powerful serve-and-volley game to win her sixth straight Wimbledon title—her eighth over-all—defeating Chris Evert in the semi-finals (6–2, 5–7, 6–4) and emerging star Steffi Graf in the finals (7–5, 6–3). The victory is proof that Navratilova isn't ready to buckle beneath the onslaught of Graf, who had won seven tournaments and 45 matches in a row.

Benchmarks   Gary Hart's monkey business destroys his candidacy

234

1987

Indiana's Keith Smart does a backwards midflight 180 for two of his 21 points in Indiana's 74–73 NCAA title win over Syracuse. The Orangemen seem to have the game in control in the final minutes as they shut out long-range gunner Steve Alford, but Smart takes up the slack, scoring 12 of Indiana's final 15 points, including a twisting 16-foot one-hander from the left side with five seconds left to win the game.

The stock market plummets on Black Monday   The Iran-contra hearings begin

1988

The Winner's Circle

Baseball: Los Angeles Dodgers
NFL: San Francisco 49ers
College Football: Notre Dame
NHL: Edmonton Oilers
NBA: Los Angeles Lakers
College Basketball: Kansas
Masters: Sandy Lyle
U.S. Open (golf): Curtis Strange
British Open: Seve Ballesteros
PGA: Jeff Sluman
Australian Open: Mats Wilander
French Open: Mats Wilander
Wimbledon: Stefan Edberg
U.S. Open (tennis): Mats Wilander
Australian Open: Steffi Graf
French Open: Steffi Graf
Wimbledon: Steffi Graf
U.S. Open (tennis): Steffi Graf
Kentucky Derby: Winning Colors
Preakness: Risen Star
Belmont: Risen Star
Indianapolis 500: Rick Mears

Jackie Joyner-Kersee skies to her second gold medal and an Olympic-record distance of 24' 3 ½" on her fifth attempt in the women's long jump in Seoul. She won her first gold with a world-record point total of 7,291 in the pentathlon. During the course of the Games, sister-in-law Florence Griffith Joyner extends the family gold cache to five with wins in the 100- and 200-meter dashes as well as a gold in the 4 x 100-meter relay.

East Germany's Katarina Witt charms the world once again with her beauty and grace, becoming the first women's singles figure skater since Sonja Henie in 1936 to win back-to-back Olympic gold medals. A disappointed Debi Thomas of the U.S. falls during her final routine and is forced to settle for a bronze. Witt will soon retire from competitive skating and begin touring professionally.

With an explosive dash, Canada's Ben Johnson breaks his own 100-meter world record with a time of 9.79 to defeat Carl Lewis of the U.S. by .13 of a second. But Johnson's triumph turns to ashes just 24 hours later when a drug test reveals traces of an anabolic steroid, stanozolol, in his system, and he is stripped of his gold medal and banned from all international meets for two years.

237

Benchmarks Benazir Bhutto becomes the prime minister of Pakistan

1988

Steffi Graf has every reason to be ecstatic, becoming the fifth player in history to win tennis's Grand Slam. She and her rifle-shot forehand defeat four different final-round opponents: Chris Evert in the Australian Open; Natalia Zvereva at the French; Martina Navratilova at Wimbledon; and Gabriela Sabatini at the U.S. Open.

Wayne Gretzky's year of living famously: In June he leads the Edmonton Oilers to their fourth Stanley Cup in five years; in July he marries movie star Janet Jones in Canada's version of a royal wedding; and in August he outrages his countrymen by being traded to the Los Angeles Kings for a slew of Oiler players and draft choices.

Jimmy Swaggart admits his sin   Wrigley Field adds lights

Orel Hershiser (below) is Mister Zero for the Los Angeles Dodgers, hurling 59 straight scoreless innings to break Don Drysdale's 20-year-old mark. Hershiser goes on to pitch a shutout against the Mets in the seventh game of the National League playoffs and allow just two runs in a pair of victories against the Oakland A's in the Dodgers' five-game triumph in the World Series.

The prefight sniping between wife Robin Givens and manager Bill Cayton doesn't distract Iron Mike Tyson from the task at hand as he takes out the woefully over-matched Michael Spinks in just 91 seconds, four fewer than it takes Jeffrey Osborne to sing the national anthem. For his brief appearance, Tyson earns between $18 million and $22 million, or roughly $220,000 per second.

1988

Magic Johnson is as good as his name, conjuring yet another NBA title for the Lakers—their fifth in the '80s and second in a row, making them the first team since the '69 Celtics to repeat as NBA champs. But the handwriting is on the hoop: The Lakers barely escape elimination by Detroit in Game 6 and win Game 7 against a hobbled Isiah Thomas. The younger Pistons are clearly on the rise.

Superman turns 50   Gorbachev is boffo at the U.N.

241

1989

The Winner's Circle

Baseball: Oakland Athletics
NFL: San Francisco 49ers
College Football: University of Miami
NHL: Calgary Flames
NBA: Detroit Pistons
College Basketball: Michigan
Masters: Nick Faldo
U.S. Open (golf): Curtis Strange
British Open: Mark Calcavecchia
PGA: Payne Stewart
Australian Open: Ivan Lendl
French Open: Michael Chang
Wimbledon: Boris Becker
U.S. Open (tennis): Boris Becker
Australian Open: Steffi Graf
French Open: Arantxa Sanchez
Wimbledon: Steffi Graf
U.S. Open (tennis): Steffi Graf
Kentucky Derby: Sunday Silence
Preakness: Sunday Silence
Belmont: Easy Goer
Indianapolis 500: Emerson Fittidaldi

Greg LeMond pulls off an amazing comeback, winning the Tour de France just two years after lying near death from a hunting accident in which he was shot in the back. He trails Laurent Fignon of France by a full 50 seconds going into the final stage of the 23-day race but rides the 24.5 kilometers from Versailles to Paris like a man possessed and completes the distance in a time of 26:57, 58 seconds faster than Fignon.

Baseball faces its darkest hour since the Black Sox scandal of 1919 as accusations of gambling swirl around the head of Pete Rose, the game's alltime hits leader. Worse yet, the charges include allegations that he bet on his own team, the Cincinnati Reds. Rose denies the charges, but commissioner Bart Giamatti concludes there is truth in them and bans Rose from baseball for life.

Soon after the Rose scandal, baseball is rocked again—this time literally—by the San Francisco earthquake, which occurs just minutes before the scheduled start of Game 3 in Oakland's four-game World Series sweep over the Giants. Pitcher Kelly Downs (left, with nephew Billy Kehl) and the Candle-stick crowd leave calmly and only later learn the tragic news: 46 people have died.

1989

After six titles and 20 brilliant seasons, Kareem Abdul-Jabbar finally turns his back and walks away from the game of basketball. His record constitutes a litany of greatness: He has appeared in more games, scored more points and played for more minutes than any player in history; six times he has been the league's MVP, 19 times he has been an All-Star. Will there ever be a more majestic sight than the unstoppable skyhook?

The Exxon Valdez befouls the Alaska seas   The Berlin Wall comes tumbling down

1990

The Winner's Circle

Baseball: Cincinnati Reds
NFL: New York Giants
College Football: Georgia Tech/Colorado
NHL: Edmonton Oilers
NBA: Detroit Pistons
College Basketball: UNLV
Masters: Nick Faldo
U.S. Open (golf): Hale Irwin
British Open: Nick Faldo
PGA: Wayne Grady
Australian Open: Ivan Lendl
French Open: Andres Gomez
Wimbledon: Stefan Edberg
U.S. Open (tennis): Pete Sampras
Australian Open: Steffi Graf
French Open: Monica Seles
Wimbledon: Martina Navratilova
U.S. Open (tennis): Gabriela Sabatini
Kentucky Derby: Unbridled
Preakness: Summer Squall
Belmont: Go And Go
Indianapolis 500: Arie Luyendyk
World Cup: West Germany

Philadelphia's Lenny Dykstra gives baseball fans a thrill by flirting with the .400 mark, remaining well above that magic number for the first nine weeks of the season before falling to the more mortal climes of the mid-.300s. Alas for Phillie fans, Dykstra's descent is mirrored by his team as Philadelphia, in second place for six weeks during the early season, loses 17 of 29 games in June and tumbles to fourth.

Hale Irwin becomes the oldest man, at 45, to win the U.S. Open. It isn't easy: Irwin needs a 45-foot putt on the final hole of regulation to force an 18-hole playoff with Mike Donald, then finishes the playoff still tied. But he gets the win quickly in sudden death, sinking an eight-foot birdie putt on the first hole.

Stacey Augmon skies for two as the Runnin' Rebels of UNLV dash to a 103–73 drubbing of Duke in the most lopsided final game in NCAA history. Anderson Hunt bombs away from the perimeter for 29 points, Larry Johnson grabs 11 rebounds and UNLV's tenacious defense hounds Duke into 23 turnovers.

1990

It looks like just another stop on Mike Tyson's parade through palookaville as Buster Douglas hardly seems a worthy challenger. After all, isn't this the guy who lost to Mike White and David Bey? But Douglas shocks the pundits, coming off the canvas in the eighth round and knocking the champion out for the first time in his career with a crashing left hook in the 10th.

Isiah Thomas streaks to the hoop for two of his 21 points in Detroit's 93–74 rout of Chicago in the seventh game of the Eastern Conference finals. Thomas, who also has 11 assists and eight rebounds in the game, will go on to lead the Pistons to their second straight NBA title, with 27.6 points and 7.0 assists per game in Detroit's five-game final-series win over Portland.

Nelson Mandela is free at last   Germany becomes one nation again

A fast bike, a beautiful day and miles and miles of desert add up to relaxation for Robin Yount, baseball's quiet hero who just keeps cranking out the hits.

S*Favorites*

MAX
Steve Wulf visits Max Patkin, the Clown Prince of Baseball

THE RYAN EXPRESS
Ron Fimrite profiles fireballer Nolan Ryan

SONS OF THE WIND
Kenny Moore examines the land of Kenya and its bounty of distance runners

THE MOURNING ANCHOR
Rick Reilly spends time with a melancholy Bryant Gumbel

THE BOXER AND THE BLONDE
Frank Deford takes a trip to the past with boxer Billy Conn and the love of his life

THE LONGEST RIDE
William Nack recounts the troubled tale of jockey Robbie Davis

THE LOSER
William Oscar Johnson and Kenny Moore report on Ben Johnson's steroid use

ROSE'S GRIM VIGIL
Craig Neff and Jill Lieber get the scoop on Pete Rose

THE COACH AND HIS CHAMPION
Alexander Wolff pays a visit on legendary coach John Wooden as he struggles alone

THE CURIOUS CASE OF SIDD FINCH
George Plimpton tells the fanciful story of a pitching prospect you just won't believe

TAKE MY GOLF GAME, PLEASE!
Jack McCallum reports on the Worst Avid Golfer competition

ALI AND HIS ENTOURAGE
Gary Smith visits Muhammad Ali and recalls the days of glory

MAX

BY STEVE WULF

Max Patkin, the Clown Prince of Baseball, has been entertaining baseball audiences with his slapstick routines for more than 40 years. In 1988, Steve Wulf spent some time with Max and came back with this memorable portrait.

Everybody in baseball knows Max Patkin. Some of them may try to hide when they see him coming, but there are probably only a handful of major leaguers in uniform who haven't seen the Clown Prince of Baseball at one time or another. And if they haven't laughed, they're not human. The funny thing about Maxie's act is that it is still funny. It's the same corny shtick that he has done for 40 years in 400 ballparks on 4,000 different days or nights over the course of four million miles. "If it was a class act, I would have been out of business a long time ago," he says.

Max is 68 now, and suffering from glaucoma, bad knees and a herniated disk in his back, but he's strong as a horse and has every intention of taking his act into the '90s, which would be its sixth decade. In all that time, and over all those miles, he has never missed a performance. He has jumped out of a burning plane, dodged tornadoes and been mistaken for a fugitive from justice—"I feel sorry for the guy if he looked like me," says

Max. He nearly bought the farm 30 years ago in Gastonia, of all paces, when he wrecked the De Soto he was driving. Still, the only time he ever had to cancel a booking (as opposed to missing a scheduled performance) was when, in a scene worthy of *I Pagliacci*, his wife at the time hit him over the head with a hammer. "True story," says Max, who always says that....

"We had some good times together," he recalls one afternoon before a performance. "God, she was a good-looking blonde. But she was leading a double life while I was on the road. I was blind. Look, I was probably no picnic to live with, but all the time I was on the road, she was fooling around...."

In *I Pagliacci* (which is based on a true story), Canio, who is Puchinello in the play within a play, discovers his much younger wife's infidelity and kills her and her lover. The last line of the opera, spoken by Canio, is "The comedy is ended."

But for Max the comedy goes on and on, night after night, flight after flight, ballpark after ballpark, Holiday Inn after Days Inn after Rodeway Inn, after International House of Pancakes. His is a life of *Addams Family* reruns at 6 a.m. when he can't get back to sleep. He could do something else for a living—he used to sell janitorial supplies and shoes in the off-season. He could even retire. Why does he go on being the Clown Prince of Baseball? He can't really explain it any more than he can explain why he always kisses the motel Bible 14 times before he leaves for the park....

[After a performance in Burlington, N.C.]

When he walks out to the parking lot, it is almost empty. Suddenly, out of the darkness, comes a rough-hewn man in a John Deere baseball cap. Max stiffens, thinking it might be a holdup.

"I just wanted to shake your hand," the man says. "God bless you. You made the kids laugh. You made me laugh."

"Thank you very much," says Max Patkin. His eyes say, "This is what I live for."

True story, by the way.

Excerpted from an original story published in
SPORTS ILLUSTRATED, *June 6, 1988*

THE RYAN EXPRESS

BY RON FIMRITE

The amazing Nolan Ryan just keeps going—as of August 1990, he had six no-hitters, 300 wins and an all-time major league high of 5,226 career strikeouts. In 1986, Ron Fimrite caught up with Ryan—then a pitcher for the Houston Astros—on his Texas cattle ranch.

Smile, Jesus loves you. Nolan Ryan smiles. "That's our street, Dezso Drive," he says, "just the other side of that Jesus sign—this is Baptist country—and I was raised in that little house there. My mom still lives in it." Ryan is in the family van conducting a tour of sorts of his hometown, Alvin, Texas (est. pop. 20,000). With him are his wife, Ruth, and daughter, Wendy, 9. His sons, Reid, 14, and Reese, 10, are tending to chores on the Ryan acreage just outside of town. "There's our church, the First Methodist, and that's where Ruth used to live, on Richard Street." The core of Alvin, its downtown, has been siphoned off into commercial centers on Highways 35 and 6, but the residential neighborhoods of spacious green lawns and brick and clapboard houses, all shielded from the merciless summer sun by spreading live oaks, are much as they were when Ryan was growing up there as the town's boy wonder. Alvin is no dusty *Last Picture Show* plains town with tumble-weed careering through its streets. It is humid and verdant, 26 miles south of Houston and 29 miles west of Galveston, smack in the path of the fierce storms that sweep inland from the Gulf of Mexico. Alvin? Now, what kind of a name is that for a town? Just the right one, say the townsfolk, named for one Alvin Morgan, a Santa Fe Railroad man who built the first house there in 1879. Baseball has taken Nolan Ryan to both coasts, but it has never taken him out of Alvin. It's what he's all about....

The fastball pitcher, the strikeout king, the kid who can throw the high hard one, the dark one, the hummer, heat, smoke, is, with the home run hitter, the glamour boy of the game, the stuff of baseball legend....

Consider the mythic status of Walter Johnson, who threw so hard he never bothered to learn to throw a good curveball and still won 416 games and led the American League in strikeouts 12 times.... Or consider Lefty Grove, of whom columnist Bugs Baer once wrote, "He could throw a lamb chop past a wolf." Or Bob (Rapid Robert) Feller. Or Van Lingle Mungo. Or Dizzy Dean. Or Dazzy Vance. Or Sandy Koufax....

But all these legends, living and dead, are so many balloon-tossers when compared with Nolan Ryan, "The Ryan Express."

Excerpted from an original story published in SPORTS ILLUSTRATED, *September 29, 1986*

SONS OF
THE WIND

BY KENNY MOORE

In 1989, Kenny Moore went to Kenya to seek an explanation for that nation's astonishing succession of brilliant distance runners. During his stay, he met Joseph Kibor, a young Kenyan runner, and traveled with him to his village. It was an illuminating trip.

The men's 10,000-meter run in Kenya's Commonwealth Games trials is a race of many departures, many rejoinings. The leaders—exuberantly, incorrigibly Kenyan—surge and slow and surge again, flying willingly into the distress such tactics cause. That they race through the thin air of Nairobi's 5,500-foot altitude seems of no consequence. Most were born and trained at even greater elevations. With their incessant passing and jostling, they seem to consider the 25 laps not as a single long contest but as dozens of shorter ones. If you don't know how excruciatingly effective this manner of racing is, you think them impatient children....

Joseph Kibor, barefoot, shirttail out, the gap in his lower teeth a mark of his Kalenjin tribal upbringing, clings to the pace. Kibor turned 17 only the day before. This is his first year of competitive running. He had to sell a goat to pay his way from his home far back in the Cherangani Hills to the preliminary trials in Kisumu, on Lake Victoria. He is barefoot because he failed in a two-day search to borrow some spikes....

His form, it happens, is the picture of the young Kipchoge Keino, Kibor's idol and an influence on almost every Kenyan runner. Keino, now 50, is the man who let the world know Kenyans could run. More to the point, he let Kenyans know Kenyans could run.

Keino's world records at 3,000 and 5,000 meters in the mid-1960s and his defeat of Jim Ryun in the '68 Olympic 1,500 gave rise to a river of superb Kenyan distance men. Since Kenya gained independence from Great Britain in '63, its athletes have won 24 Olympic medals in men's running events, despite boycotting the '76 and '80 Games. Ten of those medals were gold, a total second only to the sprinter-blessed U.S.'s....

Traditionally these magisterial runners have come from a very few tribes, notably the Kisii and the Kalenjin, which constitute only 15% of Kenya's 23 million people (52% of whom are under 15 years old). The Kalenjin are actually a group of related tribes. One of them is Kenya's historic cradle of runners, Keino's tribe, the Nandi, most of whom live at an altitude of 7,000 feet or more in a small area near the northeast corner of Lake Victoria.

Nandi athletes have won nearly half of Kenya's Olympic and Commonwealth Games medals. But in recent years, champions have begun to come from other tribes.... Kibor embodies this expanding excellence. He is Marakewt, from the mountainous district to the north of the Nandi. Though Kibor's tribe is of the Kalenjin group, there has never been a superior Marakewt runner....

With 600 meters to go, Kibor is still a close fourth. He begins to move up, a development the others find intolerable. [Ondoro] Osoro and [Kibiwott] Bitok cut him off twice, then hurl him three lanes wide. Kibor darts inside and passes, dangerously, on the rail. With a lap to go he is in the lead and sprinting with an expression of terrible anguish. A lap is too far, and he has used too much. He tightens. [Moses] Tanui passes him on the backstretch, Osoro on the last turn. But Kibor holds third to the end.

His time is 28:51.1, one of the fastest 10,000s ever run by one so young at any altitude. After a vote of the selection committee, Kibor is named to the team that will go to Auckland a month later, in January, for the 1990 Commonwealth Games. He will be the youngest Kenyan male ever to represent the country in a major competition and will finish fifth in the 10,000....

[Moore makes the trek to Kibor's village.]

The road grows steadily worse.... At a lunch stop you realize that nowhere in all these hills have you been out of the sound of human voices. They lift, soft and high, from every slope, testimony to the density of humanity here, and its youth. Sometimes kids chase the car, running with a smile and a will, staying there in the dust for long minutes until they make you nervous. After such a childhood, formal athletic training must be just polish, a final pat on the butt....

Grandmother's house is still quite far away,

however, and seems to be receding. The road is now either a sandy track or a faint depression in the animal-cropped grass. Bamboo, laid down for traction in muddy streambeds, cracks and splinters under the tires. At 10 miles an hour, you are slammed around the inside of the four-wheel-drive Isuzu Trooper as if on a small boat in a sickening six-foot chop.

You're above 10,000 feet now, and climbing. Fantastically shaped trees seem like twisted, gesturing spirits. Clouds lie down on the road....

Beyond, on a dome of green, are the tawny buildings of Kapchebau. The single approach is across a saddle, making the village seem like a medieval fortress. As you reach it, you see that there is nothing beyond but a precipice plunging a mile or more down to the desert floor of the Great Rift Valley.

At once you are surrounded by a dozen weather-burnished people. You have the honor of informing them that their native son made the team. Kibor points out his name in the newspaper account of the trials. The pages are received as if they were illuminated manuscripts....

Even descending you feel dizzy from the altitude.

After half a mile you reach a compound of seven huts perched below cypress trees on the lip of the cliff. There, ecstatic in a shiny Christmas dress, is Elizebeth Kokibor, Kibor's grandmother. She hugs you delicately, her eyes tightly shut, and gives you rich, oily tea....

[Late in his trip, Moore watches Kibor run on the Kapsabet Stadium track.]

He has never even done any track training. He has simply grown up Kalenjin in the Cherangani Hills, and come to a decision. Had you known in high school that people like this existed, it would have darkened your dreams of running.

Here, though, it has the opposite effect. The vision of Kibor in full stride has drawn a flock of kids. They watch for a while, poker-faced; then, told it's O.K. to go on the track, they fly into motion like a covey of quail, boys and girls, forming a ragged pack. They're impatient, they surge and elbow and squeal, and when it's time to go, you can't get them stopped. But never again will you quite think of them as children.

Excerpted from an original story published in
Sports Illustrated, *February 26, 1990*

THE MOURNING ANCHOR

BY RICK REILLY

When NBC announced that Bryant Gumbel would be the anchor for the network's coverage of the Seoul Olympics, SI sent Rick Reilly to meet him. Reilly came back with the story of a man obsessed by a memory.

What is it the poet said? Like muffled drums, our hearts beat a funeral march to the grave. And so it is that Bryant Gumbel, a man who is nothing if not prepared, keeps a list of his pallbearers.

Who has been true? Who has transgressed? Though only 39, he has done it many times. Gumbel hates surprises. The list changes every few months or so. He keeps track.

"I don't want to wait until something happens to see who my friends are," says Gumbel. "Or maybe I just don't want to be the guy who, when he dies, they can't find six guys to carry his coffin. Maybe this is a way to be sure I have six."

There have been days when he has wondered. Gumbel has a couple of thousand acquaintances but very few friends. Not that he couldn't have more. It's his choice. "If I'm in a room with 100

people, will I be able to find one person I'd like to have dinner with?" he asks. "Probably not," he answers....

The problem with people is that they just aren't as good as a certain Chicago probate judge who has been dead for more than 16 years—Gumbel's father, Richard. People don't try as hard as he did; they don't work as hard, achieve as much, carry themselves as tall. And who could be as heroic? Once, in the Philippines during World War II, Richard continued to march despite being obviously ill. The medic finally pulled him aside, sat him on a rock and took out his tonsils, then and there. And what did Sergeant Gumbel do? He got up and marched on. The man never let up. When he returned from the war, he put himself through Xavier University in New Orleans while working full-time to keep his family eating. He was senior-class president and yearbook editor. Then he put himself through Georgetown law school while working two jobs. He graduated second in his class.

Let's face it. Compared to Richard Gumbel, most people come off like Lumpy Rutherford. So Bryant finds it hard to be impressed; he finds himself getting let down a lot. He has more feuds than some people have friends: David Letterman, Connie Chung, Linda Ellerbee, Steve Garvey. It's not his fault. People aren't good enough. People aren't professional enough. People aren't true enough. And so he sits alone in the den of his 14-room home in Waccabuc, N.Y., making a list that weighs heavy on his mind. Who can be trusted to hold up one-sixth of his memory?

If you happen to be among the listed, consider yourself lucky. In Gumbel, you have a man of wit, style and grace. You have a man who, as anchor of NBC's *Today* show, is the only TV interviewer who might make Ted Koppel look over his shoulder. When the situation gets tense, Gumbel is a lock as the silkiest talent strapping on an earpiece....

Excerpted from an original story published in Sports Illustrated, *September 26, 1988*

THE BOXER AND THE BLONDE

BY FRANK DEFORD

It was the summer of 1941, a tumultuous time for America and for Pittsburgh's Billy Conn. It was the summer when Conn's mother, Maggie, passed away, when he married his wife, Mary Louise, and when he fought Joe Louis for the heavyweight title. Conn lost the fight, going for a knockout he didn't need, but that didn't dim the luster of the battle. Frank Deford visited Billy and Mary Louise in 1985.

The boxer and the blonde are together, downstairs in the club cellar. At some point, club cellars went out, and they became family rooms instead. This is, however, very definitely a club cellar. Why, the grandchildren of the boxer and the blonde could sleep soundly upstairs, clear through the big Christmas party they gave, when everybody came and stayed late and loud down here. The boxer and the blonde are sitting next to each other, laughing about the old times, about when they fell hopelessly in love almost half a century ago in New Jersey, at the beach. *Down the Jersey shore* is the way everyone in Pennsylvania says it. This club cellar is in Pittsburgh.

The boxer is going on 67, except in *The Ring* record book, where he is going on 68. But he has all his marbles; and he has his looks (except for the fighter's mashed nose); and he has the blonde; and they have the same house, the one with the club cellar, that they bought in the summer of 1941. A great deal of this is about that bright ripe summer, the last one before the forlorn simplicity of a Depression was buried in the thick-braided rubble of blood and Spam....

He still has his looks? Hey, you should see her. The blonde is past 60 now, and she's still cute as a button. Not merely beautiful, you understand, but schoolgirl cute, just like she was when the boxer first flirted with her down the Jersey shore....

[Deford describes the Louis-Conn fight]

It was wonderful. Men had been slugging it out for eons, and there had been 220 years of prize-

fighting, and there would yet be Marciano and the two Sugar Rays and Ali, but this was it. This was the best it had ever been and ever would be, the 12th and 13th rounds of Louis and Conn on a warm night in New York just before the world went to hell. The people were standing and cheering for Conn, but it was really for the sport and for the moment and for themselves that they cheered. They could be a part of it, and every now and then, for an instant, *that* is it, and it can't ever get any better. This was such a time in the history of games....

A few years ago Louis came to Pittsburgh, and he and Conn made an appearance together at a union hall.... Billy brought the film of the '41 fight over from Squirrel Hill in a shopping bag. As soon as the fight started, Louis left the room and went into the bar to drink brandy. Every now and then Louis would come to the door and holler out, "Hey, Billy, have we got to the 13th round yet?" Conn just laughed and watched himself punch the bigger man around, until finally, when they did come to the 13th, Joe called out, "Goodby, Billy."

Louis knocked out Conn at 2:58, just like always, but when the lights went on, Billy wasn't there. He had left when the 13th round started. He had gone into another room, to where the buffet was, after he had watched the 12 rounds when he was the heavyweight champeen of the world, back in that last indelible summer when America dared yet dream that it could run and hide from the world, when the handsomest boy loved the prettiest girl, when streetcars still clanged and fistfights were fun, and the smoke hung low when Maggie went off to Paradise.

Excerpted from an original story published in SPORTS ILLUSTRATED, *June 17, 1985*

THE LONGEST RIDE

BY WILLIAM NACK

When jockey Robbie Davis's horse killed fellow jockey Mike Venezia, no one knew the demons that the accident would unloose within Davis—demons held captive since his childhood of sexual abuse at the hand of his stepfather. William Nack talked to Davis as he prepared to return to his brilliant riding career after a hiatus of five months. His story is a testament to courage.

It happened so fast that even today Robbie Davis has trouble sorting out the whole haunting nightmare: the terrible fall and the vision of the silks flashing beneath him, the sound like a water balloon bursting at his horse's feet, his own screaming voice, the sight of the dead jockey, and then his hiding like a child in the darkened broom closet in the first-aid room at Belmont Park.

On the afternoon of Oct. 13, 1988, in the fifth race at Belmont Park, Davis, atop Drums in the Night, was moving down the backstretch of the turf course and sensing in the hollow of his bones that he could not have been in a sweeter spot on this great green earth. "It was a beautiful, gorgeous, perfect day," Davis says. "There's nothing like a fall day in New York, you know, and I had won with my horse the time before and I had all sorts of horse under me."

Davis saw the horse directly in front of him—Mr. Walker K., with veteran jockey Mike Venezia up—stumble suddenly and veer to the right, out of Drums in the Night's path. Instinctively, Davis took hold of his horse, waiting to see what would happen in front of him. "All of a sudden I seen the jockey pop up right in front of me," he says, "and I took straight back to see which way he would go, so I could miss him. I didn't want to move until he committed himself in one direction or the other. All of a sudden he lost his balance—it happened so fast, I didn't know who it was—and he kicked off the left side of his horse, and he went under my horse. My horse tried to jump, but it was too late. He clipped him and stumbled. The jockey's head was right in the path of my horse, right underneath! I looked down and seen him under me, and my horse scissored

his head with his back feet. Shattered his skull."

Davis screamed, "Oh, my God!" He looked back and saw the body lying on the grass, motionless in the sun. Caught in the hot whips of panic, Davis came undone. He looked over to his left and saw jockey Nick Santagata, and he hollered, "Nickie! Who was that! I just killed him! I just ran over him. Who was that?"

Santagata glanced at Davis over his shoulder. "Venezia!" he shouted.

The two men raced together for the far turn. Davis screamed again to Santagata: "I killed him! I swear I killed him. What do I do? Do I ride? I can't believe it. Nickie! What do I do?"

Santagata never answered, and together the two men drove their horses home. Drums in the Night finished fourth, and as Davis pulled him up at the clubhouse turn, he looked over his left shoulder and saw the ambulance already out on the backstretch. Venezia had been killed instantly, the blow from Drums in the Night's hooves having struck his head so sharply that it dislodged his right eye. But as Davis slowly walked his horse back to the unsaddling area, he didn't know that. He prayed, "God, I know I busted something, but I just hope he's O.K."

Davis had to see for himself. He pushed past the guards and looked in the back window of the ambulance. The horror was entire. "He's lying in there on a board," Davis says. "With his head turned away from me. I peeked in. All I could see was blood so thick on his face, and he was lying there motionless. I thought, Oh, no. It can't be!"

Davis bolted for the first-aid room, opened the door of the broom closet and closed it behind him, leaving himself alone in the sudden dark. He fell to his knees. His whole life flashed past him, as though it was he who was dying, and in a way he was. "It was flashing and flashing and flashing," Davis says. "If it wasn't one thing flashing, it was something else. All the violent things in my life came back to me. I was on my knees, and I was gripping my fists and saying, 'God, why me? Why does this happen to me all the time? Why do I have to take the pain all the time? Why so much pain?' My whole life was flashing."

Flashing back to those afternoons, so rich in an

oily aroma that he can smell them now. Back to when he was four and was sitting on the gasoline tank of his Uncle Tim's dirt bike, holding on to the handlebars as he and his uncle roared along at 60 miles an hour among the rock-encrusted hills outside Pocatello, Idaho. Back to the day he got the call at Eddy's Bakery, where he was stacking bread, and found when he got home that Uncle Tim, who had been like a father to him, had died of carbon monoxide poisoning in a mining accident. Back to the night that his best friend plunged to his death when the friend's truck rolled off a 60-foot cliff into a cemetery on the east side of Pocatello. Back to his own aborted suicide attempt, when at three one morning he screeched his light-blue 1968 El Camino to a stop just shy of the tree he had been aiming for at the end of Kinghorn Road. Back to the fights at home between his mother and his stepfather Thomas William Darner, the sound of the ashtray smashing through the television screen, and the nights he hid in the closet or under the bed or covered his head with a pillow and screamed to muffle the noise of the violence. Back to his terrorized childhood and the sexual abuse he suffered at the hands of his stepfather. Back to all those years of biting anger, self-loathing and shame that had sprung from that abuse, the dark little secret of his life.

And so, a week after the accident, [Davis's wife] Marguerite found him frantically packing all their belongings—winter and summer clothes, books, tapes, pictures, VCRs, golf clubs, dirt bike.... "What are you doing?" Marguerite asked.

"I just want to get out of here!" Robbie said. "I want to escape for a while. Take a vacation. I want to go home. I want to get back to myself. To my roots."

So, at age 27, riding high in his prime as one of the leading jockeys in one of the richest venues of American racing, Davis packed his family and their belongings, aimed his Suburban truck west and hit the gas. Until last week, to the dismay and confusion of all his friends, Davis did not ride in another horse race. True to his word, too, he did go home again....

Davis was carrying all that unchecked baggage from his childhood when, on that fine October afternoon, Venezia fell in front of him, Davis peered into the ambulance and then ran off to hide. As his life flickered before him in that closet, the scenes of violence and abuse, something in him seemed to die. A kind of serenity came over him, as if the accident, in catharsis, had suddenly slain all the old torments in his life. "It pulled a trigger," he says. "It shot off inside me and went through me. I never loved people more in my life than that moment right there. All the hate I had for everybody, it just all went away."

With that began the craving to head home. Davis says, "It's hard to explain, but there was something pulling me back to Pocatello—to my values. I was packing too heavy a load. There was too much I had to get off my mind."

[Finally Davis told his wife of the sexual abuse.]

It was easier than he had thought it would be. They talked about it into the night. "It just flowed out," Davis says. "We were both crying. She was so understanding. We tied the knot that much tighter. She held me all night and we went to sleep. It was such a relief. It was like a new beginning."

Excerpted from an original story published in Sports Illustrated, *March 20, 1989*

THE LOSER

BY WILLIAM OSCAR JOHNSON
AND KENNY MOORE

Over the years, SI has led the effort to bring the tools of investigative journalism into the arena of sports. In the cases of Ben Johnson, the Canadian sprinter who was stripped of his gold medal at the 1988 Olympics, and Pete Rose (see opposite page), SI played a major role in uncovering key facts. Bill Johnson and Kenny Moore teamed up for the story that told the world about the sprinter's illicit use of steroids.

In late May, Canadian sprinter Ben Johnson traveled to the Caribbean island of St. Kitts to be treated by his doctor, Jamie Astaphan. Ten days before, he had aggravated a pulled left hamstring, an injury that could ruin his gold medal chances at the Seoul Olympics. Astaphan administered a variety of therapies during the next 10 days. On Tuesday two sources told SPORTS ILLUSTRATED that Astaphan also injected Johnson with anabolic steroids.

SI's sources said that they were present during conversations in which both Johnson and Astaphan spoke of the different steroids Johnson was being given, and how Johnson could fool the doping tests in Seoul and at other meets that he might enter before the Olympics. "We can beat them," Astaphan said.

Astaphan, who lives in St. Kitts, has often been at odds with Johnson's long-time coach, Charlie Francis, over who should get credit for Johnson's accomplishments. One SI source said that while Astaphan was the one who administered the steroids in May, other members of Johnson's entourage knew about the use of the substances. "They actually bragged about it, how Ben was a skinny little kid before he got into steroids," the source said. He also said Astaphan told him that one of Johnson's corporate sponsors had promised a million dollars to anyone who could get Johnson over his injury and back on track for the gold in Seoul.

Both of SI's sources said Johnson knew that the injections he was receiving were steroids but that he spoke of his eagerness to get off the drugs after the Olympics. In the meantime, Astaphan had told them that the Americans and the Soviets did not know how to administer drugs to enhance the performance of their athletes without the drugs being detected, and that his "idols" in sports medicine were Bulgarian team doctors who were expert at this deception....

And what happened to the Bulgarians in Seoul also happened to Johnson. In the early days of the Games, two Bulgarian weightlifters, Mitko Grablev and Angel Guenchev, were disqualified by the International Olympic Committee (IOC) after they had won gold medals, and the entire Bulgarian weightlifting team went home. On Tuesday it was Johnson's turn to leave Seoul in disgrace.

He fled like a criminal, hiding his face behind a briefcase as an army of photographers and TV cameramen fought one another to take his picture. Scarcely 72 hours earlier Johnson had been the toast of the Games, a hero of truly Olympian proportions. His fall from gold and glory occurred with thundering finality.

Excerpted from an original story published in SPORTS ILLUSTRATED, *October 3, 1988*

ROSE'S
GRIM VIGIL

BY CRAIG NEFF
AND JILL LIEBER

The baseball world was rocked by the allegations in the Pete Rose scandal: that he gambled, that he gambled on baseball and, finally, that he gambled on the Cincinnati Reds, the team that he managed. SI was on the case from the very beginning as evidenced in this piece by Jill Lieber and Craig Neff written in April of 1989, four months before baseball's alltime hits leader was banned from the game for life.

On the surface Cincinnati Reds manager Pete Rose seemed his usual unflappable self. He looked out at the horde of reporters and the TV crews that descended last week on Plant City (Fla.) Stadium, the Reds' spring-training park, and joked that the super-charged, World Series–type atmosphere they had created would be a good experience for his team. "All you media people stick around," he said. But on a down note, Rose confided to reporters, "I feel like a piece of fresh meat."

And with good reason: Even as Rose worked to prepare his team for its April 3 opener in Cincinnati against the Los Angeles Dodgers, his personal and business affairs were under scrutiny by the media, federal authorities and baseball commissioner Peter Ueberroth, who on March 20 announced that his office was conducting a "full inquiry into serious allegations" about Rose....

Ueberroth's dramatic announcement seeded the media clouds, and the downpour that followed drenched Rose—and baseball—in a torrent of stories about Rose's associations with convicted felons, his alleged huge betting losses and his handling of his lucrative memorabilia sales and autograph signings. The New York *Daily News* reported that Ueberroth had publicly disclosed his investigation "only after being made aware of an upcoming Sports Illustrated story," and, indeed, SI subsequently reported in its March 27 issue that Ueberroth had received information that Rose may have bet on baseball games, behavior that, if substantiated, could result in Rose's suspension from the game and could jeopardize his election to the Hall of Fame when he becomes eligible in 1992.

The information came from Alan Statman, a lawyer for Ron Peters, a Franklin, Ohio, restaurateur whom Statman described as Rose's "principal bookmaker." Statman approached SI in hopes of selling Peters's story—the magazine declined the offer—and said he had told baseball investigators that he and Peters could supply information that Rose had bet on baseball. SI also reported that it had discussed purchasing a story about Rose with Paul Janszen, a bodybuilder friend of Rose's now serving a six-month sentence in a Cincinnati halfway house for evading taxes on income derived from the sale of steroids. Although SI didn't buy Janszen's story, a fellow weightlifter told the magazine that he had overheard Janszen using a phone at Gold's Gym in the Cincinnati suburb of Forest Park to place baseball bets, he understood, in Rose's behalf.

Rose used to work out at Gold's and even promoted the gym. He met Janszen there, but he denies ever having bet on baseball.... He also denies suggestions that he may have evaded income taxes and suffered large gambling losses. But even as Rose proclaimed his innocence, the rains continued to fall.

Excerpted from an original story published in
SPORTS ILLUSTRATED, *April 3, 1989*

THE COACH AND
HIS CHAMPION

BY ALEXANDER WOLFF

John Wooden—the Wizard of Westwood—was surely the most successful college basketball coach in history. He was also one of the most principled men in all of sport. In 1989, Alex Wolff spent some time with the coach of coaches, who was still struggling to cope with a life without his beloved wife, Nell.

John Wooden will not be in Seattle this weekend. Instead, the greatest basketball coach ever—the man who so completely made the Final Four his private reserve that the fans and the press and the rest of the college game couldn't get in on the fun until he retired—will be at home, in Encino, Calif., in what is called the Valley.

He will not stay home because he is unwelcome in Seattle. Men like Bob Knight and Dean Smith have implored him to come, to grace with his presence the annual meeting of the National Association of Basketball Coaches, which is held at the Final Four. But their entreaties have been unavailing. "We need him at our convention," says current UCLA coach Jim Harrick, who is the sixth man in 14 years to try to wear Wooden's whistle. "He is a shining light. My wife and I have offered to take him. I hounded him so much that he finally told me to lay off. The more you badger him, the more stubborn he gets. But I can see his point. The memories would be really difficult."

To most coaches, memories of 10 NCAA championships in 12 years, including seven in a row, would be sweet and easy. Indeed, this spring marks the 25th anniversary of Wooden's first title, the championship won by UCLA's tiny Hazzard-Goodrich-Erickson team, the one he likens to his first child. But beginning in 1947, when he was coaching at Indiana State, and continuing for 37 consecutive years, Wooden attended the coaches' convention and the Final Four in the company of his late wife, Nell. At 78 he's not about to start going alone, not now.

Nell was perennial, consensus All-Lobby. She knew the names that went with the faces, and she would whisper cues to her husband as well-wishers approached. He needed her with him, for she was as outgoing as he was reserved. A few coaches didn't cotton to Nell's presence, for they had left their own wives at home and knew that the usual boys-will-be-boys shenanigans would never pass unnoticed before Nell's Irish eyes. But her husband wasn't for an instant to be talked out of bringing her, just as today he isn't to be talked into going without her.

So Wooden will spend college basketball's premier weekend in much the same way he passes all his days now. The games on TV will be mere divertissements. He will take his early-morning walk, past the park, the eucalyptus trees and the preschool his great-granddaughter attends. Each evening he will speak to Nell in apostrophe before retiring. He may whisper the lines from Wordsworth that he finds so felicitous: "She lived unknown, and few could know/When Lucy ceased to be;/But she is in her grave, and, oh,/The difference to me!"

And how did you imagine John Wooden spending his later years? The mind, the values, the spring in his step—they're all still in place. He could probably take over a misbegotten college varsity, demonstrate the reverse pivot, intone a few homilies and have the team whipped into Top 20 shape in, oh, six weeks. He continues to stage summer basketball camps in which you won't necessarily meet famous players but you may actually learn the game. He answers his own mail, in a hand that you'll remember from grammar school as "cursive writing."...

The sphinx of the Pyramid of Success rests his left forearm against his stomach, parallel to the ground. His left hand is a socket for his right elbow. His right forearm forms a hypotenuse leading to his chin, where the index finger sticks upright, hovering just over his mouth. When speaking, Wooden strikes this pose frequently and unconsciously. A photograph of him in the same pose—Nell's favorite—hangs in their bedroom.

It is an enigma, that finger to the mouth. Is it the stern Midwestern schoolteacher, meting out discipline, admonishing the class? Or is it the kindly grandfather, guiding the wayward and confused young, giving them assurances that everything will be all right?

Or is it both? Wooden's greatest achievement isn't the 10 in 12, or seven in a row, although such a feat will surely never be accomplished again. It is rather that he did all this during the roily years from 1964 to '75—an era in which 18- to 22-year-old males were at their most contrary—at UCLA, a big-city campus awash in the prevailing freedoms....

By her husband's count, Nell was twice at death's door before she finally succumbed. A heart attack, which she suffered while undergoing a hip-replacement operation in 1982, put her in a coma....

"The doctors told me to talk to her," says Wooden. "They said that I might not see any signs, but in her subconscious she might be hearing me." Three months after Nell entered the coma, as her body lay suctioned and plugged with intravenous tubing, he took her hand and squeezed it, and he felt a squeeze back. There are no nets to cut down when something like that happens.

[After one more miraculous recovery, Nell finally died on the first day of spring, 1985.]

Before every tip-off back at Martinsville High, Wooden had looked up from his guard position and caught her eye in the stands, where she played the cornet in the band. She would give him the O.K. sign and he would wave back. They kept up that ritual even as Johnny Wooden (Hall of Fame, inducted as a player in 1960) became John R. Wooden (Hall of Fame, inducted as a coach in 1972). He's the only person with the old one-two combo. Few knew that he clutched a cross in his hand. Fewer knew that she clutched an identical one in hers. She took it with her to the grave....

Some people think Wooden was too deferential to [UCLA athletic director J.D.] Morgan. Certainly, the same couldn't be said of Nell. "She really thought they were taking advantage of him," says [Wooden's daughter] Nan. "And Daddy never wanted to complain, because he never wanted for anything. But Daddy didn't have to get mad. He could stay very serene, because his other half was getting it out. Nobody was his champion the way Mother was."

A few weeks ago [Wooden's great-granddaughter] Cori and Papa [Cori's nickname for Wooden] looked up as an airplane passed overhead. "See that airplane, Papa?" said Cori. "I'm going to take that airplane and fly all the way to heaven and get Mama and bring her back, so Papa won't be lonely anymore."

Gracious sakes, Cori, no. Stay right here with Papa. For later, there, he'll have Mama. For now, here, he has you and John, two previous generations of Woodens, and—should he

ever change that mind that's so hard to change once it's made up—a convention full of rudderless coaches of basketball, who desperately need to learn how to teach the game.

Before this extraordinary life gets played out, before the buzzer sounds, won't someone please call time-out to remind him? He has taught so many of us such wonderful lessons. He has one more lesson, his own, to study up on.

Excerpted from an original story published in
SPORTS ILLUSTRATED, *April 3, 1989*

THE CURIOUS CASE OF SIDD FINCH

BY GEORGE PLIMPTON

Few stories in SI history got more attention than George Plimpton's piece on Sidd Finch, a strange new pitcher for the New York Mets who could allegedly throw a baseball at 168 mph. Most readers noted that the issue carrying the story was dated April 1—the traditional day for hoaxes—but a few were genuinely fooled.

His assigned roommate [at Harvard] was Henry W. Peterson, class of 1979, now a stockbroker in New York with Dean Witter, who saw very little of Finch. "He was almost never there," Peterson told SI. "I'd wake up morning after morning and look across at his bed, which had a woven native carpet of some sort on it—I have an idea he told me it was made of yak fur—and never had the sense it had been slept in. Maybe he slept on the floor. Actually, my assumption was that he had a girl in Somerville or something, and stayed out there. He had almost no belongings. A knapsack. A bowl he kept in the corner on the floor. A couple of wool shirts, always very clean, and maybe a pair or so of blue jeans. One pair of hiking boots ... He had a French horn in an old case. I don't know much about French-horn music but he played beautifully. Sometimes he'd play in the bath. He knew any number of languages. He was so adept at them that he'd be talking in English, which he spoke in this distinctive way, quite Oriental, and he'd use a phrase like "pied-a-terre" and without knowing it he'd sail along in French for a while until he'd drop in a German word like "angst" and he'd shift to that language."...

In hopes of understanding more about him, in early March the Mets called in a specialist in Eastern religions, Dr. Timothy Burns, the author of, among other treatises, *Satori*, or *Four Years in a Tibetan Lamasery*. Not allowed to speak personally with Finch for fear of "spooking him," Burns was able only to speculate about the Mets' newest player.

According to sources from within the Met organization, Burns told a meeting of the club's top brass that the strange ballplayer in their midst was very likely a *trapas*, or aspirant monk.

A groan is said to have gone up from [owner] Nelson Doubleday. Burns said that Finch was almost surely a disciple of Tibet's great poet-saint Lama Milaraspa, who was born in the 11th century and died in the shadow of Mount Everest. Burns told them that Milaraspa was a great yogi who could manifest an astonishing phenomenon: He could produce "internal heat," which allowed him to survive snowstorms and intense cold, wearing only a thin robe of white cotton. Finch does something similar—an apparent deflection of the huge forces of the universe into throwing a baseball with bewildering accuracy and speed through the process of *siddhi*, namely the yogic mastery of mind-body....

Excerpted from an original story published in SPORTS ILLUSTRATED, *April 1, 1985*

TAKE MY GOLF GAME, PLEASE!

BY JACK McCALLUM

When the Worst Avid Golfer competition was held at the Tournament Players Club in Ponte Vedra, Fla., Jack McCallum was there to record the triumph—of sorts—of grocery store manager Angelo Spagnolo.

Years from now they will still be talking about the 66 that Angelo Spagnolo shot on the 17th hole of the Tournament Players Club at Ponte Vedra, Fla. last Wednesday. Spagnolo, the manager of a grocery store in suburban Pittsburgh, brought up the rear—no mean feat that—in the 18-hole Worst Avid Golfer tournament, which was sponsored by *Golf Digest* and, incredibly, sanctioned by the PGA, a group not generally known for its sense of humor.

Spagnolo, 31, may not be this nation's worst avid golfer—but, then again, he may be. An unbelievable 627 players were nominated for the tournament, and Spagnolo was one of four men invited to the competition. And after his 18-hole round of 257, no one doubted that he deserved the tacky, green-checked sports jacket that was presented to him. In the seven-hour round that seemed more akin to a death march than a golf match, the new patron saint of duffers knocked 27 balls into the drink at the 132-yard 17th hole, famed for its island green, before he bowed to pressure and took a circuitous route and putted up the cart path, onto the green and into immortality.

"I didn't want to do that because, darn it, the hole wasn't designed to be played that way," said Spagnolo, the un-champ, ignoring the obvious fact that the game of golf wasn't designed to be played the way he plays it, either. But what the heck....

An important point: None of the four [golfers] was sandbagging. They are that bad and, playing on a course like the TPC, bad golfers will be worse. Several axioms were proved but none more conclusively than this: If you can't get a wedge in the air, then there's no way you can play the 17th hole except by using "Angelo's Alley," as PGA Tour commissioner Deane Beman promises the cart path on 17 will be called. How long could Spagnolo have stayed there, across the lake, forlornly consign-ing balls to a watery grave? Days? Weeks? Let's talk optimism. The night before the tournament Ange had dreamed that he got on the green in one. Now, why someone who has played golf regularly for two years cannot get a ball airborne with a wedge is a question for some Ph.D.

For those in the gallery who enjoy public executions, the 15th was undeniably the day's highlight. Spagnolo did his damage in the woods, at one point hitting an iron that ricochetted off a tree and into a golf cart where PGA Tour rules official Mike Crosthwaite was sitting. Crosthwaite was vainly trying for a moment's respite in an afternoon when he made more rulings than the Warren Court—there were, after all, 124 penalties and 102 balls hit into various water hazards.

Besides being unredeemably horrible, the final four consisted of men who passionately love the game and find a silver lining in every skulled nine-iron. These guys aren't casual golfers. Each plays at least once or twice a week, and [Jack] Pulford, bless his hacker's heart, has been terrifying small animals on courses since 1975....

"You know, I'd go right out and play another round," he said after the tournament.... "In fact, I wish they would've made this a two-day event." He leaned forward conspiratorially. "I know tomorrow I could beat the hell out of these guys."

Excerpted from an original story published in
SPORTS ILLUSTRATED, *July 1, 1985*

ALI AND HIS ENTOURAGE

BY GARY SMITH

When writer Gary Smith and photographer Gregory Heisler collaborated on a 1988 story about Muhammad Ali and his entourage, the result was a memorable juxtaposition of words and pictures. The story focused on the core group that surrounded Ali most regularly throughout his career: Ferdie Pacheco, the Doctor; Gene Kilroy, the Facilitator; Lana Shabazz, the Cook; Luis Sarria, the Masseur; Pat Patterson, the Bodyguard; Herbert Muhammad, the Manager; and Drew (Bundini) Brown, the Motivator.

Around Muhammad Ali, all was decay. Mildewed tongues of insulation poked through gaps in the ceiling; flaking cankers pocked the painted walls. On the floor lay rotting scraps of carpet.

He was cloaked in black. Black street shoes, black socks, black pants, black short-sleeved shirt. He threw a punch, and in the small town's abandoned boxing gym, the rusting chain between the heavy bag and the ceiling rocked and creaked.

Slowly, at first, his feet began to dance around the bag. His left hand flicked a pair of jabs, and then a right cross and a left hook, too, recalled the ritual of butterfly and bee. The dance quickened. Black sunglasses flew from his pocket as he gathered speed, black shirttail flapped free, black heavy bag rocked and creaked. Black street shoes scuffed faster and faster across black moldering tiles: Yeah, Lawd, champ can still float, champ can still sting! He whirled, jabbed, feinted, let his feet fly into a shuffle. "How's that for a sick man?" he shouted.

He did it for a second three-minute round, then a third. "Time!" I shouted at the end of each one as the second hand swept past the 12 on the wristwatch he had handed to me. And then, gradually, his shoulders began to slump, his hands to drop. The tap and thud of leather soles and leather gloves began to miss a quarter-beat ... half-beat ... whole. Ali stopped and sucked air. The dance was over....

He entered the long driveway of his farm, parked and left the car. He led me into a barn. On the floor, leaning against the walls, were paintings and photographs of him in his prime, eyes keen, arms thrust up in triumph, surrounded by the cluster of people he took around the world with him.

He looked closer and noticed it. Across his face in every picture, streaks of bird dung. He glanced up toward the pigeons in the rafters. No malice, no emotion at all flickered in his eyes. Silently, one by one, he turned the pictures to the wall.

Outside, he stood motionless and moved his eyes across his farm. He spoke from his throat, without moving his lips. I had to ask him to repeat it. "I had the world," he said, "and it wasn't nothin'." He paused and pointed. "Look now...."

Black blobs of cows slumbering in the pasture, trees swishing slowly, as if under water rather than sky. Merry-go-rounds, sliding boards and swings near the house, but no giggles, no squeals, no children.

"What happened to the circus?" I asked.

He was staring at the slowly swishing trees, listening to the breeze sift leaves and make a lulling sound like water running over the rocks of a distant stream. He didn't seem to hear....

[Smith visits Ferdie Pacheco, the Doctor.]

In one way, Ferdie Pacheco was just like his former patient Muhammad Ali: He needed laughter and applause. He led people to each of his paintings, lithographs, cartoons and manuscripts the way Ali once led them to continents to watch him talk and fight. Both worked on canvas: Ali, when his was not near to dance on, used parlor magic tricks to make eyes go bright and wide; Pacheco, when his was not near to dab on, told long tales and jokes, dominating a dinner party, from escargots to espresso, with his worldliness and wit.

In another way, they were not alike at all. Ali lived for the moment and acted as he felt, with disregard for the cord between action and consequence. This allured the doctor, whose mind teemed with consequence before he chose his action. "In an overcomplicated society," he says, "Ali was a simple, happy man."...

[Smith visits Bundini Brown, the Motivator.]

People'd see us back then and say, "It's so nice seein' y'all together." We made a lot of people happy. I was a soldier. *(His hands are shaking. He reaches down to the floor, pours a glass of rum as his*

eyes begin to fill with tears.) I was happy then. It'd be good for Muhammad if I could be with him again. Be good for me, too. Then I wouldn't drink as much. By me being alone I drink a lot. Always did say I could motivate him out of this sickness, if me and the champ was together. He needs the medical thing, too, but he needs someone who truly loves him. If we were together again, more of the God would come out of me. *(His voice is almost inaudible.)* Things used to explode in my head ... I'm kind of runnin' out now....

Don't see my kids like I want to. Can't go back to my babies till I got somethin' to give 'em. Right now, I'm broke. I said, broke, not poor, there's a difference. *(He glances across the room and speaks softly.)* I know one thing. You get used to good food and a clean bed, hard to get used to somethin' else. Why don't you leave now? Please?

(He rises and goes to the door, shredding a piece of bread and tossing it outside to the pigeons.) People don't know it, but feedin' the birds is like paintin' a picture.... Some people think Muhammad's broke, too. He ain't broke. He's brokenhearted. He hasn't found himself in what he really want to do. Maybe he just be in the freezer for a few years. Maybe he's going through this so he has time to think. Last time I was with him, his 15-year-old son said to him, "Daddy, Bundini is your only friend, the only one that doesn't give up on you." Muhammad looked at me, and we started cryin'....

See this bald spot on my head? Looks like a footprint, don't it? That come from me walkin' on my head. Don't you think I know I'm my own worst enemy? I suffer a lot. If my kids only knew how I hurt. But I can't let 'em know, it might come out in anger. And 'fore I see 'em, I gotta have somethin' to give to 'em. I owe $9,000 'fore I can get my stuff out of storage. *(He bites his lip and looks away.)* One storage place already done auctioned off all the pictures of Ali an' me, all my trophies and memories from back then. Strangers have 'em all...

A few days later, Bundini Brown fell in his motel room and was found paralyzed from the neck down by a cleaning woman. And then he died.

Seven years ago, when the group broke camp at Deer Lake for the final time, everyone contributed money for a plaque that would include all their names. They left the task to Bundini Brown and departed.

Today the camp is a home for unwed mothers. In front of the log-cabin gym, where babies squeal and crawl, stands a tall slab of gray granite, chiseled with 16 names and surrounded by flowers. Bundini Brown had bought a tombstone.

Excerpted from an original story published in
SPORTS ILLUSTRATED, *April 25, 1988*

PHOTOGRAPHY CREDITS

COVER

Neil Leifer

BACK COVER

Top left Neil Leifer, bottom left Manny Millan, middle right, UPI/BETTMAN NEWSPHOTOS

FRONT MATTER

1, Art Daley; 2-3, Walter Iooss, Jr.; 6, Neil Leifer

THE GOLDEN AGE

8-9, UPI/BETTMAN NEWSPHOTOS; 11, Cornell Capa; 12, Marvin E. Newman; 13, Phil Bath; 14, (copyright) New York Daily News, Inc.; 15, (2) AP/Wide World Photos; 16, Oxford Mail; 17, UPI/BETTMAN NEWSPHOTOS; 18, Ralph Morse/LIFE; 19, top Hy Peskin, bottom Mark Kauffman; 20, Maurice Jarnoux; 21, Rich Clarkson; 22, Art Daley; 23, top Los Angeles Times, bottom AP/Wide World Photos; 24, UPI/BETTMAN NEWSPHOTOS; 25, John G. Zimmerman; 26, top Joern Gerdts/LIFE, bottom Richard Meek; 27, James Whitmore/LIFE; 28, Hy Peskin; 29, top AP/World Wide Photos, bottom c. Jerry Cooke; 30, Hy Peskin; 31, Richard Meek; 32, John G. Zimmerman; 33, top no credit, bottom John G. Zimmerman; 34, Garry Winogrand; 35, Hy Peskin; 36, John G. Zimmerman; 37, top Mark Kauffman, bottom Marvin E. Newman; 38, Marvin E. Newman; 39, Milwaukee Journal; 40, John G. Zimmerman; 41, top John G. Zimmerman, bottom no credit; 42, Marvin E. Newman; 43, John G. Zimmerman; 44, Mark Kauffman/LIFE; 45, John G. Zimmerman; 46, John G. Zimmerman; 47, top c. Jerry Cooke, bottom Marvin E. Newman; 48, Herb Scharfman/LIFE; 49, AP/Wide World Photos; 50, Neil Leifer; 51, top Hulton Deutch Collection, bottom Phil Bath; 52, Lee Balterman; 53, AP/Wide World Photos; 54, Ozzie Sweet; 57, Whitney Tower; 58, Grey Villet/LIFE; 59, Mark Kauffman; 60, Charlie Ott, N.A.S./Photo Researchers; 62, David Goodnow; 63, Mark Kauffman/LIFE; 65, Lee Friedlander; 67, Marc Simont (illustrator); 69, Marvin E. Newman

THE AGE OF AUDACITY

70-71, Walter Iooss, Jr.; 73, Neal Barr-Larry Burrows/LIFE; 74, Neil Leifer; 75, John G. Zimmerman; 76, Rich Clarkson; 77, top Hy Peskin, bottom Rich Clarkson; 78, James Drake; 79, top Neil Leifer; 80, Walter Iooss, Jr.; 81, top Herb Scharfman, bottom Neil Leifer; 82, Herb Scharfman/LIFE; 83, Peter Custer; 84, top George Silk/LIFE, bottom c. Jerry Cooke; 85, Arthur Rickerby/LIFE; 86, Marvin E. Newman; 87, top Marvin E. Newman, bottom Bruce Roberts; 88, James Drake; 89, Walter Iooss, Jr.; 90, c. Jerry Cooke; 91, top Neil Leifer, bottom Rich Clarkson; 92, Bill Eppridge/LIFE; 93, James Drake; 94, Neil Leifer; 95, top Neil Leifer, bottom Neil Leifer; 96, Walter Iooss, Jr.; 97, Neil Leifer; 98, Walter Iooss, Jr.; 99, top Neil Leifer, bottom Herb Scharfman; 100, Rich Clarkson; 101, Richard Meek; 102, top Neil Leifer, bottom John G. Zimmerman; 103, Tony Duffy/Allsport; 104, Neil Leifer; 105, top Walter Iooss, Jr., bottom James Drake; 106, top Neil Leifer, bottom Neil Leifer; 107, Walter Iooss, Jr.; 108, Eric Schweikardt; 109, top Walter Iooss, Jr., bottom Herb Scharfman; 110, Gerry Cranham; 111, John G. Zimmerman/LIFE; 112, Walter Iooss, Jr.; 113, top Tony Triolo, bottom James Drake; 114, top Walter Iooss, Jr., bottom Neil Leifer; 115, Heinz Kluetmeier; 116, Tony Triolo; 117, top Sheedy & Long, bottom Sheedy & Long; 118, Dick Raphael; 119, Sheedy & Long; 120, top Co Rentmeester/LIFE, bottom Co Rentmeester/LIFE; 121, Neil Leifer; 122, Melchior Di Giacomo; 123, top Neil Leifer, bottom Neil Leifer; 124, John D. Hanlon; 125, Neil Leifer; 126, James Drake; 127, top Neil Leifer, bottom Heinz Kluetmeier; 128, Tony Triolo; 129, Heinz Kluetmeier; 130, Heinz Kluetmeier; 131, top Eric Schweikardt, bottom Heinz Kluetmeier; 132, Rich Clarkson; 133, Neil Leifer; 134, c. Jerry Cooke; 137, Charles Trainor; 138, Tony Triolo; 139, c. Jerry Cooke; 141, MIchael Ramus (illustrator); 142, Herb Scharfman; 143, James Drake; 145, c. Jerry Cooke; 146, Walter Iooss, Jr.; 147, Stuart Smith; 149, Walter Iooss, Jr.; 151, David Noyes (illustrator); 152, left Neil Leifer, right Neil Leifer; 153, Herb Scharfman

THE ERA OF FREEDOM

154-155, Walter Iooss, Jr.; 157, Walter Iooss, Jr.; 158, James Drake; 159, Heinz Kluetmeier; 160, Neil Leifer; 161, top Walter Iooss, Jr., bottom Tony Triolo; 162, James Drake; 163, Neil Leifer; 164, top Heinz Kluetmeier, bottom Dick Raphael; 165, Walter Iooss, Jr.; 166, Hank de Lespinasse; 167, top Eric Schweikardt, bottom Co Rentmeester; 168, Neil Leifer; 169, Manny Millan; 170, Tony Duffy/Allsport; 171, top c. Jerry Cooke, bottom John Iacono; 172, George Tiedemann; 173, Harry Benson; 174, Rich Clarkson; 175, top James Drake, bottom Walter Iooss, Jr.; 176, top Heinz Kluetmeier, bottom Manny Millan; 177, James Drake; 178, Heinz Kluetmeier; 179, top Heinz Kluetmeier, bottom Heinz Kluetmeier; 180, John Iacono; 181, Walter Iooss, Jr.; 182, top Peter Read Miller, bottom Walter Iooss, Jr.; 183, Heinz Kluetmeier; 184, Tony Duffy/Allsport; 185, top Manny Millan, bottom Russell/Kelley; 186, Eric Schweikardt; 187, Walter Iooss, Jr.; 188, Ronald C. Modra; 189, top Jerry Wachter, bottom Joe DiMaggio; 190, top George Tiedemann, bottom Heinz Kluetmeier; 191, Steve Goldstein; 192, Walter Iooss, Jr.; 193, top Trevor Jones, bottom Peter Read Miller; 194, Manny Millan; 195, Bill Eppridge; 196, William Campbell; 199, Rich Clarkson; 200, Carl Skalak; 201, Helen Williams/Photo Research, Inc.; 203, John Papanek; 205, Walter Iooss, Jr.; 206, Nancy Moran/Sygma; 207, Arthur Shilstone (illustrator); 209, Eric Schweikardt; 210, Ronald C. Modra; 211, Richard Mackson

THE SELLING OF SPORT

212-213, Lane Stewart; 215, Mickey Pfleger; 216, Lee Crum; 217, Caryn Levy; 218, Heinz Kluetmeier/ABC Sports; 219, top David Burnett/Contact Press Images, bottom Tony Tomsic; 220, John Iacono; 221, John Iacono; 222, top John Iacono, bottom Manny Millan; 223, Richard Mackson; 224, Trevor Jones/Allsport; 225, top Ronald C. Modra, bottom Ronald C. Modra; 226, top Jeff Schultz/Gamma-Liaison, bottom Heinz Kluetmeier; 227, Carl Skalak; 228, Chuck Solomon; 229, top c. Jerry Cooke, bottom Lane Stewart; 230, Michael O'Bryon; 231, top Jacquelin Duvoisin, bottom John Iacono 232, John Biever; 233, top Jon Wright, bottom Anthony Neste; 234, Manny Millan; 235, Manny Millan; 236, Heinz Kluetmeier; 237, top Manny Millan, bottom Ronald C. Modra; 238, Bongarts Sportspressbild; 239, Paul Bereswill; 240, top Manny Millan, bottom Heinz Kluetmeier; 241, Richard Mackson; 242, AFP/World Wide Photo; 243, top David Walberg, bottom John Iacono; 244, Andy Hayt; 246, John Iacono; 247, top John W. McDonough, bottom John Iacono; 248, Kyodo News Service; 249, Manny Millan; 250, Ronald C. Modra; 252, Lane Stewart; 253, Ronald C. Modra; 255, Heinz Kluetmeier; 256, George Lange; 257, no credit; 259, Craig Molenhouse; 260, Peter Read Miller; 261, Chuck Solomon; 263, Peter Read Miller; 264, Lane Stewart; 265, Bill Eppridge; 267, c. Gregory Heisler

INDEX

AFL 13, 77, 98
Aaron, Henry 10, 11, 28, 39, 127, 153
Abdul-Jabbar, Kareem 75, 95, 101, 115, 166, 182, 210, 217, 245
acid precipitation 200
Adcock, Joe 39
Affirmed 157, 171
Alabama, University of 15, 47, 227
Alaska 60, 61
Alaska, Game Division of the State of
Albright, Tenley 27
Alcindor, Lew (see Abdul-Jabbar, Kareem)
Alexeyev, Vasili 139
Alford, Steve 235
Ali, Muhammad 11, 72, 73, 75, 83, 97, 129, 132, 142, 148, 152, 157, 158, 181, 257, 266, 267
Allen, Richie (Dick) 75, 148
All-Star Game (baseball) 159
Altobelli, Alessandro 190
Alydar 157, 171
America's Cup 108, 159, 167, 195. 233
Anderson, Jon 143
Anderson, O.J. 158
Andretti, Mario 106, 226
Andujar, Joaquin 158
Arcaro, Eddie 19, 56
Arlington Classic 90
Arts and Letters 106
Ashe, Arthur 101
Astaphan, Jamie 260
Atlanta Braves 105, 127, 153, 157
Auburn University 47
Audobon, James 60
Auerbach, Red 75, 105
Augmon, Stacey 247
Austin, Tracy 158, 159
Australia II 159, 195
Australian Open 23, 101, 239

Baeza, Braulio 90
Baker, W. Thane 26
Baldwin, James 151
Ballard, Sarah 210
Ballesteros, Seve 158
Baltimore Bullets 115
Baltimore Colts 12, 13, 38, 81, 98, 109, 150
Baltimore Orioles 93, 105, 109, 176
Banks, Ernie 10
Bannister, Dr. Roger 17, 59
Basilio, Carmen 31
Bauer, Hank 33
Baylor, Elgin 11, 151
Beamon, Bob 103
Beathard, Pete 51
Beban, Gary 97
Becker, Boris 224
Belmont Stakes 19, 29, 106, 124, 168, 171
Beman, Deane 265
Bench, Johnny 164
Benitez, Wilfred 177
Benoit, Joan 218
Benson, Kent 163
Berra, Yogi 24
Berry, Ray 38
Bertrand, John 195
Bey, David 249
Bias, Len 229
Big Ten 69, 198
Bikila, Abebe 44
Biletnikoff, Fred 165
Bird, Larry 159, 175, 217
Bislett Games 174
Bitok, Kibiwott 255
Blackledge, Todd 189
Black Sox scandal 243
Bleier, Rocky 91
Bold Arrangement 229
Bolt, Tommy 34
Bonham, Ron 77
Borg, Bjorn 162, 184, 204
Boros, Julius 34
Boston Bruins 32, 75, 110, 118, 129, 167
Boston Celtics 12, 31, 46, 75, 76, 87, 105, 108, 150, 229, 241
Boston Marathon 183
Boston Patriots 77
Boston Red Sox 49, 58, 130, 157, 228
Bowman, Kirk 189
Boyle, Robert H. 200
Bradley, Bill 73, 87
Brett, George 159

Brigham Young University 157
British Empire Games 17, 59
British Open 157, 231
Brocklin, Norm Van 40
Brooklyn Dodgers 12, 13, 18, 24, 33, 58
Brooks, Herb 209
Brooks, James 60
Brown, Drew (Bundini) 266, 277
Brown, Freddie 190
Brown, James 73
Brown Jim 11, 81, 150
Brumel, Valeri 47
Brundage, Avery 143
Bryant, Bear 47, 227
Buckner, Bill 153, 228
Buckpasser 90, 91
Budd, Zola 206, 219
Budge, Don 51
Burdette, Lew 39
Bush, Guy 153

Cameron State College 150
Campanella, Roy 33
Campbell, Earl 202
Campbell, Milt 11
Canseco, Jose 215
Carlos, John 73, 102
Casals, Rosie 110
Cauthen, Steve 157, 171
Cayton, Bill 240
Chamberlain, Wilt 11, 87, 118, 151
Chanfreau, Gail l 149
Charbonneau, Joe 159
Cheevers, Gerry 167
Chicago Bulls 216, 249
Chicago Cubs 105, 171
Chicago Blackhawks 113
Chung, Connie 256
Cincinnati Bengals 186
Cincinnati Reds 109, 116, 130, 158, 164, 243, 261
Cincinnati Royals 76
Cincinnati, University of 77
Citation 56
Clarke, Bobby 129
Clark, Dwight 186
Clark, Will 215
Clay, Cassius (see Ali, Muhammad)
Cleary, Billy 41
Cleary, Bobby 41
Cleveland Browns 12, 81, 89, 150
Cobb, Ty 227
Coe, Sebastian 49, 157, 174, 179
Coghlan, Eamonn 174
Comaneci, Nadia 156
Conn, Billy 257
Conn, Mary Louise 257
Conn Smythe Trophy 167
Connolly, Maureen 17
Connor, Dennis 195, 233
Connors, Gloria Thompson 204
Connors, Jimmy 192, 204, 205
Cooney, Gerry 189
Cope, Myron 142
Corso, Lee 199
Cosell, Howard 74, 97, 142
Cotton Bowl 15
Courageous 167
Court, Margaret Smith 110
Cousy, Bob 12, 76
Craig, Jim 159
Creamer, Robert 58
Crenshaw, Ben 220
Crosthwaite, Mike 265
Cruguet, Jean 168
Curren, Kevin 226
Cy Young award 79, 105

Dallas Cowboys 84, 109, 114, 131, 156, 186
Dancer's Image 99
Davis Cup 148
Davis, Ernie 37
Davis, Robbie 258, 259
Davis, Roger 37
Dawson, Len 104
Dayton, University of 95
Daytona 500 83
Dean, Dizzy 99, 253
Dean, Ted 40
Decker, Mary 206, 219
Deford, Frank 144, 198, 204, 257
Dempsey, Jack 10, 176
Denver Broncos 231, 232
Detroit Lions 12
Detroit Pistons 241, 249
Detroit Red Wings 19
Detroit Tigers 99, 157, 221
DiMaggio, Joe 171
Dr. J (see Julius Erving)
Donald, Mike 247

Dorias, Gus 68
Doubleday, Nelson 264
Douglas, Buster 249
Downs, Kelly 243
Downing, Al 127, 153
Driesell, Lefty 229
Dryden, Ken 113
Drysdale, Don 240
Duke University 247
Dundee, Angelo 83, 181
Duran, Roberto 158, 182
Dykstra, Lenny 246

Edmonton Oilers 191, 239
Edwards, Harry 151
Ellerbee, Linda 256
Emerson, Roy 51
environment 200
Eruzione, Mike 178, 208
Erving, Julius 72, 159, 195
Esposito, Phil 118
Evert, Chris 124, 156, 158, 170, 222, 234, 239
Ewing, Patrick 223

Fairly, Ron 88
Faulkner, William 56
Feller, Robert 253
Ferdinand 229
Ferrari 36
Ficker, John 108
Fidrych, Mark 159
Fignon, Laurent 242
Fimrite, Ron 10, 153, 253
Final Four 87, 262
Finch, Sidd 264
Fingers, Rollie 116
Finsterwald, Dow 50
Fischer, Bobby 75, 148
Floyd, Raymond 156
Fonda, Jane 148
Ford, Whitey 81
Foreman, George 123, 129
Forward Pass 99
Forest Hills 204
Foyt, A.J. 127, 217
Francis, Charlie 260
Frazier, Joe 75, 123, 132, 152
French Open 124, 163, 239
Frenn, George 143
Frick, Ford 12
Fullmer, Gene 31
Fuqua, Frenchy 75
Futch, Eddie 132

Gainford, George 64
Gallant Man 29
Garvey, Steve 256
Georgetown University 190, 222, 227
Georgia, University of 189
Giacomin, Eddie 118
Giamatti, Bart 243
Gibson, Althea 11, 29
Gibson, Kirk 221
Gilbert, Bil 201
Givens, Robin 240
Golf Digest 265
Gooden, Dwight 215
Gossage, Rich 159
Grablev, Mitko 260
Graebner, Clark 149
Graf, Steffi 222, 234, 239
Graham, Michael 223
Grambling University 227
Granatelli, Andy 106
Grand Prix 148
Grand Slam 23, 51, 107, 110, 239
Grange, Red 10
Grateful Dead 202
Green Bay Packers 12, 40, 74, 89, 95
Greenwood, L.C. 126
Gretel II 108
Gretzky, Wayne 158, 191, 217, 239
Grove, Lefty 253
Guenchev, Angel 260
Guidry, Ron 159
Gumbel, Bryant 256
Guthrie, Janet 157

Haddix, Harvey 12, 39
Hagberg, Roger 43
Hall of Fame 262
Hammill, Dorothy 156, 161
Hanratty, Terry 91
Hard, Darlene 29
Harkness, Jerry 77
Harrelson, Ken 73
Harrick, Jim 262
Harris, Danny 193
Harris, Franco 126, 175

Harris, Jimmy 24
Harris, Percy 150
Hartack, Bill 106
Hayes, Bob 84
Hayes, Elvin 101, 151
Hayes, Woody 68, 69, 157
Hearst, Patty 203
Heiden, Eric 158, 179
Heisler, Gregory 266
Heisman Trophy 37
Henderson, Rickey 188
Henie, Sonja 237
Hershiser, Orel 240
Hill, Phil 36
Hoad, Lew 11, 23
Holmes, Larry 158, 181, 189
Hood, Ted 167
Hornung, Paul 89
House, Tom 153
Houston Aeros 122
Houston Astros 253
Houston, University of 101, 150, 223
Howard, Percy 156, 159
Howe, Gordie 19, 122
Howe, Mark 122
Howe, Marty 122
Hull, Bobby 93, 122
Hunt, Anderson 247

Iditarod Sled Dog Race 226
Indianapolis Motor Speedway 106
Indianapolis 500 113, 127, 157
Indiana State 175, 262
Indiana, University of 97, 163, 235
International Basketball Federation 217
International Olympic Committee 260
Intrepid 108
Iron Constitution 168
Iron Liege 29
Irving, Clifford 148
Irwin, Hale 247

Jackson, Reggie 49, 75, 116, 156, 157, 210
Jacobs, Tommy 80
Jagger, Mick 148
Janszen, Paul 261
Jenkins, Dan 140, 146, 147
Jenner, Bruce 156
Johansson, Ingemar 11, 37
John Hancock Bowl 216
Johnson, Ben 217, 237, 260
Johnson, Bill 219
Johnson, Larry 247
Johnson, Magic 158, 159, 175, 182, 217, 241
Johnson, Mark 209
Johnson, Marques 132
Johnson, Rafer 11, 63
Johnson, Walter 253
Johnson, William Oscar 139, 260
Jones, Bobby 10, 41
Jones, Janet 239
Jones, K.C. 112
Jordan, Michael 72, 159, 190, 216, 217
Joyner, Florence Griffith 236
Joyner-Kersee, Jackie 236

Kansas City Chiefs 104
Kansas City Royals 158, 159, 181
Kauai King 90
Keeler, Wee Willie 171
Keino, Kipchoge 254
Kempes, Mario 173
Kentucky 47
Kentucky Derby 56, 57, 19, 29, 90, 99, 124, 229
Kenya 254
Kibor, Joseph 254, 255
Kiick, Jim 117
Killy, Jean-Claude 102
Kilroy, Gene 266
King, Billie Jean 72, 110, 124, 134, 158, 210
Kirkpatrick, Curry 148
Klammer, Franz 160
Knievel, Evel 75
Knight, Bobby 198, 199, 262
Knight, Ray 228
Kookaburra III 233
Koppel, Ted 256
Korbut, Olga 206
Koufax, Sandy 79, 253
Kram, Mark 152
Kramer, Jerry 95
Kulikov, Yevgeny 179

LPGA 35, 173
Lafleur, Guy 167
Landy, John 17, 59
Larsen, Don 12, 24
La Salle 21
Lavegh, Pierre 21

Laver, Rod 11, 51, 107
Lefebvre, Jim 88
Lema, Tony 78
LeMans Grand Prix 21
Lemon, Bob- 157
LeMond, Greg 242
Lendl, Ivan 192
Lenglen, Suzanne 210
Leonard, Sugar Ray 158, 177, 182, 257
Letterman, David 256
Lewis, Carl 237
Lewis, Tommy 15
Liberty 159, 195
Lieber, Jill 261
Lincoln, Keith
Liston, Sonny 53, 83
Littler, Gene 34
Lombardi, Vince 12, 95
Lopez, Nancy 173
Los Angeles Dodgers 13, 79, 88, 93, 127, 153, 168, 240, 261
Los Angeles Kings 239
Los Angeles Lakers 13, 76, 105, 118, 158, 166, 182, 195, 216, 241
Louisiana Tech 193
Louis, Joe 257
Loyola (Chicago) 77
Luce, Clare Boothe 62
Luce, Henry 62
Luciano, Ron 158
Lundgren, Birgit 37
Lynn, Fred 159

MacPhail, Lee 159
Mahre, Phil 185
Mahre, Steve 185
Majestic Prince 106
Mallon, Bill 75
Mantle, Mickey 11, 22, 72, 205
Marciano, Rocky 12, 257
Marcos, Imelda 152
Maris, Roger 12, 49, 72, 153
Martin, Billy 159, 157
Massachusetts, University of 72
Masters 11, 49, 50, 78, 86, 158, 220, 230, 231
Maule, Tex 63
May, Lee 109
May, Scott 163
Mays, Willie 10, 11, 14, 150
Mazeroski, Bill 43
McCallum, Jack 265
McCarty, George 150
McCarver, Tim 81
McEnroe, John 158, 184
McKay, John 51
McLain, Denny 99
McLain, Gary (Gizmo) 227
McNally, Dave 157
McTear, Houston 159
McVea, Warren 150
Medich, Doc 188
Messersmith, Andy 157
Meyran, Octavio 182
Miami Dolphins 74, 75, 114, 117, 222
Michigan State 91, 175
Michigan, University of 72, 87, 163
Miller, Cheryl 193
Milwaukee Braves 12, 28, 33, 39
Milwaukee Brewers 188
Milwaukee Bucks 115
Minneapolis Lakers 13
Minnesota Twins 88
Minnesota, University of
Minnesota Vikings 104, 126, 165
Mix, Ron 77
Moegle, Dickie 15
Monday Night Football 142
Montana, Joe 186, 217, 222
Montreal Canadiens 12, 19, 32, 113, 167
Montville, Leigh 72
Moore, Kenny 143, 254, 260
Morgan, J.D. 263
Morgan, Joe 130
Morris, Jack 221
Morrow, Bobby 26
Morton, Craig 109
Moses, Edwin 193
Motley, Marion 10
Muhammad, Herbert 266
Mulligan, Martin 51
Mulvoy, Mark 207
Mungo, Van Lingle 253
Munich tragedy 143
Murray, Eddie 176
Musial, Stan 11

NBA 11, 12, 13, 46, 74, 115, 159, 215
NBA Finals 31, 118, 158, 182

NBA Players Association 215
NCAA 21, 203, 215, 216
NFL 10, 12, 13, 40, 81, 117, 156, 215, 217
NHL 12, 19, 158
Naber, John 161
Nack, William 211, 258
Namath, Joe 72, 73, 75, 98, 147, 148
Nashua 19
Nastase, Ilie 148, 149, 163
National Association of Basketball Coaches 262
Navratilova, Martina 170, 210, 222, 234, 239
Nebraska, University of 189
Neff, Craig 214
New England Patriots 74, 207
New Mexico, University of 150
New York Cosmos 131
New York Giants (baseball) 13, 14
New York Giants (football) 12, 13, 38, 40, 231
New York Jets 98, 123
New York Knicks 87, 118
New York Marathon 176, 186
New York Mets 53, 105, 228, 264
New York Rangers 118
New York Yankees 12, 18, 22, 24, 28, 33, 43, 58, 79, 81, 157, 159, 168, 221
Nicholson, Jack 216
Nicklaus, Jack 11, 41, 78, 81, 86, 112, 146, 158, 196, 217, 230
Nielsen, Gifford 157
Nike 216
Norman, Greg 231
North American Soccer League 131
North Carolina, University of 190
Notre Dame 24, 51, 91

Oakland A's 73, 116, 188, 240, 243
Oakland Raiders 95, 165, 207
O'Brien, Jim 109
Ohio State 68, 69
Okker, Tom 101
Oklahoma, University of 24
Olajuwon, Akeem 223
Olsen, Jack 150
Olympics
 1932 23
 1956 11, 26, 27
   slalom 26
   giant slalom 26
   downhill 26
   100-meter dash 26
   200-meter dash 26
 1960 11, 41, 44, 63
   decathlon 63
   100-meter dash 44
   200-meter dash 44
   1,500-meter run 63
   4x100-meter relay (track) 44
   marathon 44
 1964 84, 85
   100-meter dash 84
   800-meter run 84
   1,500-meter run 84, 254
   100-meter freestyle 85
   400-meter freestyle 85
   4x100-meter relay (swimming) 85
   4x200-meter relay (swimming) 85
 1968 102, 103, 254
   downhill 102
   long jump 103
 1972 120, 143
   100-meter freestyle 120
   200-meter freestyle 120
   100-meter butterfly 120
   200-meter butterfly 120
   marathon 121, 143
 1976 160, 164, 214, 254
   figure skating 161
   100-meter backstroke 161
   200-meter backstroke 161
 1980 158, 178, 208, 214, 254
   1,000-meter race (speed skating) 179
   1,500-meter race (speed skating) 179
   5,000-meter race (speed skating) 179
   10,000-meter race (speed skating) 179
   800-meter run 179
   1,500-meter run 179
 1984 193, 214, 218, 219,
   400-meter hurdles 219
   downhill 219
   Los Angeles Olympic Organizing Committee 214
   women's marathon 218
 1988 217, 236, 237, 256, 260,
   100-meter dash 236, 237
   200-meter dash 236
   4x100-meter relay (track) 236
   figure skating 237
   pentathlon 236
   women's long jump 236
 1992 217

Olympic trials 94
1967 94
  pole vault 94
Orange Bowl 156
Orosco, Jesse 228
Orr, Bobby 75, 110, 129
Osborne, Jeffrey 240
Osoro, Ondoro 254
Ott, Ed 176
Ovett, Steve 179
Owens, Jesse 26

PGA 158, 265
Pacheco, Ferdie 266
Padilla, Carlos 177
Palmer, Arnold 11, 15, 41, 49, 50, 86, 146, 210
Papanek, John 202
Pappas, Milt 93
Parker, Jim 150
Passarella, Daniel 173
Paterno, Joe 189
Patkin, Max 252
Patterson, Floyd 11, 37, 53
Patterson, Pat 266
Patterson, Reggie 227
Pavelich, Mark 208
Payton, Walter 159, 217
Pele 131
Pender, Paul 64
Penn State 189
Perry, Joe 10
Peters, Ron 261
Petty, Richard 83
Philadelphia Eagles 40, 138, 158
Philadelphia Flyers 129, 158
Philadelphia Phillies 181, 246
Philadelphia 76ers 87, 158, 182, 195
Phinizy, Coles 60
Pinckney, Ed 227
Pittsburgh Pirates 12, 39, 43, 58, 157, 159, 176
Pittsburgh Steelers 74, 75, 126, 131, 156, 175
Plante, Jacques 32
Player, Gary 11, 34, 49, 50, 86
Plimpton, George 264
Plymouth 83
Podres, Johnny 58
Polo Grounds 14
Pope, Edwin 136, 159
Portland Trail Blazers 166, 203, 249
Prairie View (A&M) 227
Preakness 19, 90, 106, 124, 168, 171
Princeton 73, 87
Pulford, Jack 265

Quisenberry, Dan 159

Reagan, Ronald 215
Reese, Don 158
Retton, Mary Lou 214
Revson, Peter 113
Rice University 15
Rice, Grantland 68
Richardson, Jerry 38
Richey, Cliff 149
Riddles, Libby 226
Robertson, Oscar 11, 115, 151
Robinson, Brooks 109
Robinson, Eddie 225
Robinson, Frank 10, 93
Robinson, Jackie 10, 18, 74
Robinson, Sugar Ray 31, 54, 64, 65
Robisch, Dave 75
Rockne, Knute 68
Rodgers, Bill 176, 183
Rogin, Gilbert 64, 66
Roller Derby 12
Rose Bowl 51, 69, 97
Rose, Pete 130, 171, 217, 225, 243, 260, 261
Rosewall, Ken 11, 23
Ross Trophy 191
Rossi, Paolo 190
Rossovich, Tim 138
Rozelle, Pete 13
Rouse, Vic 77
Rudolph, Wilma 11, 44
Rupp, Adolph 198
Russell, Bill 11, 12, 21, 31, 46, 87, 105, 150
Russell, Cazzie 73
Russi, Bernhard 160
Ruth, Babe 10, 58, 127, 153
Rutherford, Johnny 127
Ryan, Nolan 217, 253
Ryun, Jim 91

Sabatini, Gabriela 239
Sabol, Steve 138
Sailer, Toni 26, 102

St. Louis Cardinals 28, 81, 158
St. Louis Hawks 31, 46
Salazar, Alberto 186
Sambito, Joe 72
Sampson, Ralph 159
Sande, Earl 56
Sanderson, Derek 148
San Diego Chargers 77
San Diego Clippers 203
San Diego Padres 221, 227
San Francisco, University of 21
San Francisco 49ers 186, 222
San Francisco Giants 11, 243
San Francisco Warriors 87
San Jose State College 151
Santagata, Nick 258
Sarazen, Gene 140
Sarria, Luis 266
Savage, Steve 143
Schmidt, Mike 181
San Francisco, University of 21
Schlichter, Art 159
Schneider, Buzzie 208
Schollander, Don 85
Scott, Jack 203
Seagren, Bob 94
Seattle Slew 157, 168
Seaver, Tom 105
Sebring 36
Secretariat 75, 124
Seidler, Maren 206
Seitz, Peter 157
Shabazz, Lana 266
Sharman, Bill 12
Shoemaker, Ruby 211
Shoemaker, Bill 11, 29, 211, 217, 229
Shorter, Frank 121, 143
Show, Eric 227
Shutt, Steve 167
Silk, Dave 209
Simmons, Ted 188
Simpson, O.J. 97, 123, 158, 210
Smart, Keith 235
Smith, Dean 262
Smith, Gary 266
Smith, Robyn 144, 145
Smith, Tommie 73, 102, 151
Smith, Walker Jr. (see Robinson, Sugar Ray)
Snead, Sam 78
Snell, Matt 98
Snell, Peter 84
Snider, Duke 18
Southwestern State 151
Spagnolo, Angelo 265
Spinks, Leon 157, 240
Spitz, Mark 120
Sports Illustrated 157, 158, 159
Sports inc. 216
Sportsman of the Year 17, 58, 208
Stabler, Ken 165
Stallard, Tracy 49, 153
Stallworth, John 175
Stanley Cup 19, 32, 75, 110, 112, 118, 129, 158, 167, 239
Stansfield, Andrew 26
Stargell, Willie 157, 159
Starr, Bart 89
Stars & Stripes 233
Statman, Alan 261
Staubach, Roger 114, 156
Steinbrenner, George 159
Stengel, Casey 24, 53
Stenmark, Ingemar 185
Stern, David 215
Stingley, Darryl 207
Stones, Dwight 164
Strawberry, Darryl 228
strike (football) 233
Suggs, Louise 35
Sullivan, Danny 226
Sun Bowl 216
Super Bowl 74, 95, 98, 109, 114, 117, 126, 131, 158, 165, 175, 186, 189, 222, 231
Swann, Lynn 131
Swaps 19, 56
Swift, E.M. 208
Syracuse University 37, 150, 235

Tanui, Moses 254
Tardelli, Marco 190
Tarkenton, Fran 126
Tasmanian devil 201
Tatum, Jack 207
Taylor, Jim 89
Tenace, Gene 116
Terrell, Roy 68
Terry, Ralph 43

Texas A&M 47
Texas at El Paso, University of 150
Thomas, Debi 237
Thomas, Duane 114, 148
Thomas, Frank 53
Thomas, Isiah 241, 249
Thompson, John 223
Throneberry, Marv 53
Tilden, Bill 8
TIME 62, 215
Tinling, Ted 210
Tiriac, Ion 149
Tkaczuk, Walter 118
Tour de France 242
Trammell, Alan 221
Trevino, Lee 112, 146
Triple Crown (baseball) 22, 93
Triple Crown (horse racing) 90, 124, 157, 168, 171
Turner, Ted 157, 167
Tyler, Wendell 222
Tyson, Mike 217, 240

UCLA 95, 97, 101, 117, 132, 203, 263
UNLV 247
Ueberroth, Peter 214, 261
Underwood, John 136, 138
Unitas, Johnny 38
U.S. Amateur 15, 41
U.S. hockey team 11, 158, 178
U.S. Open (golf) 34, 41, 80, 112, 146, 158, 231, 247
U.S. Open (tennis) 23, 29, 101, 110, 124, 148, 149, 158, 192, 222, 239
University of San Francisco 10
University of Southern California 51, 94, 97, 138, 193
Unser, Al 113

Valenzuela, Fernando 158, 185
Vance, Dazzy 253
Velasquez, Jorge 171
Venezia, Mike 258, 259
Venturi, Ken 80
Vezina Trophy 113
Villanova 227

Wagner, Hans 58
Waitz, Grete 176
Walton, Bill 75, 117, 166, 202
Warmath, Murray 43
Warren, Mike 117
Washington Redskins 117, 232
Watson, Tom 220
Weaver, Earl 158, 159
Wepner, Chuck 73
Wertz, Vic 14
West Point 199
Whirlaway 56
White, Mike 249
Whitman, Walt 148
Whittingham, Charlie 229
Wide World of Sports 142
Wichita State 87
Wiley, Harry 65
Wilkins, Mac 206
Williams, Ted 11, 136, 137, 153, 232
Wills, Maury 10, 88
Wilson, Marc 157
Witt, Katarina 237
Wimbledon 11, 17, 23, 29, 51, 101, 110, 124, 148, 149, 156, 158, 163, 170, 184, 205, 226, 234, 239
Wisconsin, University of 51
Wolff, Alexander 262
Women's Open 35
Wooden, John 132, 262, 263
Wooden, Nell 262, 263
Woodward, Otis 65
World Cup (skiing) 185, 190
World Cup (soccer) 173
World Hockey Association 122
World Series 12, 14, 18, 23, 28, 33, 43, 58, 79, 81, 88, 93, 105, 109, 116, 130, 157, 158, 164, 168, 176, 181, 221, 228, 243, 240
Worst Avid Golfer 264
Worthy, James 190
Wottle, Dave 143
Wright, Mickey 35
Wulf, Steve 156, 252

Yancey, Bert 146
Yang, Chuan Kwang 63
Yepremian, Garo 117
Yosemite National Park 202
Young, Cy 58
Yount, Robin 250

Zachary, Tom 153
Zaharias, Babe Didrikson 23
Zvereva, Natalia 2392

Sports Illustrated